sprinkled? → polenta?

→ savoury crumble

Oats

CRUNCH CRUSTED

The dressed leaf
fresh
· acidity.

The Parmesan
Blanket
Pecorino.

Sourdough Bruschetta

filled.

The fragrant sprinkle. Herb/pomegranate tasty

Chilly toppings. → Aftertaste
- the oft. underra

Milk

Rollap

Fruit Bread

Brioche

CRUSTY

Dusted

T.gered.

...re! for drawing 10 ideas!

Crackle crusty rolls

Whatever is this?

How about individual stunners?

T0304585

BAKE WITH JACK

BREAD EVERY DAY

All the best breads and simple, step-by-step
recipes to use up every crumb!

JACK STURGESS

EBURY
PRESS

CONTENTS

INTRODUCTION 6

-1-
SIMPLE LOAVES & ROLLS
28

•••

-2-
WET DOUGHS & FLATBREADS
84

•••

-3-
FLAVOURED BREADS
130

•••

BREAD, BREAD, BREAD...

I love it. I love eating it, I love the pride and satisfaction that comes with making it, I love the aroma when I'm baking it, I love that it takes effort and I love that it's always worth it.

I'm Jack Sturgess, professional chef turned bread maker and educator on a mission to SMASH bread-making myths to smithereens, remove the worry and fear of baking a 'live' dough and give you the knowledge you need to be able to make amazing bread at home without overcomplicating things. This is exactly what we have been doing in my bread-making classes for over ten years now and on the *Bake with Jack* YouTube channel for so long. Chatting and discussing the finer points of making your home bread a roaring success every single time; and serving it all up alongside some tasty dishes.

But before we continue, I need to come clean with you ...

This is not the 'easy' way to make bread. This is not a 'shortcut' way to make 'quick' bread. This book is SO MUCH MORE than that. It's your **guide to understanding** how to make incredible bread at home in the proper way, and with that knowledge comes PRACTICALITY too!

I know you are busy, I get it. And bread is a true craft that relies on time. Time is the all-important, game-changing, irreplaceable factor that we don't want to remove at all costs because every time we take a shortcut, every time we speed things up to make our bread 'easier' or 'quicker' or more 'convenient', we are compromising on the final texture and flavour of the bread. Always. That's why the majority of the bread that we buy, 'modern' bread, is tasteless, bland and floppy.

But here is the secret part nobody ever talks about: once you truly understand the PRINCIPLES of what you are doing, you'll be knocking out amazing bread with ease. Tailoring your bread to the requirements

of your life, instead of fitting life in and around your bread, because bread may take some time from start to finish, but the ACTUAL time you spend DOING it is minimal.

Throughout this book, we'll go through each recipe with as many useful photos of the process as possible to help you get your head around things. We'll be talking a lot about the all-important PRINCIPLES of homemade bread just as if we were in class together. Like WHY we knead the dough in the first place? WHY it is important NOT to dust the dough with flour along the way? It's so important to understand WHY things happen the way that they do because with that comes confidence, let me explain ...

Fixing a car is beyond me. Sure, I can change a headlight bulb like a pro (after consulting the manual for at least 25 minutes and finding the correct screwdriver), but when it comes to things like spark plugs and [insert the name of other such mystery car parts here], I have no idea what I am doing at all. And so, if I tried to fix something by myself, I would wonder all along if I was actually doing it right, and it would no doubt go a little wrong, leading me to become upset and frustrated, not ONLY because I probably made things worse, but also because the process was a pretty stressful one and I STILL would have no idea why I ended up with what I did. Let us not stop here! Next, I may even begin to question whether it was a good idea to embark upon that journey in the first place, decide that it probably wasn't and that cars are clearly not for me, so let's not do this ever again. BUT what if I built a solid understanding of how a car works and what all the bits and bobs are actually there to do? With the hows and the whys answered, I'd probably stand a better chance of getting it right. Is any of this making sense yet? Hold on ...

This same principle applies to a lot of things, and bread is certainly one of them. The point I am trying to make is that you can't go steaming ahead into making bread with a twelve-step instruction plan for the first time and expect everything to come out just perfect. You need a little bit MORE. There are plenty of nuances and unspoken technicalities, which are often NOT written into recipe books at all. On the other hand, there are also plenty of unnecessary safety nets written into recipes that probably cause more harm than good. If only you knew the areas of potential stitch up along the way, then you'd sidestep a TON of potential failures. With knowledge and understanding, you'll confidently make your own judgement calls and, believe me, it's probably not as hard as you think.

In my YouTube videos, I have touched upon and discussed these nuances for years to educate and inspire home bakers all over the world. If you get stuck, you'll find plenty of help on the *Bake with Jack* channel with so much more to come.

Bread-making is a craft, a real learning journey to get excited about and EVERY bread in this book holds a lesson. Whether it is the super-wet focaccia dough that enables us to skip kneading entirely for an even BETTER result, the RULE-BREAKING nature of the classic bagel, or the fact that the sourdough making process is actually made EASIER by the length of time that the dough is left unattended, enabling us to get on with other things while we wait.

I've tried to present the breads here in such a way that you are taken on a journey. Not necessarily from 'easy' to 'tricky', but to introduce you to different processes and practices in a logical order on the quest to raise your bread game.

In this book, you'll find my classic go-to bread recipes and alongside each one, I've included a few recipes for dishes I think work really well with them. From Breakfast Tacos (see page 78) to Things on Toast (see page 39) and a warming Spiced Split Pea Bowl to serve with your homemade naan (see page 106). If you are planning ahead for an evening meal with friends, celebrate the bread centre table as the real star of the show by carefully constructing a complementary meal around it; mixing and matching a few dishes together. You could bake some Focaccia (see page 109) and match it with the Mint Ricotta, Green Bean Salad (see page 116), the Cured Meats antipasti board (see page 92) and an easy-to-assemble salad, like the Tomato, Mozzarella, Basil & Fresh Chilli (see page 96) or perhaps a Baked Camembert (see page 168). The bread will likely take up most of the attention, and it doesn't take much to turn it into a showstopping meal to share with friends and family.

And as your bread gets past its best, you'll also find ideas for using up every single crumb in interesting and exciting ways, like a Hot Cross Bun 'Pancake' Stack (see page 246), Beef Shin Chilli Nachos – yes please! (see page 82) or garlicky crispy breadcrumbs to top off a Leek & Brie Risotto (see page 98), which will have you reaching for more.

And the rest is up to you: practise, patience and persistence. There's no substitute, believe me, so start falling in love with the bread-making process. I have complete unconditional belief that with the not-so-secret secrets I share with you here, you'll get your first epic win, and then you'll be on a roll (sorry, pun intended).

Whatever happens from here on in, you'll have those wins, and you might have a couple of losses and that's all part of the process. It's my hope that with what I share with you in the following pages, you'll know exactly why things may not have turned out how you wanted them to in the past, and with that knowledge you'll feel encouraged to continue on and tweak things for next time.

In the life of *Bake with Jack,* I have met so many people who became frustrated with failures because they didn't know why they happened and where to go next. They failed once or twice seven years ago and then they gave up, deciding it was just another thing they simply 'can't do'. That is such a shame and breaks my heart every time I hear it because a simple lack of knowledge was the reason they haven't been baking and eating amazing bread, week after week, for the last seven years. That's exactly why *Bake with Jack* began years ago. Those people never knew how close they came to cracking it and then often in class, there will be just one thing, one discussion, one single penny drop moment where they 'get it'. I've seen it with my own eyes time and time again. Everything changes in a moment. Crusty baguettes, lighter-than-air focaccia, buttery brioche – they are ALL completely achievable in your kitchen at home, baked in your oven, crafted with your own two hands.

I want this for you so much: to discover your ability to effortlessly crack out weekly breads for yourself, your family and friends. To look upon the process without worry, or fear, or feeling overwhelmed because **bread-making is SO POWERFUL, it requires the development of skills essential for LIFE, not just LUNCH.** It's practise and patience, it's trial and sometimes error, it's persistence, care and attention. It's effort rewarded.

Please, please, please, if your bread doesn't come out spot on the first-time round, do it again. Anybody can make a terrible loaf and give up, that's easy. But it takes real courage to do it again and again and when you do, you'll realise with EVERY SINGLE attempt you're learning and growing as a home baker. Even if you feel like you're not sometimes, you already ARE winning the game by simply doing. It is so worth it. Just like our bread dough, give it time.

Maybe you bought this book as a complete beginner ready to take your first steps into homemade bread. Maybe you've had a good crack, some have been okay and others mysteriously fail. Perhaps you are on the cusp of throwing in the towel and this is a last-ditch attempt to cobble together a loaf before giving it up forever, or maybe we've known each other for YEARS, having baked bread together way back in the olden days of *Bake with Jack.*

Whatever your story, it is my hope that within these pages that follow, you gain a MASSIVE sense of enjoyment, satisfaction and appreciation for the value a humble homemade loaf brings. I hope you enjoy making, eating and sharing everything here as much as I've enjoyed creating it.

Thank You!

Jack

INGREDIENTS

While reading this book, I hope you'll begin to recognise that the foundations of all these breads are made from very similar ingredients, the BIG FOUR being flour, water, salt and yeast, with SOURDOUGH being JUST flour, water and salt with no yeast at all – isn't that crackers?! You *could* go to the ends of the earth with flour varieties from all over the globe, but the point I am trying to get across here is that the real skill of homemade bread is in the PROCESS and PRINCIPLES. So I have tried to keep the ingredients simple and accessible. No trawling the internet for a specific type of flour you've never heard of; just simple stuff to be found in almost any supermarket …

THE BIG FOUR

FLOUR

This will be your foundation. Flour is the cause of bread's existence, the reason WHY bread is what it is. ALL bread flours are different, even one strong white bread flour can vary hugely to the next strong white bread flour, so try to stick with the same brand as you are learning.

Strong white bread flour
You'll be using this as the base for the majority of these recipes. White flour for white bread, often cut with one of the below flours for texture and flavour. It is the wheat grain smashed into flour with the brown parts sifted out, and so it is the strongest most glutenous of them all. It allows for the LIGHTEST of bread textures in focaccias, ciabattas and soft sweet buns, for example.

Wholemeal (whole wheat) bread flour
This one is the (WHOLE) wheat grain, smashed WITHOUT removing the bran (brown bits). A heavier flour for heavier bread, with a MASSIVE wholemealy flavour, often combined with white for a wholesome bread that retains its lightness.

Wholemeal rye flour
The flavour of rye is unmistakable, and it provides a ROBUST starter for your Sourdough Loaf (see page 264). Used in combination with strong white bread flour, a little goes a long way, while used by itself in a bread like the Rye Sourdough (see page 281), it provides little to no structure at all, resulting in a super-heavy, wholesome bread, which equally has its place.

WATER

The Liquid Part is the simplest part of the recipes. Without this, your bread will be a little … dry. Get it from the tap. Temperature here is important since water is a large part of the recipe in most cases. For beginners, I ALWAYS recommend using water at room temperature, i.e. the same temperature as your room. It's important. For more on this, see *The Importance of Temperature* on page 18.

SALT

For flavour and structure. Bread WITHOUT salt (we've all done it!) tastes like cardboard and ends up crumbly and hard to slice. For one reason or another, the structure just doesn't develop properly. I try to keep salt to a minimum where possible, while still producing a tasty loaf.

YEAST

Yeast makes gas and gas PUFFS up our dough! (Principle number 1). It also ferments the dough, making FLAVOUR. The recipes here call for fresh or fast-action dried yeast, roughly 2 parts fresh to 1 part dry. I feel like fresh yeast brings a little more character to the party but if it's tricky to get hold of where you are, don't let that be a barrier, just get dry. Fresh yeast keeps for weeks in the fridge in a lidded plastic box lined top and bottom with parchment paper. You'll see signs of it getting old – it may go dry and crumbly or turn into a puddle. Fast-action dried yeast keeps for ages, but opened it gives you NO sign of whether it will work or not. If you're worried about freshness, pop some in a glass of warm water with a pinch of sugar and if it moves around making bubbles, it's a good sign it'll puff up your dough.

EXTRAS

Sugar and honey

'Hold on, shouldn't this be in the ESSENTIALS section?' I hear you cry. No. Sugar is actually NOT an essential ingredient in bread. It is not NEEDED, though it is often unnecessarily INCLUDED as a booster for your yeast. I use it to sweeten, in the case of sweet buns, for example, and also as a BONUS it helps the final bread retain its moistness for longer.

Fat – butter and oil

Fat is NOT an essential ingredient. You can completely make bread without it, but its presence does bring a little something. Adding oil or butter to a dough makes it SILKIER and brings SOFTNESS both to the dough AND to the final bread. At times it can help us a little with kneading, as a dough with fat incorporated tends to stick a little less to the table. Also, it brings FLAVOUR. Imagine a buttery brioche or olive oil focaccia. Steer well clear of margarine and other spreads – they're not real food. Try to use the good stuff when you can. ADDED BONUS! Fat also brings additional shelf-life to the final bread. As fresh bread gets old, it dries out and goes hard. I like to think of the fat as the moisture that doesn't evaporate, therefore keeping your bread softer for longer.

Milk

AHA! Another source of fat, and … milkiness. You'll find milk in the Enriched section of this book as we bring more softness and lightness to the party. Just be aware that adding milk tends to slow the rise, so expect milky doughs to take a little longer to puff up.

Eggs

All the eggs I use here are UK medium, meaning around 50g (1¾oz) without the shell! A source of fat and therefore silky softness once again but ALSO a great source of LIFT. Imagine the overcooking of an omelette, or the PUFF of a soufflé. Eggs bring VOLUME INCREASE, making the most egg-laden of breads, the brioche, the lightest and fluffiest it can be!

ADDITIONAL INGREDIENTS

This part is where you can let your imagination run wild. I'm talking about FLAVOUR! Nuts, seeds, dried fruits, olives, CHEESES of all descriptions, onions, spices, peels, marzipan, salami, fresh herbs, CHOCOLATE.

Stick to the same quantities I show in the recipes and you can happily swap a raisin for a dried blueberry, or dark chocolate for white chocolate, or an olive for a sun-blushed tomato, for example … have a PLAY.

EQUIPMENT

I'm not really a gadget guy, you may be surprised to hear. I deal with flour and water mostly. But when learning something (anything!) for the first time, I think it's important to shell out for just a few bits and bobs. PROPER kit will make your life EASY and increase your chances of success, which is exactly what you need when you're starting out. You'll have enough to get your head around without compromising with makeshift equipment …

BASIC KIT

With just these things, you'll have enough stuff to confidently and comfortably knock out your weekly loaf, rolls, bloomers and sweet buns. These are the essentials and really, it doesn't take much to get started!

Scales

I measure EVERYTHING on scales, even my morning coffee … Get digital ones that go up 1 gram (or ⅛ ounce) at a time. The ones I like best have the buttons that are NOT on the actual weighing surface. Oh, and stash a spare battery in your kitchen drawer too.

Dough scraper

You'll be using this for EVERYTHING! Mixing dough, lifting, cutting, turning out, unsticking, scraping bowls, cleaning the table, tiling the bathroom, defrosting your windscreen in winter – lacking one, I have even used an egg slice or loyalty card in desperation. Small ones, large ones, metal ones, whatever you fancy. I like flexible plastic ones with a short and long side for cutting, and a rounded edge for cleaning my bowl.

A stack of mixing bowls and a couple of jugs

BIG bowls are always handy for really getting in there and mixing well. We'll be measuring liquids in grams (fluid ounces), but jugs are always handy for getting your water to the right temperature before weighing the quantity into another.

Trays and baking parchment

Flat trays are great for rolls, buns and free-standing breads like bloomers. Always line them with baking parchment so that nothing sticks and you can also reuse it a couple of times. Don't confuse parchment paper with greaseproof, which sticks to bread like CRAZY!

Loaf tins and pie tins

I use 900g (2lb) box folded loaf tins with a 450g (1lb) one for the rye loaf. Enamel pie dishes of all shapes and sizes are lovely to bake inside of too. Line with baking parchment or grease each time you use them just to be sure, and yes, even the 'non-stick' ones.

Proving cloths

These are cotton cloths or tea towels for covering resting dough and using as a couche – creating a pleated bed for stone baked breads to rest before they bake. Mine are natural cotton tea towels kept only for bread-making and NOT washing up. When washing these, try NOT to use too much detergent or perfumed softener because your dough WILL take on the aroma, resulting in bread that tastes like potpourri (learnt from experience!).

Bread knife

When the work is done and the bread is a triumph, all that's left to do (after a victory dance) is slice it. So, get a decent knife to avoid hacking a loaf into door wedges or tearing a baguette to shreds! A SMOOTHLY serrated knife will slice your bread with ease without destroying the top and scattering shrapnel all over your kitchen.

Small serrated knife

For the classic pre-puff slash you'll be doing on your simple sandwich loaf, bloomer and wholemeal. Tomato knives are perfect!

Steam tray and kettle

MOST of the breads in this book are baked with STEAM! For this, you'll need a deep roasting tray in the bottom of the oven, and a kettle of water to tip into it.

Pencil and notepad

I can't stress enough how important it is to take notes when you are making bread if you really want to nail it! Record things like the temperature on the day; how the bread went; what you may have found tricky; what you liked or didn't. You can then tweak things for the next time, for example, reducing the water in a dough you may have found tricky to handle. ALWAYS keep a pencil handy, preferably behind your ear.

USEFUL EXTRAS

Timers

I have these EVERYWHERE. As much as I always THINK I'll remember what to do and when, in reality I never do. Set them for resting and baking times.

Thermometers

It's NICE to know your temperatures, though if you are a beginner, please don't get overwhelmed by this idea. I have a thermometer on my kitchen wall to let me know what temperature the room is, and one I pop into the water (or milk) to get them just where I want them to be. More on this later (see *The Importance of Temperature* on page 18).

Water spray

GREAT for making steam in the oven with a quick spritz. Fill with tap water for CLEANING up the mess after you've baked (liberally spray the doughy table, let it soak, wipe it up) and essential for spritzing your table to create a non-stick surface for folding sourdough.

Cotton thread and metal ruler

It's very, very pleasing to slice your cinnamon buns with cotton thread for the perfect swirl. And fun. And I always have a metal ruler on hand when following recipes EXACTLY.

Scoopy spatula and wooden spoon, spoon measures, rolling pin

You'll likely have these things if you're baking or cooking at home already – very useful to have around!

PRO KIT

Venturing further, into the realms of stone baked breads and sourdough, these are the things you'll need to raise your game.

Grignette and spare blades

A tomato knife will do well for a pre-puff slash, but as you venture into stone baking territory, you'll be slashing your baguettes and other breads AFTER they have puffed. At this stage, your dough will be delicate and it's WAY too risky to slash with a knife – it will likely collapse at the final hurdle! A grignette is a handle that holds super-sharp razor blades. Use the blade straight or bent for a swift slash across the top of your puffy dough.

Baking stone

You can get baking stones made out of granite, cordierite, steel and probably many other materials, but the point is always the same … it's something HOT and HEAVY (to HOLD the heat) to bake on top of. Like in the bottom of a pizza oven. You can get round ones with fancy handles to get them out, but I like a rectangle stone the EXACT size of my oven shelf and it pretty much lives in there 24/7.

Banneton baskets

If you're on the quest for the perfect sourdough loaf, you'll need a proving basket. For straight yeasted doughs, you can get away with proving up a free-standing loaf on a tray, but sourdough is a much wetter dough and needs to prove for WAY longer before being slid onto a hot stone and baking bare to the wind! It NEEDS something to hold its shape as it rests up for the final time so it doesn't turn into a puddle. Enter a breathable banneton basket to offer support and create the all-important outside 'skin' for scoring.

Peels

Yes, you may already have guessed that I like peels – a piece of wood used to slide the naked bottom of bread dough directly onto a hot stone. A rimless upturned flat baking tray will do the trick if you have nothing better around! As you get into it, you may discover that it makes SO MUCH SENSE to have different peels for different things. A large one for round loaves and pizzas; long wide ones if you're baking two sourdough loaves side by side like me; and four baguette sized ones for … er … baguettes. Loading them into the oven one by one sure beats lining them all up on a MASSIVE peel, only to find that one sticks and you destroy the others in your attempts to release it!

THE PRINCIPLES OF BREAD

It's one thing to have and follow a collection of bread recipes, but when you have a true understanding of the principles that run through all yeasted baking, the world of homemade bread is blown wide open. **Principles are your POWER.** As you commence upon your learning journey, you'll begin to see and FEEL those principles in action. With them, failures of the past will be explained, future efforts will yield incredible triumphs – it's like peeping behind the curtain of a magic trick. Then you experience true freedom. Freedom to tweak recipes to your liking, making them work for you; to adjust timescales to your lifestyle; and the freedom to simply PLAY and create your very own amazing bread recipes, as nobody has ever thought or imagined them before.

   Don't skip this part. The following four principles are INTERLINKED. They all rely upon each other and when you've got all four working together, all four working in your favour, you've already won the game and your bread will be a great success every single time. They may not make sense right away, but I promise that every single time you make bread things will get a little clearer until one day everything just clicks! These principles will be part of you, they will become your instincts, and you won't even need to think about them any more, you'll just be cracking out triumphant breads with ease.

PRINCIPLE 1: PUFF!

This is the name of the game. We WANT our dough to PUFF UP or else our loaf will be a heavy, dense brick. Perhaps you have experienced that before … Call it puff, or rise, or prove, or proof, the point is that the YEAST plays its part in creating gas inside of the dough and it PUFFS UP. **A puffed-up dough BAKED is a light, fluffy bread.** Hundreds and thousands of teeny, tiny bubbles grow inside and the bigger the puff, the lighter the bread, but dough does have its limits. Dough starts firm and bouncy to the touch, and the more gas it takes on, the more delicate it will become until it becomes super-fragile, but it can't puff forever! At some point there will be too much gas for the dough to hold and it will start to deflate, the bubbles will start to burst and the dough will collapse. The idea is that we bake it when it is at MAXIMUM PUFF before it gets too far. A collapsed dough doesn't always spell disaster though. In the simplest of yeasted bread doughs it can simply be reshaped and left to puff once more or turned into something else, but I digress … yeast makes our dough PUFF and for our dough to be able to hold all that gas, we need principle number 2 …

PRINCIPLE 2: STRENGTH

Your dough needs to be STRONG so that when the yeast gets to work, the dough can hold all the gas it produces and PUFF UP. **Strength is key** because without it, your dough won't puff up properly, it will begin to puff, be too weak to hold the gas, crinkle and collapse WAY SOONER than you would have wanted.

   It takes one or BOTH of the following seemingly contradictory things to build STRENGTH in our dough: WORK and REST, otherwise known as KNEADING and DOING NOTHING for a bit. GLUTEN is responsible for the strength in our dough and that's as technical as we are going to get. **Gluten is the elastic bands inside the dough that knit the whole structure together.** They start off short and tight and become LONG and STRETCHY and STRONG, bringing our dough ELASTICITY, BOUNCE and SNAP BACK. Working your dough, that eight to ten minutes kneading in the beginning, develops the strength and elasticity, then when you are resting the dough, gluten develops even further just sitting in the moisture while you do NOTHING. In some of the recipes that follow, we do both, and in others, we extend the rest to develop the strength WITHOUT kneading, instead employing principle 3 to even greater effect …

PRINCIPLE 3: STRUCTURE

Strength and puff combined makes a great loaf – success – however, IDEALLY, we'd like our loaf to puff up NICELY in the right direction and where we INTENDED it to go, and we have to build structure to make that happen. **Structure is everything YOU DO inbetween kneading and baking**, I'm talking about balling the dough nicely before you put it in the bowl, pre-shaping, final shaping, all those deliberate folds and rolls responsible for building the TENSION correctly across the top of the dough so that your round loaf comes out like a round loaf, or your bloomer comes out like a bloomer, so that they rise up nice and tall and proud, instead of lopsided or a little skew-whiff. Structure is not spoken about enough in the world of bread-making and it is SO IMPORTANT. We can't just tear off a chunk of dough, roll it into a sausage and call it a baguette. We fold it, deliberately, arranging the dough with care and attention in the best way we know, so that it holds a nice shape when we come to bake it and the cuts on the top burst open beautifully, just as we intended. Building structure is something that WE do, this principle is OUR GLORY alone, but amazing bread is a result of COMBINED EFFORT between us and the dough, which brings us nicely to principle number 4 …

PRINCIPLE 4: TIME … THE LINK BETWEEN THEM ALL

Your dough NEEDS time to do what it needs to do. PUFF happens over TIME, it HAS to. Given time, the yeast goes to work making bubbles and the dough PUFFS UP. STRENGTH comes over TIME too: the gluten soaks in the moisture, making even more STRENGTH to be able to puff up properly and to allow us to build a better STRUCTURE. You SEE? Time is the link between them all and if that wasn't already enough, TIME also makes FLAVOUR. As your yeast is fermenting over time, it develops more flavour in the final bread, and this all happens while you are sitting on the couch doing NOTHING. That is the magic of it all! It's PATIENCE rewarded and patience on your part is NOT to be confused with WAITING. Waiting is BORING, nobody likes waiting. Take yourself away, have a cup of tea, mow the grass, pop back later … The TIME inbetween the 'doing' stages of your bread is a luxury, NOT a chore. Use it to your advantage and your bread will thank you for it.

Without TIME, your dough is nothing. Your bread is dense, tasteless, structureless and pointless and that's where modern bread falls a little short. Modern bread is sped up, removing some of the TIME from proceedings and replacing it with magical powders and hocus pocus and ALWAYS sacrificing flavour and texture.

Following these principles will make your homemade bread a roaring success to be shouted from the rooftops. You see, the true success of your bread is a combination of effort on your part and the natural process the dough needs to go through over time. It could be seen as the dough doing its thing, while we give it a helping hand along the way, nurturing it into the best it can be. You and your dough are in this together. You play your part and allow the dough some time to do its thing too, and when your joint efforts come together, THAT'S where amazing bread lies.

THE IMPORTANCE OF TEMPERATURE

Temperature is something that's often fluffed about in bread-making recipes. When referring to water temperature, you'll read words like 'tepid' or 'lukewarm' or 'body temperature' or 'blood heat', but WHAT DO THEY MEAN?

I don't know either, and that's exactly the point!

Without knowing, we make our best guess. Then wonder why things didn't play out exactly how we expected. And NO WONDER they didn't because:

Bread dough is *temperature sensitive*

Inside our bread dough, the baker's yeast (in the case of a yeasted dough) and natural yeasts (in the case of sourdough) are making the gas we need for our dough to rise. The warmer they are, the faster they produce gas and therefore the faster the rise, while the cooler they are, the slower it all happens.

All these recipes were written and tested in the kitchen in my home and again at the *Bake with Jack* studios. Here in Surrey, England, as a rule I always prove my bread out on the kitchen side at *room temperature*. Let me clarify …

Room temperature = the temperature of my room, on the day.

Generally, my room temperature lies somewhere around 21°C (70°F).

If your 'room temperature' falls a couple of degrees above or below what I would consider to be 'normal', your dough will happily rise, and you can follow my recipes expecting similar results to me. This doesn't mean that you *can't* make bread in your kitchen if it's not the same temperature as mine, it just means that timings might be a little different for you.

Don't feel like you need to play with your thermostat to make sure your room is the same temperature as mine. It's not important what the temperature is, after all, when you are

baking regularly, your room temperature will fluctuate throughout the year and you'll develop the ability to adapt. Your dough will rise in temperatures outside of my range, but I feel what is important is to KNOW what the temperature is, because then you'll know what to expect from your dough and you won't be left scratching your head if rising takes ages!

Consistency is KEY

Over the years, I've heard so many stories of epic bread fails. Things like doughs rising the first time and not the second time; thick, dry skins forming over doughs; loaves collapsing in the slightest of breezes; or bread that's puffy on the top and dense in the middle. A lot of the time the problem is not necessarily temperature, but INCONSISTENCY of temperature.

It's the CHANGE in temperature that CAUSES problems more often than the actual temperature itself.

Moving the dough from one place to another; attempting to speed up the puff by stashing the dough somewhere warm; starting with warm water – all these things cause the temperature to change. For beginners, I ALWAYS recommend doing everything at the temperature of your room. Room-temperature flour, room-temperature water – then the dough will stay a consistent temperature throughout the whole process. You may need to adjust timings if your kitchen is warmer or colder than mine, but it is certainly the most reliable way when you are starting out.

Having said all this, I DO appreciate there may be a few cases where you need to take matters into your own hands. If you are baking bread in extremes of temperatures, below 14°C (57°F), or above, say, 30°C (86°F), you can, of course, still bake amazing bread at home.

Here are a few suggestions to get that consistent temperature wherever you are:

Too hot?

If you live somewhere particularly hot, here are a few things you can do to help your dough and stop it from rising too fast!
1. Have a think, is there somewhere in your home you can leave your dough to prove that is cooler?
2. Perhaps you can adjust the amount of yeast in a recipe, taking some away. Less yeast will mean that your dough rises up slower.
3. Start with cool water or chilled water. Your dough will warm up over time, but at least it will have a cool start.

Too cold?

If your 'normal' temperature is a little on the chilly side, here are a few suggestions of what you can do.

1. Maybe there is somewhere in your home that is a little warmer, and at a consistent temperature, where your dough will quite happily tick along. Some people use the oven when it is off but the light is on. Pop a thermometer in there and find out if it would be suitable.
2. Start with liquid a little on the warm side. This is a bit risky as the dough will constantly be trying to dry out on the surface. You'll need to cover your dough with cling film or an upturned bowl to prevent this from happening.
3. Try a gadget. Proving boxes are available that create a consistent temperature and humid environment for your dough to prove in.

BASIC TECHNIQUES & SPECIAL MOVES

Bread recipes have the potential to be LONG. If I put every tiny detail into each recipe, they would be SO LONG that it would only take a quick look at one to put the average person off bread-making FOR EVER. For that reason, I'd like to outline the basic universal bread techniques here in this section for you to refer to each time to MAXIMISE your chances of success. If at any point you're not sure what to do, you should find the answer here.

KNEADING

Kneading your dough starts the all-important process of developing its strength (see bread principle 2, page 16) and I ALWAYS do it by hand because that way you really get a feel for what is happening in your dough. Turn out your dough onto the table with ZERO flour. With the heel of your hand, push the furthest part of your dough up ALONG the kitchen work surface as opposed to down *into* it, lift it, pull it back towards you over the top and repeat. If it sticks (which it probably will), continue on and use your dough scraper every once in a while to release the dough from the surface. The more

you work it, the less sticky it will become, so employ some patience here and it will come together nicely. In my recipes, I knead for eight minutes normally, or ten minutes for enriched doughs. You'll get a little messy, so expect that. Best practice is to knead with one hand and have a dough scraper in the other for releasing/unsticking/cleaning up every once in a while.

Try not to stress about what your dough 'looks like' along the way or even at the end. Just relax into it and go with it. In class, we all knead for the same time and everything comes out just nice. If you have ANY worries by the end of kneading as to whether you think it is 'done' or not, it won't hurt to squash your worries with a couple of extra minutes' work. Just don't keep on going for an hour, there's really no knead (Ha Ha!).

You can, of course, knead dough in a mixer with a dough hook, but there is no 'one size fits all' piece of advice I can give here, other than to spend some time with your mixer. They are ALL different and may require your dough to be a specific consistency for it to be worked sufficiently. Check with the makers on their best advice and adjust moisture levels in recipes if you need to.

When is my bread dough fully kneaded?

BEFORE YOU KNEAD your dough, just after you've mixed it, take a good look at it. You'll see it's kind of lumpy, it's wet in places and dry in others, and it breaks into pieces REALLY EASILY. AFTER you've finished kneading, ball it up and take a look for the FIVE signs that it is ready:

1. It will no longer stick to everything in sight like it did in the beginning.

2. Although it may not be completely smooth on top, it has a smoothness to it that was not present earlier.

3. It is much stronger and won't break easily when stretched like it once did. When pressed with your fingers it is more responsive now, more elastic and bouncy, trying its best to return back into the ball shape after you've let go.

4. If you cut a wedge out of the ball of dough with your dough scraper, it stays as a definite wedge shape with an evident clean cut.

5. The WINDOW PANE TEST is a thing you may have seen. The idea is that your dough should be so strong that it is able to be stretched super-thin before it breaks, so thin in fact that you can see light through it when held up to a window. Dust a decent-sized chunk of dough and hold it up. Tease it out, stretching it under its own weight, until it is so thin you can see the light BEFORE it breaks.

DISCLAIMER ALERT

I NEVER spend any time wondering whether or not my dough is 'ready'. I knead for the required time and call it a day, knowing I've put in the work and everything will be fine. However, these five signs are interesting to try to help you understand what is happening and build your instincts as to when things are ready. Also, they are REALLY EVIDENT in a recipe using only white flour. The more brown or rye or other ingredients, the trickier it is to see, so do take these signs with a pinch of salt.

RESTING

When your dough rests, three things happen: it PUFFS UP, amazing FLAVOUR develops AND the gluten, which is the STRENGTH, continues to develop further, even after kneading. All these things happen all by themselves while you do NOTHING. Isn't that cool?

The most IMPORTANT thing to note when resting your dough is that draughts are your enemy. Movement of air from a window or a heat source will dry out your dough. There's no real need to find somewhere warm to put it either and I've heard them all … placing your dough on top of a boiler, near the Aga (or INSIDE!), on a stepping stool next to a

radiator or in the classic airing cupboard will likely create problems and cause it to rise inconsistently inside. I leave mine on the kitchen work surface ALWAYS. In a draught-free place it is enough to simply dust with flour and cover with a clean, dry cloth. In the case of the enriched doughs, I normally cover these with another upturned bowl or cling film as they are more at risk of drying out on the top on their final rest.

DIVIDING

When you need to cut the dough into pieces, turn it out onto a lightly dusted kitchen work surface, sticky side up. Use the flat side of your dough scraper and push straight down into the dough all the way to the work surface. Don't saw it like a knife, just push down and use your other hand to peel the dough apart so that it doesn't re-stick together when you lift the scraper ready for the next cut.

--------- TIP ---------

KNEAD WITH ZERO FLOUR

As tricky as it may be, do not dust with additional flour while you are kneading the dough. Added flour will be absorbed and the dough will then become sticky again. Repeated dusting will add additional flour to the dough, making it dry and tightening it up, leading you to believe it is fully worked when it really isn't. The resulting underworked, dry, tight dough won't puff up properly and that's how you bake a brick! Use all your powers of patience to resist dusting until the very end.

THE FUNDAMENTALS OF SHAPING

**Your dough has a sticky side
and a non-stick side**
And it will stay that way all the time until
your dough hits the oven. We deliberately
create a non-stick side with the use of flour
and turn dough out of the bowl upside down.
With the non-stick side touching the work
surface, it will NEVER stick and the sticky
side is where all the folds, joins and seams
go, so they STICK TO THEMSELVES, right?
The non-stick side becomes your nice smooth
'top' and all joins and seams are tucked away
UNDERNEATH and out of sight.

Always build tension across the top
Every time you fold, roll and shape your dough,
you are building structure and creating tension
across the TOP of the dough. That's what holds
a great shape and helps your dough prove up
tall and proud as you intended it to. It takes
practise and a real feel for the dough, but
over time you'll crack it!

Use MINIMUM flour, one side only
We don't want our dough to STICK to the work
surface, right? But we also don't want it to slip
and slide all over the place. For most shaping,
we need GRIP, halfway between stick and slide.
Flick a fine film of flour ACROSS the table,
just enough flour to stop things from sticking.
If they still do, employ the TACTICAL DUST
technique, sprinkling flour round the edges
and shimmying it underneath with your
dough scraper.

Work with nimble fingers
A light but firm touch is required for shaping.
We don't want to stretch the dough beyond
its means. Your dough has a natural resistance
point and it's our job to recognise that and not
pull it too far, ripping and tearing it. Be nimble
fingered, whipping away your fingers from
the sticky side so that you don't get stuck
there for good.

Pre-shape vs final shape
Sometimes (most of the time) you'll see
a pre-shape stage, which is the shape BEFORE
the final shape. This is often balling up the
dough to create an additional layer of structure
and uniformity before the final shape. It's WAY
easier to shape a nice bloomer from a ball, for
example, than from some randomly cut shape.
That's how the pros do it in a bakery, lining
them all up nicely, allowing some time to relax,
and THEN commencing the all-important final
shape, getting it spot on and giving it the best
chance of puffing up well.

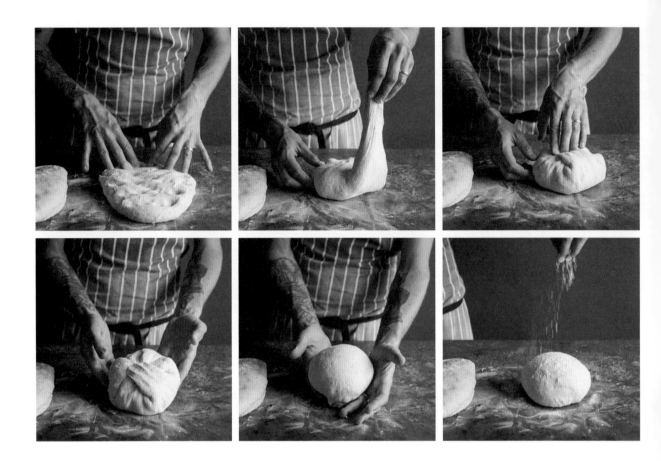

BALLING

You'll notice certain shapes come up again and again in this book. Even with those shapes that are unique to a specific recipe, like baguettes, bloomers and batards (my FAVOURITE), the principle of shaping holds true. The most universal shape is the ball, so let's take a look at the process of creating it to best illustrate the principles above.

Large balls

For creating a large ball, place the dough down onto the flour, non-stick side underneath, sticky side up. Pinch a piece of dough from the edge, lift it and fold it over the top, sticking it down just past the centre point of the dough. Work your way around the dough, folding in all sides until you have a nice ball with all the joins and seams in one place. Roll the dough over, revealing your new, nice smooth, non-stick dome 'top'. With your palms facing up at either side of the dough, commence the classic 'cup and turn' manoeuvre. Tuck them underneath, squeeze the bottom and turn the ball to tighten it up nicely.

Small loose balls

The process for this is exactly the same as the first part of creating a large ball, only this time we do it on a teeny, tiny scale. Pull out an edge piece and fold it over the top, working your way around sticking them all down, then roll over to reveal the smooth side. The more folds you do, the tighter the ball will become. Five or six folds will likely be enough when you are asked to make loose balls.

Small tight balls

For this we take the loose ball a little further, perhaps ten to twelve folds. Then turning it over, smooth side up, seam underneath, we place a clawed hand over the top. With the side of our palm and pinky in contact with the work surface at all times, move your hand in large circles and with pressure on the top and sides of the dough, combined with grip on the work surface, you should feel the dough tightening in your hand. Go clockwise if you are left-handed or anticlockwise with your right hand. Stop when your ball is tight and bouncy.

BAKING

Baking with steam

Baking bread with steam works for bread on SO MANY LEVELS. It's the condensation on the outside of your bread dough combined with high heat that makes crusty bread crusty, while it's the humid environment combined with a low heat that keeps soft bread soft. Steam keeps the outside of the bread softer for longer, allowing it to rise to its full potential before the crust sets the shape and stalls the puff and, as if by magic, brings amazing, vibrant golden colour to your final bread.

Steam is a game changer and here is the best way I find to get it into your oven at home.

Preheat your oven with a deep roasting tray on the bottom shelf or even the oven floor. When you are ready to load the bread, boil half a kettle of water. Load the bread into the oven, very, very carefully pour the hot water from the kettle into the tray beneath, then shut the oven door, keeping the initial burst of steam in the oven as much as possible.

All home ovens are different. You might find that yours is really good at ejecting steam from the oven, which is not great for your bread. If you struggle to get the steam to stay inside and you have the space for it, try doubling up your trays for MAXIMUM steam production.

Getting to know your oven

The idea with bread, certainly for the savoury recipes, is to bake it at as high a heat as possible so long as nothing burns. That's how you get a great crust and good oven spring (that initial JUMP and increase in volume as the dough goes in). And that's ANOTHER reason why steam is useful – it's like a burn buffer. Professional bakers bake at temperatures our ovens at home don't even reach, and they can get away with it because the inside space is small, like a letterbox, and they are injecting in LOADS of steam. And if that wasn't enough,

they are also loading TONS of bread in one go, thereby creating their own steam ON TOP, and NOTHING BURNS. However, in our home ovens things are a little different. The recipes here were all baked in my fan oven, which is great at keeping steam in, but as I say, ALL ovens are different and I've baked in HUNDREDS of professional and home ovens over the years. The point I am trying to make here is this: don't take the baking instructions here as gospel. Don't load up the oven and set a timer for 40 minutes and walk away. Keep an eye on things along the way. If things are colouring up a little early on, you may need to turn the oven down a touch and continue to bake on a lower heat to ensure your bread is baked all the way through. The more you do, the more you'll learn the nuances of your own home oven and the less you'll need to worry about later down the line.

When is my bread ready to bake?

I WISH I could give you a straight answer for this one but, alas, things aren't as clean cut as that with bread.

Over-proofed and under-proofed are terms created by TV judge hosts to instil fear into ANYBODY who dares make a loaf. BUT the reality is that if your dough has puffed up and you bake it, it'll be tasty and a success. What you DON'T want to do is puff up your loaf SO MUCH that the structure breaks down and the whole thing collapses. And so, the answer to this question is: follow your instincts!

'Ahh… but I don't have any instincts yet!' I hear you say, 'I am a beginner, I have nothing to go by'. Yes, you are quite right, and this is WHY I keep going on about the importance of time. Trying and trying again – practise is experience.

Here are a few things you can do to build your instincts:

* Shape your loaf and touch it with your finger: it'll be firm and bouncy. Now, let it rest and puff perhaps halfway, then touch it again. See how it's becoming lighter, possibly more responsive to the touch, more bounce back, more resistance to your finger? Keep going the rest of the way. The further you go, the softer it'll become, so keep popping back and really pay attention to the change. If at any point it begins to get delicate, as though it is so fragile that if you were to touch it with any force it may well collapse, then get it into the oven. GENTLY.

* If you are making rolls, spread them across two or three trays. Then, when you think they are ready, bake one tray. Leave the rest and bake them later down the line at intervals, making a note of your timings. Touch them as you go along and get a feel for the change here, then after they are baked, try them all and see which one you like the best!

* Getting a real 'feel' for your dough is really tricky/impossible to explain in words. By far the best way to get experience is to GET EXPERIENCE. Try things, observe what you are doing and how the dough responds and build up your instincts.

How can I tell if my bread is FULLY BAKED?

Tap, tap, tap.

You'll have heard a lot about that elusive 'hollow' sound that lets us know when a bread is fully baked. Tapping a loaf on its bottom will reveal a 'drum-like' resonance when held to the ear that says 'I'm READY' and it is MOST obvious in a large loaf of all-white flour. If this is something you'd like experience of, bake the Simple Sandwich Loaf (see page 33) for 30 minutes, then pop it out of the tin, tap the base and listen. At this point, it'll sound like a kind of dull thud. Finish off the baking and try it again and you should appreciate the difference between the sound of underbaked bread and the hollowness everyone refers to.

In this scenario, the hollow sound can help us, but when you are filling breads with cheese, fruit, nuts, whatever you like, things get a little trickier and the sound becomes dampened by everything else going on inside. Where necessary, you'll find notes on 'doneness' throughout the recipes that follow.

… And there you have it. From here on in it's time to roll up your sleeves and GET CRACKING. Have fun!

CHAPTER ONE

SIMPLE
LOAVES
& ROLLS

LET THIS BE THE BEGINNING OF YOUR JOURNEY...

In this chapter, I'd like to introduce you to the very basics of bread-making. Here you'll find your weekly standards: loaves for sandwiches and toast and rolls for filling. Everything is made from our four foundation ingredients: flour, water, salt and yeast, in varying quantities and, with the exception of the Soft Flour Tacos (see page 77) since they are the only ones without yeast, they all follow a very similar formula:

Knead the dough > rest it > shape it > rest it > bake it.

Here you'll begin to get a feel for things – that all-important development of strength and structure. Practise your shaping with the Simple Sandwich Loaf (see page 33). Since it is enclosed in a tin, you really can't go too far wrong. Then have a play with shapes with the Seeded White Rolls & Knots (see page 47).

We'll then begin to introduce a little wholemeal flour here and there and break the rules of bread-making entirely by making a slow-moving (minimum yeast) dry dough for the Bagels (see page 65), which are always fun to boil before baking and so satisfying to make at home.

There is so much to learn with these breads. To go alongside them, I've created plenty of quick-and-easy breakfast and lunch dishes to keep things fresh, as well as some main meals, making sure every single crumb is made use of by adding breadcrumbs to the Meatballs (see page 41) and turning soft tacos into the crispiest tortilla chips for a Beef Shin Chilli Nacho sharer (see page 82).

And when you're done making the bread, have a crack at making your own butter. It's such a cool process to see for real and as close to magic as you can get. It takes only a couple of minutes to do it and serving homemade bread with homemade butter is the best.

Remember to refer back to the introduction for everything you'll need to know about kneading and those other bread-making principles – it's time to see them in action.

Have fun!

SIMPLE SANDWICH LOAF

MAKES 2 LARGE LOAVES

When starting out on your bread-making journey, it's really important to choose something simple and functional to bake first – something you'll want to bake again and again and, more importantly, eat time after time. As the dough here is baked in a loaf tin with nowhere to go but UP, you're pretty much guaranteed a good-looking loaf even if you fluff the shaping slightly.

Consider this your go-to fresh bread recipe, but it comes with a word of warning: once you crack your first loaf, pull it out of the oven with so much pride and eat it for the very first time, there is no going back to shop-bought bread.

This bread will be at its best on the day of baking once it has cooled completely. Expect two to three days of sandwich bread out of it and from then on it will make the best toast of your life.

=== EASY TO MAKE, EASY TO BAKE / TOTAL TIME: 3½–4¾ HOURS ===

You'll need: 2 x 900g (2lb) loaf tins (see my tip on page 35) – mine measure 10 x 16.5cm (4 x 6½in) base, 13 x 20cm (5 x 8in) top, 9cm (3½in) deep

640g (1lb 7oz) room-temperature water
24g (1oz) fresh yeast, crumbled, or 14g (½oz) fast-action dried yeast
900g (2lb) strong white bread flour, plus extra for dusting

100g (3½oz) strong wholemeal bread flour
16g (½oz) salt
30g (1oz) olive oil
butter or extra olive oil, for greasing

Making the dough: 15–20 minutes
1. In a large mixing bowl, mix together the water and yeast until the yeast has dissolved.
2. Add the flours and salt, then mix with a dough scraper until the mixture starts to come together. Add the olive oil and mix again into a rough dough.
3. Turn your dough out onto a clean work surface and knead without any additional flour for 8 minutes.

Resting: 1–1½ hours
4. Shape the dough into a ball and place it back in the bowl. Sprinkle the top with a little flour, cover with a clean cloth and rest at room temperature for 1–1½ hours.

Dividing and pre-shaping: 5 minutes
5. Dust the top of the dough lightly with flour and use your dough scraper to turn it out upside down onto the work surface, sticky side up.

6. Use your fingertips to flatten the dough gently and cut in half with your dough scraper. Fold and roll each piece of dough into a ball, then cup slightly to tighten (see page 24).

Resting: 15 minutes
7. Line up your dough balls on the work surface. Dust only the tops lightly with flour, cover with the cloth and rest for 15 minutes to relax and spread slightly.

Final shaping: 5–10 minutes
8. Dust the work surface lightly with flour. Working with one at a time, slide your dough scraper underneath a dough ball to release it and flip sticky side up onto the dusted surface.
9. Press with your fingertips and knuckles to flatten and spread the dough into a circle. Slide your fingers, palms up, underneath each side of the circle. Grip the dough and pull to stretch it sideways. At an angle, fold one side two-thirds of the way over the dough

Recipe continued overleaf

and fold the other side in the same way so that it overlaps the first fold and you have a kind of 'A' shape. Roll up the dough from the point towards you into a tight sausage and press the seam to stick it together, then turn the dough over, seam side down.

10. Using a serrated knife, make 5 or 6 diagonal cuts across each loaf about 5mm (¼in) deep.

11. Grease your loaf tins lightly with butter or oil and drop a loaf into each, seam side down.

Resting: 1–1½ hours

12. Cover your loaves with the cloth and rest for 1–1½ hours.

13. Towards the end of resting, preheat your oven to 200°C fan/425°F/Gas Mark 7 with a shelf in the middle and a deep roasting tray on the oven floor. Half fill a kettle.

Baking: 40–50 minutes

14. Boil the kettle.

15. Place your loaf tins on the oven shelf and carefully pour the hot water into the tray below. Bake your loaves for 40 minutes. I bake mine without checking because I know my oven really well, but if this is your first loaf, set a timer for 30 minutes and take a peek. If the loaves are taking on too much colour, turn the oven down to 180°C fan/400°F/Gas Mark 6 for the final 10 minutes.

16. Pop the loaves out of their tins, and if the undersides feel soft and steamy, sit them right way up directly on the oven shelf and bake for another 5–10 minutes.

17. Let them cool completely on a wire rack.

TIPS

TURNING-OUT TROUBLESHOOTING

If your loaf is stuck in its tin, the first thing is NOT to panic and the second is NOT to slide a knife down the edge and try to wrench it out because that will surely destroy it. If you greased your tin, your loaf will release itself when it's ready. However, if the heat in your oven is uneven (often hotter at the top than the bottom), the top may look ready but the bottom will still be moist and doughy, and therefore clinging to your tin. Flip your loaf upside down in its tin and bake it for another 10 minutes or so, which will toast up the base and allow it, with a swift tap on all sides on the work surface, to pop out easily. It may be a little crispier than normal, but rather that than ruined!

THE LOAF TIN OF CHOICE

Not ALL 900g (2lb) loaf tins were created equal – they may all hold that weight of dough but some are long, some are wide and shallow and some are deep like mine. I like my loaf to rise up tall and proud, which is why I opt for a traditional old-school folded loaf tin. But consider the slice size you are after – I often use a LONGER, narrower two-pounder that is perfect for making small sandwiches for the kiddies.

PARMESAN POACHED EGGS WITH ROSEMARY CROUTON SOLDIERS

SERVES 1

Boiled eggs have their place, I understand that. But for dipping? It seems like a bit of a gamble to me. POACHED eggs, on the other hand, may initially seem tricky, but at least you can SEE what's going on while they're cooking, making them so much more reliable for creating the PERFECT dippy eggs.

These are buttered, generously topped with shaved Parmesan and served with the crispiest crouton soldiers made from your stale white loaf leftovers.

2 thick slices of stale
   Simple Sandwich Loaf
   (see page 33)
40g (1½oz) unsalted butter,
   plus extra to serve
1 fresh rosemary sprig
2 super-fresh medium eggs
   (see method)
Parmesan cheese, for grating
sea salt flakes and cracked
   black pepper

Making the croutons

1. Preheat your oven to 180°C fan/400°F/Gas Mark 6. Line a baking tray with baking parchment.

2. Slice your bread into soldiers 1.5–2cm (½–¾in) thick and line them up neatly on your lined tray.

3. Melt the butter in a small pan and add the leaves picked from the rosemary sprig.

4. Pour the butter over the soldiers and toss them to coat nicely. Spread them back out on the tray with plenty of room in between and season with sea salt flakes.

5. Bake for 15–20 minutes until golden and crisp. Set aside.

Poaching the eggs

6. Bring a small saucepan of water to the boil.

7. Crack each egg into a small ramekin or bowl. Poached eggs are best made with super-fresh eggs because that's when the egg white is more 'together'. But if you notice a large amount of runny white around the edge, drain off the excess really carefully into a colander to avoid making a mess of your water later on.

8. Remove the pan from the heat, carefully slide your eggs into the water and return the pan to a VERY LOW heat, just enough to bring the water back to boiling point but not erupt like a hot tub, tossing your eggs all over the place. My eggs took 2½ minutes to be perfectly runny inside, but keep your eyes peeled so yours don't overcook.

9. Remove the eggs, one by one, from the water with a slotted spoon and rest the spoon on folded kitchen paper to drain off the excess water before transferring the eggs to a small bowl.

Putting it all together

10. Top your poached eggs with a thin slice of butter and let it melt. Finely grate over a generous amount of Parmesan, add a pinch of cracked black pepper and serve alongside your croutons for dipping.

THINGS ON TOAST...

SERVES 1

We can ALL put jam on toast, or butter, or butter AND jam (steady on!) but if we put a little thought into it, we can make something pretty special-tasting (and LOOKING) by just matching a few carefully considered ingredients, transforming a once quite-standard weekly loaf into an exceptional lunch/breakfast/brunch in as little as a few minutes!

Here are a few tasty ideas that I like to take your toast to the NEXT LEVEL.

DRESSED COURGETTE & BOCCONCINI

1 slice of Simple Sandwich Loaf (see page 33)
olive oil
½ courgette (zucchini)
4–5 bocconcini (mozzarella balls)
1 teaspoon lemon juice
pinch of dried chilli (hot pepper) flakes
3–4 sun-blushed tomatoes
sea salt and cracked black pepper

1. Chargrill your bread in a hot griddle pan. Drizzle with olive oil and season with sea salt.
2. Use a peeler to peel the courgette into ribbons and place them in a large mixing bowl. Tear the bocconcini in half and add them too. Dress with 1 teaspoon of olive oil, lemon juice and a pinch of salt and some pepper, tossing everything together really well.
3. Pile up on top of your toast and finish with a pinch of dried chilli flakes. Serve with sun-blushed tomatoes.

CINNAMON TOAST WITH BERRY YOGHURT & CRUNCHY PEANUT BUTTER

1 slice of Simple Sandwich Loaf (see page 33)
1 generous tablespoon (30g/1oz) Cinnamon
   Sugar Butter (see page 60)
50g (1¾oz) fresh raspberries
50g (1¾oz) fresh blackberries
3 tablespoons thick set yoghurt
1 tablespoon crunchy peanut butter

1. Toast one side of your bread underneath the grill (broiler). Flip it over and butter the soft side with your cinnamon butter. Toast this side until bubbling and crispy.
2. Mash your berries together in a mixing bowl with the back of a fork. Add your yoghurt and fold it through.
3. Serve your toast with the berry yoghurt and topped with the peanut butter. Yesssssssssss.

SMASHED PARSLEY PEAS, CHORIZO & SOFT-BOILED EGG

1 slice of Simple Sandwich Loaf (see page 33)
1 medium egg
60g (2¼oz) frozen peas or petits pois,
    if you're fancy like me
½ teaspoon lemon juice
½ teaspoon olive oil
½ tablespoon chopped fresh flat-leaf (Italian)
    parsley leaves and stalks
butter (optional)
4 slices of chorizo
sea salt and cracked black pepper

1. Toast your bread. Carefully lower your egg into a small pan of boiling water to cook for 5 minutes.
2. Put your peas into a jug and pour over enough boiling water from the kettle to cover. Let them sit for 20 seconds, then drain, returning the peas to the jug.
3. Add a pinch of salt, the lemon juice, olive oil and parsley. Mix together and smash and squash with the back of your spoon.
4. Butter your toast if you wish and pile your peas on top. Tuck your thin chorizo slices in and around the peas. Lift your egg from the water and rinse in cold water to make it cool enough to handle. Peel the shell, cut the egg in half and place it on top of the peas. Finish with a pinch of cracked black pepper.

Pictured on page 38

BRESAOLA, PECORNIO, ROCKET & BALSAMIC

1 slice of Simple Sandwich Loaf (see page 33)
olive oil
½ garlic clove
a handful of rocket (arugula)
1 teaspoon balsamic vinegar
3–4 slices of bresaola
pecorino cheese shavings
1 walnut, finely grated
sea salt and cracked black pepper

1. Toast your bread or chargrill it in a griddle pan till scorched. Drizzle with olive oil, season with salt and rub it with the cut side of your garlic, bruschetta-style.
2. Place your rocket leaves in a mixing bowl, season with salt and add the balsamic vinegar and 1 teaspoon of olive oil. Toss together.
3. Top your toast with the dressed rocket, tucking the bresaola slices in and around. Finish with some hefty pecorino shavings, grated walnut and a little extra drizzle of olive oil.

Pictured on page 38

STALE BREAD MEATBALLS
WITH PAPPARDELLE

SERVES 4

You may feel a little weird about this concept – I sure did at first – but soaking stale bread in water, squeezing it out and making meatballs with it is wicked delicious, and it certainly beats blitzing rock-hard bread ends in a food processor! The bread really helps to BIND your meatballs together, meaning when they cook they keep the moisture (and flavour!) INSIDE, instead of the juiciness leaking out and turning the meatballs into dry rubber bullets.

It's an easy way to use up leftover bread, it's a smart way of bulking up the meat content and therefore using (and spending) less and it's a bowl of top-notch meatballs, so it's a proper win-win situation.

I'm using a classic tomato sauce here (the chilli is optional) and my pasta of choice is pappardelle because … why not?

For the meatballs
150g (5½oz) stale bread, crusts and all
500g (1lb 2oz) minced pork (10% fat)
30g (1oz) Parmesan cheese, finely grated, plus extra to serve
1½ tablespoons chopped fresh thyme leaves
½ garlic clove, finely grated

For the sauce
2 garlic cloves, sliced
½ red bird's eye chilli, sliced (optional)
3 tablespoons olive oil, plus extra for drizzling
2 x 400g (14oz) tins of good-quality chopped tomatoes
pinch of sugar, if needed

To finish
300g (10½ oz) dried pappardelle pasta
4 tablespoons crème fraîche or sour cream

salt and cracked black pepper

Soaking the bread

1. Tear or chop your stale bread into chunks and place it in a large mixing bowl. Cover with cold water and soak until soft.

Making the sauce

2. Put the sliced garlic and optional chilli into a medium-sized saucepan and add the olive oil. Place over a medium heat, bring up to a healthy sizzle and cook out the rawness of the garlic for a couple of minutes or so.

3. Add the tomatoes. Fill one empty can nearly to the top with water, rinse it out into the second can and tip the water into the pan, leaving both cans nice and clean.

4. Bring to the boil, then simmer for a good hour. The added water should buy you enough time to cook the tomatoes nicely without the sauce thickening too much, but keep your eye on it and top it up as needed.

5. After an hour the sauce should have changed from a pinky red to a deep orange-red. Remove from the heat, taste it and season with salt. Some tomatoes are more acidic than others, so you may find that they benefit from a pinch of sugar, just to take the edge off. Taste, adjust, taste again and adjust until you are happy. Set aside.

Making the meatballs

6. Drain the bread in a colander set over the sink and put the bowl back underneath to catch the drips as you transfer it to the work surface. Pick up a handful of wet bread at a time and squeeze it

Recipe continued overleaf

really hard to extract as much moisture as possible, then pop it into a clean large mixing bowl as you go.

7. To the soaked bread add the pork, Parmesan, thyme and garlic, and season generously with salt. Mix everything together really well with your hands or a wooden spoon.

8. Before you roll ALL your meatballs, it's a good idea to have a taste and make sure everything is fine before you're past the point of no return. So, get a small frying pan (skillet) over a medium heat, shape a small piece of the meat mixture into a flat patty and cook on both sides, then taste. Adjust the seasoning of the uncooked batch if you need to.

9. With your hands moistened with water to prevent sticking, roll the meat mixture into balls slightly smaller than a ping-pong ball, arranging them as you go, nice and snug in a large cold frying pan – mine is 26cm (10½in) wide into which they all fit perfectly.

10. Place the frying pan over a medium heat and bring up to a gentle sizzle. Your meatballs are at their most delicate now, so let them cook for a couple of minutes until golden and sealed on the underside. Then go round with a spoon and turn them all over. The idea here is to brown all sides and they will take around 18–20 minutes to cook through and get a good crust on the outside. Keep turning, and as they cook they will shrink slightly and become firmer, allowing you to toss them without fear of breaking them.

Cooking the pasta

11. Bring a large pan of water to the boil and season really well with salt – make it taste like the sea.

12. Add the pasta and cook for a little less than the packet instructions recommend, just to be sure it doesn't overcook. Check a ribbon for doneness and continue to cook to your liking, then drain in a colander.

Putting it all together

13. Reheat the sauce and pour it into a large bowl, followed by the pasta. Toss it all together and add the meatballs.

14. Give it one final toss to coat everything in the sauce, then use a pair of tongs to divide the pasta between 4 warm bowls. Top with the meatballs, which should have remained at the bottom of the bowl. Spoon over the remaining sauce.

15. Top each bowl with a tablespoon of crème fraîche or sour cream, a blanket of finely grated Parmesan, a drizzle of olive oil and a pinch of cracked black pepper.

BREAD-AND-BUTTER PUDDING

SERVES 6

There is a richly historical, widely quoted saying here, passed down through generations, and it goes like this … 'If it ain't broke, don't fix it'.

I ummed and ahhed over a bread-and-butter pudding for AGES. Should I put some clever spin on things? Make it chocolate or add some 'wacky' fruit, and then I thought, no. Bread-and-butter pudding is a triumph in itself and the success of it comes down to a few things combined.

It needs to be a sweet, custardy, set-in-the-middle pudding, crispy and crunchy on the top and BUTTERY, with plenty of nutmeg and sultanas. The only thing I have done here is made it a touch more practical for us because, and this may surprise some of you about me, I have absolutely ZERO interest in buttering both sides of sliced white bread triangles. Instead, I've taken a more faff-free, rustic approach, ripping the bread into chunks, which actually rather helpfully brings a rocky, rubbly texture to the top for even more crunch.

In theory, you can use any bread for this, but I've used the Simple Sandwich Loaf (see page 33). The Chocolate Brioche (see page 200) would work really well too. Serve with fresh double cream or CLOTTED cream.

580ml (about 1 pint)
   whole milk
3 medium eggs
   (about 150g/5½oz)
½ teaspoon vanilla
   bean paste
80g (2¾oz) golden caster
   (superfine) sugar
480g (1lb 1oz) stale bread,
   crusts and all
100g (3½oz) butter
½ orange
½ nutmeg
40g (1½oz) sultanas
   (golden raisins)
40g (1½oz) demerara sugar
double (heavy) cream or
   clotted cream, to serve

1. In a large mixing bowl, whisk together the milk, eggs, vanilla and golden caster sugar, then set aside.
2. Rip up your bread into 3cm (1in) chunks and place in a large mixing bowl. Melt the butter and pour it over the bread chunks, tossing to coat every piece.
3. Finely grate over the orange zest and nutmeg and toss together again. Place an even layer in the bottom of a round 21cm (8¼in) baking dish – half of the bread should be enough for this first layer. Sprinkle over two-thirds of the sultanas, being careful not to have them bunch up together in the gaps between the bread. Cover with the rest of the bread and then the remaining sultanas.
4. Carefully pour the egg and milk mixture over the bread, pressing down with your fingers to do your best to submerge the top pieces, then leave to soak for 30 minutes. Preheat the oven to 180°C fan/ 400°F/Gas Mark 6.
5. Before baking, sprinkle liberally with the demerara sugar, place into the oven on the middle shelf and bake for 50–60 minutes until nicely set and golden and crispy on top. Peep into the middle using a knife to make sure it is set and there is no runny milk there and it's done.
6. Let it sit for 10 minutes or so before cutting and serving with cream or clotted cream.

SEEDED WHITE ROLLS & KNOTS

MAKES 8 LARGE OR 12 SMALL ROLLS

Once you have nailed the making of your dough, you can start experimenting with shaping it. This is a great way to get some practise using simple rounds and knots to create rolls that look pretty special. But just because these are the shapes I've made, don't feel you have to follow them EXACTLY. Use your knowledge of balls and ropes to create your own signature rolls. You could even shape these into a four strand plait from page 237 like I have in the photo.

The larger-size rolls are perfect for filling or make smaller rolls to serve with soup.

═══ EASY TO MAKE, EASY TO BAKE / TOTAL TIME: 2½–3¾ HOURS ═══

310g (11oz) room-temperature water 12g (½oz) fresh yeast, crumbled, or 7g (¼oz) fast-action dried yeast	500g (1lb 2oz) strong white bread flour, plus extra for dusting 8g (¼oz) salt 15g (½oz) olive oil	seeds of your choice for topping, such as poppy, sesame, linseed (flaxseed), sunflower or pumpkin

Making the dough: 15–20 minutes

1. In a large mixing bowl, mix together the water and yeast until the yeast has dissolved.

2. Add the flour and salt, then mix with a dough scraper until the mixture starts to come together. Add the olive oil and mix again into a rough dough.

3. Turn your dough out onto a clean work surface and knead without any additional flour for 8 minutes.

Resting: 1–1½ hours

4. Shape the dough into a ball and place it back in the bowl. Sprinkle the top with a little flour, cover with a clean cloth and rest at room temperature for 1–1½ hours.

Dividing and shaping: 10–20 minutes

5. Line a baking tray with baking parchment.

6. Dust the top of the dough lightly with flour and use your dough scraper to turn it out upside down onto the work surface, sticky side up.

7. Press with your fingertips and knuckles to flatten the dough slightly and cut into 8 or 12 equal-sized pieces with your dough scraper. If you want them all to be exactly

the same size, weigh the dough as a whole, divide by 8 or 12 and then weigh out each piece accordingly.

ROUND

8. Working with one at a time, turn a piece of dough sticky side up and flatten it slightly. Fold and roll it into a tight ball (see page 24). Place on the lined tray.

KNOT

9. Turn a piece of dough sticky side up and flatten it slightly. Roll it up into a sausage and press the seam to stick it together. Roll the sausage with your palms on the work surface until it is about 25cm (10in) long, then apply a little extra pressure on the ends to make them pointy. Tie the sausage into a knot and tuck the ends in. Place on the lined tray.

Topping: 5 minutes

10. Spray or brush the top of each roll with water and dip them into your chosen seeds in a bowl, or sprinkle them on top for a less dense coverage. Arrange them on the lined tray with plenty of space in between so that they can puff up nicely. If they are still a little wet on

Recipe continued overleaf

top, let them dry for a few minutes, or dust with a little flour.

Resting: 45 minutes – 1 hour
11. Cover your rolls with the cloth and rest for 45 minutes–1 hour.
12. Towards the end of resting, preheat your oven to 200°C fan/425°F/Gas Mark 7 with a shelf in the middle and a deep roasting tray on the oven floor. Half fill a kettle.

Baking: 15–25 minutes
13. Boil the kettle.
14. Place your baking tray on the oven shelf and carefully pour the hot water into the tray below. Bake your rolls for 15–25 minutes, depending on their size, until golden.
15. Let them cool completely on a wire rack.

—— TIP ——
PART-BAKING TO FREEZE

Because these rolls are small, you can part-bake and freeze them, then whenever you like take them straight from the freezer and they'll come back to life as if you've just baked them. The rolls will be baked through to the middle before they are golden brown, so bake them initially for 10–12 minutes for the small rolls or 12–15 minutes for the large rolls until they hold their shape. Leave them to cool, then freeze them in a reusable freezer bag. When you're ready to bake, place your frozen rolls directly on the oven shelf and bake at the same temperature as before with steam for 12–15 minutes to make sure they are baked through to the middle and get a lovely colour.

ROASTED BUTTERNUT, BULGUR WHEAT, PICKLED FENNEL & POMEGRANATE

SERVES 3–4 AS AN ACCOMPANIMENT

This has been a Bake with Jack standard for a long time, refined over many years. It's part of our meal on the Introduction to Homemade Bread Class. Sweet roasted squash, fresh mint and parsley, pickled fennel (one of my favourite things ever) and fresh pomegranate bring a party of flavour to our wholesome bulgur wheat base.

This one is so tasty, there's no real need for a dressing to bring everything together. Instead, just a little olive oil and pickling liquor from our fennel is enough.

Peeling butternut squash is a thing of personal preference I find. Here, I peel the top half and leave the seeded part skin-on because I like the two textures. Feel free to peel, or not, as you would like.

For the pickled fennel
1 fennel bulb
80ml (2½fl oz) red
    wine vinegar
50g (1¾oz) golden caster
    (superfine) sugar
1 teaspoon caraway seeds
pinch of sea salt

For the rest
1 butternut squash
olive oil
100g (3½oz) bulgur wheat
juicy seeds from
    ½ pomegranate
2 tablespoons finely chopped
    fresh flat-leaf (Italian)
    parsley leaves and stalks
2 tablespoons finely chopped
    fresh mint leaves
sea salt
Seeded White Rolls & Knots
    (see page 47)

Making the pickled fennel: A day ahead

1. Top and tail the brown parts from your fennel and discard them. Slice the bulb in half down the middle, place each half cut side down onto the chopping board and slice lengthways as thinly as possible.

2. Mix together everything else in a small bowl to make the pickling liquid.

3. Place the fennel in a re-useable freezer bag, pour over the liquid and do your best to squeeze out as much air as you can. Seal up the bag and gently shake it, squeeze it, scrunch it to get all the fennel in part of the liquid.

4. Place the bag in a bowl or plastic box in case of any leaks and refrigerate overnight.

Cooking the squash

5. Top and tail your butternut squash, then cut it in half horizontally into the seedy part and the other part. Place the seedless piece cut-side down on the work surface and work your way round, peeling the skin off. Cut it into 3cm (1in) fingers and then random shaped chunks.

6. Halve the seeded part down the middle, scoop out the seeds and discard, and wedge the flesh into half-moons.

7. Put all the butternut into a large mixing bowl, toss in 2 tablespoons of olive oil and season with salt.

8. Spread it out in one layer onto a baking parchment-lined roasting tray and roast in a preheated oven at 180°C fan/400°F/ Gas Mark 6 for 40–50 minutes until soft and sweet. Set aside.

Recipe continued overleaf

Bringing it all together

9. Cook your bulgur wheat in a medium-sized saucepan of well-salted boiling water for 6 minutes. Drain and leave to cool.

10. Place the butternut, bulgur wheat, pomegranate and chopped herbs into a large mixing bowl.

11. Lift the fennel from its pickling liquid and add that too, tossing everything together.

12. Add 2 tablespoons of pickling liquid to the bowl and 2 tablespoons of olive oil. Toss again.

13. Taste and adjust the seasoning with salt if you need to and drizzle over a little extra oil. Serve with the rolls.

MULTISEED BLOOMER

MAKES 2 MEDIUM LOAVES

Shaping a bloomer is EXACTLY the same as shaping a loaf for a tin, only you put it on a baking tray. You'll need to be more precise when shaping, as without the tin to support the rise, any small errors will show, BUT don't let that put you off. This makes two manageable-sized bloomers, so it's double the practise.

Here we are adding seeds INTO the actual dough itself, and because I have opted for SMALL seeds, we can put these in with the flour instead of incorporating them after kneading.

Just like the tin loaf on page 33, this will make great sandwiches for a couple of days, then toast.

=== EASY TO MAKE, EASY TO BAKE / TOTAL TIME: 3¼–4½ HOURS ===

325g (11½oz) room-temperature water
12g (½oz) fresh yeast, crumbled, or 7g (¼oz) fast-action dried yeast
400g (14oz) strong white bread flour, plus extra for dusting

100g (3½oz) strong wholemeal bread flour
75g (2½oz) small seeds of your choice, such as poppy, sesame, linseed (flaxseed) or sunflower, plus extra for topping

8g (¼oz) salt
15g (½oz) room-temperature butter, broken up into pieces

Making the dough: 15–20 minutes
1. In a large mixing bowl, mix together the water and yeast until the yeast has dissolved.
2. Add the flours, seeds and salt, then mix with a dough scraper until the mixture starts to come together. Add the butter and mix again into a rough dough.
3. Turn your dough out onto a clean work surface and knead without any additional flour for 8 minutes.

Resting: 1–1½ hours
4. Shape the dough into a ball and place it back in the bowl. Sprinkle the top with a little flour, cover with a clean cloth and rest at room temperature for 1–1½ hours.

Dividing and pre-shaping: 5 minutes
5. Dust the top of the dough lightly with flour and use your dough scraper to turn it out upside down onto the work surface, sticky side up.
6. Use your fingertips to flatten the dough gently and cut it in half with your dough scraper. Fold and roll each piece of dough into a ball, then cup slightly to tighten (see page 24).

Resting: 15 minutes
7. Line up your dough balls on the work surface. Dust the tops with flour, cover with the cloth and rest for 15 minutes to relax and spread slightly.

Final shaping and topping: 5–10 minutes
8. Line a baking tray with baking parchment.
9. Dust the work surface lightly with flour. Working with one at a time, slide your dough scraper underneath a dough ball to release it and flip sticky side up onto the dusted surface.
10. Press with your fingertips and knuckles to flatten the dough into a circle. Slide your fingers, palms up, underneath each side of the circle and pull to stretch it sideways. At an angle, fold one side two-thirds of the way over the dough and the other side in the same way so that it overlaps the first fold and you have an 'A' shape. Roll up the dough from the point towards you into a tight sausage and press the seam to stick it together, then turn the dough over, seam side down.
11. Moisten the top of each loaf with water (see my tip on page 52) and roll the tops in

Recipe continued overleaf

a shallow tray of your chosen seeds, or sprinkle them on top for a less dense coverage.

12. Using a serrated knife, make 6 to 8 diagonal cuts across each loaf about 5mm (¼in) deep and place on the lined tray. If there are any wet patches on the surface, let them dry or dust with a little flour.

Resting: 1–1½ hours

13. Cover your loaves with the cloth and rest for 1–1½ hours.

14. Towards the end of resting, preheat your oven to 200°C fan/425°F/Gas Mark 7 with a shelf in the middle and a deep roasting tray on the oven floor. Half fill a kettle.

Baking: 30–35 minutes

15. Boil the kettle.

16. Place your baking tray on the oven shelf and carefully pour the hot water into the tray below. Bake your loaves for 30–35 minutes.

17. Let them cool completely on a wire rack.

─────────────── **TIPS** ───────────────

THE J-CLOTH TRICK

This is BY FAR the easiest way to coat your loaf with seeds exactly where you want them to be. Moisten a new J-cloth with water and lay it on the work surface. Spread your seeds out on a separate tray. Pick up your loaf and roll the top on the cloth, then roll it in your seeds and hey presto, job done!

BLOOMER BLOWOUT!

If your bloomer burst itself open somewhere unexpected, like at the side or underneath, you're not alone! It's pretty common, and let me tell you why … It's the pressure inside your loaf that will bust open the crust. On a loaf like this, the weakest part is where the moisture builds up between dough and tray during resting and baking. If this happens, next time let the dough rest longer and get softer and puffier before baking so it has less 'push' inside.

MULTISEED TOAST, SWEET POTATO, CHARRED TENDERSTEM & FETA

SERVES 2

Broccoli roasted and lightly charred is delicious. It's the same principle as grilled (broiled) asparagus (an excellent substitute if you fancied it!) but it's those toasty blackened florets that really make it for me.

Here we have bread packed with goodness, a fresh and healthy toast topping with a touch of salty feta and when you're slicing your bread, don't just dust that seeded bread crust shrapnel from the board into the bin or toss it out for the birds. Keep it to one side and sprinkle it over the top when you're done!

---

1 medium sweet potato
   (mine was 380g/13½oz)
olive oil
100g (3½oz) Tenderstem
   broccoli (broccolini)
20g (¾oz) blanched
   hazelnuts (filberts)
1 orange
sea salt

To finish
2 thick slices of your
   Multiseed Bloomer
   (see page 51)
olive oil
1 garlic clove (optional)
100g (3½oz) feta cheese
sea salt flakes

1. Preheat the oven to 200°C fan/425°F/Gas Mark 7.
2. Cut the sweet potato in half lengthways and rub both pieces all over with a ½ teaspoon of olive oil. Season with salt and place them on a small baking tray, cut side down.
3. Bake in the oven for 1–1½ hours until soft and sweet.
4. Trim and discard the very ends of the broccoli. Roughly chop the hazelnuts, placing them in a large mixing bowl with the broccoli.
5. Grate over the zest of ½ your orange before adding 1 teaspoon of olive oil and a pinch of salt and tossing everything together nicely.
6. Line the broccoli up on a parchment-lined baking tray and sprinkle with the chopped nuts. Use a spatula to get the remaining zest and oil out of the bowl onto the tray. Keep the bowl to one side.
7. Roast in the oven at 200°C fan/425°F/Gas Mark 7 for 8–10 minutes until the broccoli is charred and the nuts are browned.
8. While you are waiting, slice off the top and bottom of the orange. Place it cut side down on the chopping board and peel the skin and pith from the edge with a small knife. Segment the orange by carefully cutting down each side of each segment, removing it from its walls. Do your best to keep each intact as they come out. Place into your mixing bowl and squeeze in any juice from the peelings and middle part of the orange before discarding those parts.
9. Remove the broccoli from the oven and add it along with the nuts to the bowl of orange segments and juice. Toss together.
10. Slice 2 thick slices of your seeded bloomer, keeping the seeds that fall off for later. Toast both slices of bread, both sides. Drizzle each with 1 teaspoon of olive oil, season with sea salt flakes and rub with the cut side of a garlic clove, if you like. Put the toast on 2 plates.
11. Scoop the sweet potato from their halves and smash with a fork on top of your toast. Season with salt and a little drizzle of olive oil.
12. Divide your dressed broccoli and orange between the 2 toasts and crumble over the feta cheese. Then sprinkle over a little seed and bread crust shrapnel reserved from earlier.

100% WHOLEMEAL LOAF

MAKES 2 ROUND LOAVES

It's important to note that the higher the ratio of wholemeal to white flour, the heavier the bread will be. Think of it this way. White flour is just wholemeal flour with the bran (brown) part sifted out. All the STRENGTH is in the white part, which is responsible for gluten development and the all-important elasticity of your dough, so a wholemeal dough can never reach the soft and fluffy heights of a white loaf because it doesn't have the strength to hold all those bubbles.

But once we acknowledge that, we can begin to appreciate and learn to love wholemeal bread for what it is – a heartier and more substantial loaf JAM-PACKED with flavour and goodness. Wholemeal flour sucks up more water too, so I've upped the moisture level here to make a manageable dough able to hold as much gas as possible.

=== EASY TO MAKE, EASY TO BAKE / TOTAL TIME: 3¼–4½ HOURS ===

480g (1lb 1oz) room-temperature water
20g (¾oz) fresh yeast, crumbled, or 10g (½oz) fast-action dried yeast

700g (1lb 9oz) strong wholemeal bread flour, plus extra for dusting

12g (½oz) salt
30g (1oz) olive oil

Making the dough: 15–20 minutes
1. In a large mixing bowl, mix together the water and yeast until the yeast has dissolved.
2. Add the flour and salt, then mix with a dough scraper until the mixture starts to come together. Add the olive oil and mix again into a rough dough.
3. Turn your dough out onto a clean work surface and knead without any additional flour for 8 minutes.

Resting: 1½ hours
4. Shape the dough into a ball and place it back in the bowl. Sprinkle the top with a little flour, cover with a clean cloth and rest at room temperature for 1½ hours.

Dividing and pre-shaping: 5 minutes
5. Dust the top of the dough lightly and use your dough scraper to turn it out upside down onto the work surface, sticky side up.
6. Use your fingertips to flatten the dough gently and cut it in half with your dough scraper. Fold and roll each piece of dough into a ball, then cup slightly to tighten (see page 24).

Resting: 15 minutes
7. Line up your dough balls on the work surface. Dust only the tops lightly with flour, cover with the cloth and rest for 15 minutes to relax and spread slightly.

Final shaping: 5–10 minutes
8. Line a baking tray with baking parchment.
9. Dust the work surface lightly with flour. Working with one at a time, slide your dough scraper underneath a dough ball to release it and flip it sticky side up onto the dusted surface. Shape as before into a nice tight ball.
10. Place the loaves seam side down on the lined tray as far apart as possible so that they won't touch when they puff.
11. Dust them really well with flour. Using a small serrated knife, carefully and steadily make 5 or 6 diagonal cuts across each loaf about 5mm (¼in) deep. Then give the tray a turn and repeat to create a diamond pattern.

Recipe continued overleaf

Resting: 1–1½ hours

12. Cover your loaves with the cloth and rest for 1–1½ hours.

13. Towards the end of resting, preheat your oven to 200°C fan/425°F/Gas Mark 7 with a shelf in the middle and a deep roasting tray on the oven floor. Half fill a kettle.

Baking: 30–35 minutes

14. Boil the kettle.

15. Place your baking tray on the oven shelf and carefully pour the hot water into the tray below. Bake your loaves for 30–35 minutes.

16. Let them cool completely on a wire rack.

— TIP —

WHY THE PRE-SHAPE?

Pre-shaping the dough into balls before finally reshaping in exactly the same way may seem a bit pointless here, BUT it really isn't. It's this double shaping that brings an additional layer of tension and structure to the loaf, which is EVEN MORE important with a wholemeal dough, since it has less strength than a white dough, PLUS we are leaving it free-standing with zero support while it puffs up. So the extra shaping will help it greatly as it rises UP, tall and proud.

HOMEMADE BUTTER

MAKES 100G (3½OZ)

There is plenty of butter in the supermarket, I get that. There are also lots of things pretending to be butter and most of them aren't real. Real butter is made out of cream. The end. Okay, a little bit of salt too, but the point I'm trying to make here is that it's the REAL thing. You can make it in about 2 minutes and the only specialised equipment you need is a jam jar.

The process is fun and so simple it often stops people in their tracks. You'll get some butter and bonus buttermilk too – it's like a magic trick! One thing goes in the jar, two things come out …

You don't HAVE to make your own butter for the following flavoured butters but it's pretty cool.

200ml (7fl oz) double (heavy) cream, left at room temperature for a couple of hours
pinch of sea salt flakes, to taste

1. Pour your cream into a jam jar with room for it to move. A half to one-third full works well.
2. Screw the lid on tight and shake it up and down so that it hits the lid and then the bottom of the jar for 2–3 minutes. Here's what should happen as you go along:
3. When you begin, take a look at the cream. It should be clinging all the way round the edges of the jar. As you carry on shaking it'll get thick – now you've made whipped cream.
4. Next, it'll start turning a little yellow, parts of it will start to come away from the edges and you'll be able to see inside the jar. Keep shaking – the cream is thicker now so give it some welly.
5. Shake, shake, shake, up and down, and at some point you'll hear a splash inside the jar. The cream will be freely moving up and down. Shake a few more times, then tilt the jar on its side and look inside.
6. You should see yellow butter swimming in white buttermilk.
7. Mind now sufficiently blown, it's time for the next part. Unscrew the lid, hold the butter back with a fork and pour out the buttermilk into a small pot. Keep this in the fridge for later use in something. Normally I chill it down and drink it because it's wicked tasty.
8. Get 2 measuring jugs and fill one with cold water.
9. Top up your butter jar with cold water and replace the lid. Shake it vigorously again and tip the water into the empty jug. Repeat a further 2 to 3 times until the water that you're tipping out is clear. The butter is now clean of buttermilk and will keep for longer.
10. Fold up a square of kitchen paper and put it on a small plate to the side. Scoop the butter from the jar onto the empty side of the plate with the fork. Lift the side of the plate with the butter on and mash the butter with your fork so that any excess moisture trickles down the tilted plate and is absorbed by the paper.
11. When nothing else will come out, discard the paper and mash through a sprinkling of sea salt flakes. Taste and adjust the seasoning if you need to. Serve with your fresh homemade bread and enjoy the most delicious flavour combination of all time.

FLAVOURED BUTTERS

These measurements are based on 100g (3½oz) of butter, but you can make a bigger batch if you like. Make sure the butter is very soft and you'll be able to incorporate your flavours really well. Just mix the other ingredients into the butter.

You can make the butters into a fancy shape and wrap them in cling film. They'll keep well in the fridge for a couple of weeks or you can cut them into slices and freeze them in a reusable bag.

Spread them on toast, pop a slice on a steak, top a soup, toss in some pasta or boiled potatoes, melt a slice on pancakes, stir into mash or polenta (cornmeal) – use your imagination! I feel like flavoured butters are one of those things I have to hand that I wonder how I ever lived without!

POSH ROASTED GARLIC BUTTER

1 bulb of garlic
25g (1oz) Parmesan cheese, grated
½ tablespoon chopped fresh rosemary leaves
100g (3½oz) butter

1. Wrap the garlic in tin foil and roast in the oven for 30 minutes at 180°C fan/400°F/Gas Mark 6 until soft. Cool and squeeze the flesh out.
2. Spread your Parmesan on a baking tray and bake in the oven until golden and crisp. Leave to cool then crunch into crumbs.
3. Mix the Parmesan and garlic along with the rosemary into the butter.

SOFT HERB BUTTER

100g (3½oz) butter
4 tablespoons finely chopped fresh herbs, such as mint, parsley and dill
pinch of salt, to taste

SUN-DRIED TOMATO & THYME BUTTER

100g (3½oz) butter
2 tablespoons sun-dried tomato purée (paste)
1 tablespoon chopped fresh thyme leaves

GARLIC & PARSLEY BUTTER

100g (3½oz) butter
1 garlic clove, finely grated
2 tablespoons finely chopped fresh flat-leaf (Italian) parsley leaves and stalks
pinch of salt, to taste

CHIPOTLE BUTTER

100g (3½oz) butter
2 teaspoons chipotle chilli paste

SMOKED SALT & CRACKED BLACK PEPPER BUTTER

100g (3½oz) butter
1 teaspoon smoked salt
½ teaspoon cracked black pepper

LEMON & CHIVE BUTTER

100g (3½oz) butter
3 tablespoons chopped fresh chives
zest of 1 lemon
pinch of salt, to taste

CINNAMON SUGAR BUTTER

100g (3½oz) butter
½ teaspoon ground cinnamon
3 tablespoons soft brown sugar

STREAKY BACON WITH A LEMON PEA SHOOT & SUGAR SNAP SALAD

SERVES 2

A lesson in flavour matching: peas and pea shoots go together. Because they're both pea.

Wholemeal bread is properly ROBUST and a nice slice feels well-matched here with fresh peas, a zingy lemon dressing and salty bacon. Sunflower seeds bring a little crunch to the party and we can bring out their nuttiness in a low faff way by toasting lightly in the residual heat of the bacon pan. No mess, no stress.

There are many ways to crisp bacon. If it's cooked for too long though, I find it becomes flavourless but salty. Lately, I've been lightly grilling (broiling) it to remove excess moisture and frying it quickly in a pan with no additional fat to crisp it up nice – try it!

---

6 slices of smoked
    streaky bacon
1 tablespoon sunflower seeds
2 pinches of sea salt
100g (3½oz) sugar snap peas
40g (1½oz) pea shoots
1 lemon
olive oil

To serve
2 thick slices of your
    100% Wholemeal Loaf
    (see page 57)
butter or Flavoured Butter
    (see page 60)

1. Lay your bacon slices on a tray and grill (broil) them on a medium heat for 3–5 minutes until the excess moisture comes out. Turn off the grill (broiler) and transfer the bacon to a large preheated frying pan (skillet) over a medium heat. Cook at a happy sizzle for 2 minutes or so on each side until crisp. Turn off the heat, remove the bacon from the pan and rest on kitchen paper.

2. Add the sunflower seeds to the leftover bacon fat. Thirty seconds of swishing them around should be enough to turn them a lovely golden brown. Remove them from the pan with a slotted spoon and place on the paper next to the bacon to drain. Season with a pinch of salt.

3. Slice your sugar snap peas lengthways nice and thinly and place them in a large mixing bowl with the pea shoots. Squeeze over some lemon juice and drizzle with olive oil. Season with a pinch of salt before tossing everything together.

4. Divide your salad evenly, piling it high to the side of 2 plates. Top with the bacon and a sprinkle of sunflower seeds.

5. Serve with a thick slice of bread, buttered well.

BAGELS

MAKES 6 BAGELS

Bagels are a rule breaker. Remember the saying 'the wetter the dough, the better the bread'? Well, it doesn't apply here.

The key characteristics of a classic bagel are chewiness and a fine crumb texture, i.e. SMALL HOLES. To achieve the right texture, we have to knead the dough really well. And to get that chewy crust, the bagels must be BOILED before they are baked. Therefore, the dough needs to be drier and tighter than white bread dough, and SLOW-MOVING, meaning minimum yeast. Otherwise, it would be too soft and puffy, and on contact with the hot water, it would get crinkly on the outside instead of plump and glossy.

Using exactly the same ingredients as regular white bread dough but in slightly different ratios along with a unique method is what makes the humble bagel so special and something we can learn so much from. Isn't that cool?

══ EASY TO MAKE, EASY TO BOIL AND BAKE / TOTAL TIME: 3–3¾ HOURS ══

You'll need: a large, wide saucepan for boiling 2 or 3 bagels at a time, if possible

210g (7½oz) room-temperature water
5g (1 teaspoon) fresh yeast, crumbled, or 3g (1 teaspoon) fast-action dried yeast
375g (13oz) strong white bread flour, plus extra for dusting
5g (1 teaspoon) salt
10g (½oz) olive oil, plus extra for oiling

To finish
1 tablespoon bicarbonate of soda (baking soda)
poppy and sesame seeds, for sprinkling
sea salt flakes

Making the dough: 15–20 minutes
1. In a large mixing bowl, mix together the water and yeast until the yeast has dissolved.
2. Add the flour and salt, then mix with a dough scraper until the dough starts to come together. Add the olive oil and mix again into a rough dough.
3. Turn your dough out onto a clean work surface and knead without any additional flour for 8 minutes – expect it to be a little drier and tougher than regular white bread dough.

Resting: 1–1½ hours
4. Shape the dough into a ball and place it back in the bowl. Sprinkle the top with a little flour, cover with a clean cloth and rest at room temperature for 1–1½ hours.

Dividing and shaping: 5–15 minutes
5. Line a baking tray with baking parchment and oil the paper lightly.
6. Dust the top of the dough lightly with flour and use your dough scraper to turn it out upside down onto the work surface, sticky side up.
7. Use your fingertips to flatten the dough gently into a circle and cut into 6 equal-sized wedges with your dough scraper.
8. Roll up each wedge of dough from the point into a sausage. Then roll each sausage with your palms on the work surface until it is about 30cm (12in) long. Bring the ends together, overlap and press to stick them together to form a ring, then roll the join on the work surface to seal.

Recipe continued overleaf

9. Place your bagels well-spaced out on the oiled paper and brush lightly with oil.

Resting: 45 minutes–1 hour
10. Cover your bagels loosely with cling film and let them rest for 45 minutes–1 hour to rise slowly until they are only slightly puffed – this is the key stage.
11. Towards the end of resting, preheat your oven to 200°C fan/425°F/Gas Mark 7 with a deep roasting tray on the oven floor. Bring your large saucepan filled with water to the boil, and half fill a kettle.

Boiling and baking: 30–40 minutes
12. When you are ready to bake your bagels, boil the kettle and add the bicarbonate of soda to the boiling water in the pan.

13. Gently lower 2 or 3 bagels at a time (if your pan is big enough) into the boiling water and boil them for 30 seconds. Flip and boil for another 30 seconds on the other side. Using a spider or slotted spoon, remove the bagels, one at a time, from the water and place back on the tray.
14. As you remove each batch of bagels, sprinkle them with the seeds and sea salt so that they stick.
15. Place your baking tray in the oven and carefully pour the hot water from the kettle into the tray below. Bake your bagels for 15–20 minutes until golden.
16. Let them cool completely on a wire rack.

BAGEL FILLINGS

Split and toast your bagel before filling it with one of the three ideas below.

CHICKEN & BACON WITH CHIPOTLE MAYO

Fry 3 slices of smoked streaky bacon until crispy. Make a chipotle mayonnaise by mixing together 2 tablespoons of mayonnaise and 1 teaspoon of chipotle paste. Spread both sides with the mayo, then layer up leftover roast chicken, the bacon, crisp lettuce, sliced Gouda cheese and a squeeze of lime juice.

WHIPPED FETA

Spread each side with the Whipped Feta Cheese from page 157, then layer slices of seasoned avocado with a squeeze of lemon, sun-blushed tomatoes and fresh spinach leaves.

CRUNCHY VEGGIE

Smear both sides generously with cream cheese, then season with a little salt and pepper inbetween each layer of thinly sliced carrot, cucumber, red (bell) pepper, tomato, iceberg lettuce and red cabbage. Finish with a sprinkle of defrosted frozen sweetcorn, fresh coriander (cilantro) leaves and a dash of hot sauce.

——— TIP ———

FRESH BAGELS FOR BREAKFAST

Because bagel dough is slow moving and doesn't NEED to puff up all that much, it makes it an ideal candidate for trying overnight proving in the fridge. After shaping, traying up and covering with cling film, place the tray in the fridge until the following day to puff SUPER slowly. Then in the morning you could potentially boil and bake straight from the fridge. This will take a little practise, depending on what time you put them in the fridge and what temperature your fridge is, but with less risk of over-proving, the slow-moving bagel dough is a pretty safe bet for this technique.

PASTRAMI & SWISS CHEESE SALAD WITH A GARLIC & MUSTARD DRESSING & BAGEL CROUTONS

SERVES 3–4

This salad is a take on a classic bagel filling and, of course, you can serve it that way, layering up the pastrami, leaves and cheese inside like a sandwich. But if your bagels are past their best, turn them into little round croutons. They'll go crunchy on the outside and stay chewy on the inside and go perfectly with this salad.

One bagel will be enough to make croutons for the salad, but chances are everybody will want extra! So do two and serve some on the side for topping up.

---

1 red chicory (endive)
1 white chicory (endive)
1 baby gem lettuce
1 pack of sliced pastrami
100g (3½oz) Swiss cheese
   (I used Gruyère), sliced
   or thinly shaved
3–4 sliced gherkins
cracked black pepper

For the croutons
1–2 stale Bagels (see page 65)
2 tablespoons olive oil
pinch of sea salt

For the dressing
2 tablespoons plain yoghurt
2 tablespoons mayonnaise
1 teaspoon Dijon mustard
1 teaspoon wholegrain
   mustard
½ garlic clove, finely grated
1 tablespoon chopped
   fresh dill
2 teaspoons pickle juice

1. Cut your stale bagels into little rounds. Place the rounds in a mixing bowl and toss with the olive oil and a pinch of sea salt. Spread in a single layer on a large baking parchment-lined baking tray and bake in the oven at 180°C fan/400°F/Gas Mark 6 for 15–20 minutes until golden, crisp on the outside and chewy on the inside.
2. Mix together the yoghurt, mayonnaise, mustards and garlic. Add the dill and adjust the consistency with a couple of teaspoons of vinegar from your gherkin jar. Taste and season with salt if you need to.
3. Trim the root end from the chicory and gem lettuce and discard any dodgy leaves from the outside. Cut your gem into wedges and arrange on a large plate. Pick the leaves from the chicory and place them in and around the gem wedges.
4. Drape over your pastrami, tucking it in and around the leaves, and follow with the cheese and gherkins. Top with your croutons and dress everything with a generous drizzle of your dressing and a sprinkle of pepper.

CHOPPED SALAD

SERVES 2

There's nothing particularly fancy about this salad, nothing to cook or faff about with, just fresh, crunchy salad, chopped with care and dressed nicely with a simple red wine vinaigrette. I regularly knock up salads like this to accompany a sandwich or top toast and use up what I have in the fridge to great effect. Feel free to add things like sliced sugar snaps, spring onions (scallions) or grated carrot if you have them kicking around too.

Here I've used finely chopped olives as a sort of 'seasoning' to bring great flavour to the salad and make it really moreish. The leaves and stalks of parsley bring a punch of flavour and crunch too.

½ iceberg lettuce
1 plum tomato
1 red (bell) pepper
1 stick of celery
100g (3½oz) defrosted
   frozen sweetcorn
1 tablespoon chopped fresh
   flat-leaf (Italian) parsley
   leaves and stalks
50g (1¾oz) pitted black
   olives, finely chopped

For the dressing
1 teaspoon Dijon mustard
1 tablespoon red
   wine vinegar
pinch of sea salt
½ teaspoon sugar
3 tablespoons olive oil

1. Thinly slice your lettuce and place it in a large mixing bowl.
2. Quarter your tomato, cut out the seeds and discard, leaving just the flesh. Chop into 1cm (½in) squares.
3. Slice the sides, top and bottom from your pepper, discarding the stalk and seeds. Chop the pepper into squares exactly the same size as the tomato.
4. Slice the celery into 1cm (½in) pieces.
5. Add the chopped vegetables to the bowl along with the sweetcorn, parsley and finely chopped olives. Mix everything together really well.
6. Put the mustard, red wine vinegar, salt and sugar in a small jam jar. Put the lid on tightly and shake it up. Add the olive oil, replace the lid and shake to emulsify.
7. Pour the dressing over the salad and toss well together. Taste and adjust the seasoning with a little sea salt if you need to.

ENGLISH MUFFINS

MAKES 12 ENGLISH MUFFINS

Ah, the English muffin … not ACTUALLY English but hey, I'll take it!

These are yet another deceptively simple-looking bread. While the dough is as straightforward as any to make, the tricky part is the actual 'baking' of the muffin itself, LOW AND SLOW, either on a flat griddle pan or in a heavy frying pan.

Be prepared to burn a couple if you are making these for the first time, but what you'll learn from those first two will set you in good stead for the rest. That's the reason why I normally make 12 at a time. The baking process does take time though, so you can just halve the recipe if you wish.

Super-soft and close-textured inside, to cut these in half with a knife before you toast them is a kitchen crime. Instead, push the prongs of a fork in around all the edges before prising them open to expose a craggy surface that when toasted makes for the crispiest if slightly torched texture just calling out for a cold slice of salty butter.

EASY TO MAKE, TRICKY TO BAKE / TOTAL TIME: 3–5 HOURS

You'll need: a large flat griddle pan or large, heavy frying pan (skillet)

320g (11¼oz) room-temperature milk
12g (½oz) fresh yeast, crumbled, or 7g (¼oz) fast-action dried yeast
500g (1lb 2oz) strong white bread flour, plus extra for dusting

8g (¼oz) salt
25g (1oz) room-temperature butter, broken up into pieces
coarse semolina or polenta (cornmeal), for coating

Making the dough: 15–20 minutes

1. In a large mixing bowl, mix the milk and yeast together until the yeast has dissolved.
2. Add the flour and salt, then mix with a dough scraper until the mixture starts to come together into a rough dough. Add the butter and dimple it all over into the dough with your fingertips.
3. Turn the dough out onto a clean work surface and knead without any additional flour for 8 minutes.

Resting: 1–1½ hours

4. Shape the dough into a ball and place it back in the bowl. Sprinkle the top with a little flour, cover with a clean cloth and rest at room temperature for 1–1½ hours.

Dividing and shaping: 25–30 minutes

5. Dust the top of the dough lightly with flour and use your dough scraper to turn it out upside down onto the work surface, sticky side up.
6. Use your fingertips to flatten the dough gently and cut into 12 equal-sized pieces with your dough scraper. If you want them all to be exactly the same size, weigh them out at about 70g (2½oz) each. Fold and roll each piece of dough into a tight ball (see page 24).
7. Dip each dough ball, one at a time into a bowl of coarse semolina or polenta, pressing the dough into it until it's nicely coated all over.
8. Line up your 12 semolina-coated rolls on a large tray, but not too large to fit in your fridge (or use 2) and let them rest for 15 minutes. Then roll each one firmly on the work surface with a rolling pin to flatten slightly and return

Recipe continued overleaf

to the tray. This helps to stop them puffing too high and taking even longer to bake through *and* being too fat to fit into your toaster!

Resting: 1 hour

9. Cover the muffins with the cloth and rest for 1 hour. Twenty minutes before your muffins are fully puffed up, preheat your griddle over a low heat to make sure it is as evenly heated as possible (for they never truly are!) – a heavy frying pan, if using instead, will take less time to heat up evenly.

Baking: 20 minutes–1½ hours

10. Once your muffins are ready to 'bake', unless you have a griddle or pan big enough to bake them all in one go (see my tip right), stash them in the fridge. The cool environment will put the puff pretty much on pause, allowing you to bake them in batches low and slow without the remainder rising too far.

11. It's a good idea to start with a tester muffin. Place one on the preheated griddle or in the pan, set the timer for 8 minutes (per side) and keep an eye on it – if it browns too fast, turn the heat DOWN for the next ones.

12. When you are happy and ready to commit, load up your griddle or pan with a manageable amount of muffins, 3 or 4 (keep the remainder in the fridge), and bake for 8 minutes on each side until golden, keeping your eyes peeled for burning.

13. Let them cool completely on a wire rack.

TIPS

SINGLE-BATCH BAKING

I have a griddle big enough for all 12 muffins (show off, I know!) and it goes over 2 burners, a small one and a big one, so one side is always hotter than the other – the hot side is too hot and the cool side is too cool, but that's just life! I preheat the griddle for 20 minutes on minimum heat before adding ALL the muffins. I set a timer for 4 minutes, then check on the muffins and move the pale-looking ones on the cooler side to the hot side and the darker-looking ones to the cooler side, and set the timer again for 4 minutes. When that time is up, I flip them all over with a small angled (cranked) palette knife, set the timer again for 4 minutes and repeat the check 'n' shuffle technique when the beeper goes off. Then I bake for the final 4 minutes, lifting and peeping to make sure no muffins are turning black.

RESCUE STRATEGY

If your griddle or pan is too hot and the heat won't go lower, your muffins will brown too fast. If you reduce the baking time, they will be perfect on the outside but raw on the inside, and if you continue baking for the full time, the inside will be delicious but the outside will be black and your home full of smoke. If you sense this happening, here's what to do. Preheat your oven to 180°C fan/400°F/Gas Mark 6. Toast up all your muffins in your griddle or pan so that they are perfect on the outside, then transfer them to a baking tray lined with baking parchment and bake in the oven for 10–12 minutes to make sure they are done on the inside.

HOT-SMOKED SALMON & EGGS

SERVES 1

I'd take hot-smoked salmon over cold-smoked salmon any day. Hot-smoked salmon cooks in the heat as it is smoked, making it enticingly flaky. In one of my (many) jobs, we'd trim a whole side into very specific rectangles to fit nicely onto a starter plate, saving the trimmings for staff lunch. SERIOUSLY ... We must have been the classiest chefs in the country, eating hot-smoked salmon for lunch, what a luxury.

I like to call these eggs 'ribbon eggs' because they are cooked very flat in the pan with gentle encouragement from a spatula to create buttery ribbon layers.

For the eggs
2 medium eggs
1½ teaspoons finely chopped
    fresh chives, plus a little
    extra to serve
pinch of sea salt
10g (½oz) butter

To finish
1 English Muffin (see page 73)
1 tablespoon crème fraiche
    or sour cream
a handful of watercress
60g (2oz) hot-smoked salmon

1. Crack your eggs into a jug. Add the chives and a pinch of salt and whisk them well. When you think they are done, whisk them a little more to make sure they are properly whisked. Set aside.
2. Working all the way around your muffin, insert the prongs of a fork into the side right to the middle. When you get back around to where you started, you should be able to pull the 2 halves apart, revealing the craggy crumb texture on the cut side. Toast your muffin in the toaster (if it fits) or under the grill (broiler).
3. Bring a large non-stick frying pan (skillet) up to a medium heat. Add the butter, melt it and swirl it all around the base of the pan.
4. Pour in the egg and give it some time to set on the bottom. Gently encourage the sides into the middle with a silicone spatula, allowing any raw egg to flow from the sides, making a new thin layer in the empty part of the pan. Remove the pan from the heat a little sooner than you think as the residual heat continues to cook the egg.
5. With a swift mix, manoeuvre the egg to the side of the pan and onto your plate, followed by a tablespoon of crème fraîche, your muffin and a handful of watercress and the hot-smoked salmon.

SOFT FLOUR TACOS

MAKES 20 SOFT FLOUR TACOS

Talk about FAST! These teeny tiny flat flour tacos are a massive hit at the dinner table in my house. They require no yeast, no proving time and hardly any time to 'bake' on a hot flat griddle pan, so you can make them at the drop of a hat. They only really need enough time to rest and relax so that you can roll them out SUPER-THIN. And when they are done, they're your blank canvas for anything you would like to wrap, fold or roll up inside.

SUPER-EASY TO MAKE, EASY TO BAKE / TOTAL TIME: 1–1¼ HOURS

| **You'll need:** a flat griddle pan or heavy frying pan (skillet) | 350g (12½oz) strong white bread flour, plus extra for dusting
5g (1 teaspoon) baking powder
5g (1 teaspoon) salt | 35g (1¼oz) olive oil or butter or lard, cut into pieces
190g (6¾oz) warm water |

Making the dough: 5–10 minutes

1. In a large mixing bowl, mix together the flour, baking powder and salt.
2. Add your fat of choice and whisk it in with a balloon whisk or fork if using oil or rub it in with your fingertips if it's butter or lard.
3. Add the water and mix with a dough scraper until the mixture forms a rough dough.
4. Turn your dough out onto a clean work surface and knead without any additional flour for 3–4 minutes.

Dividing: 10 minutes

5. Cut the dough into 20 equal-sized pieces.
6. Fold and roll each piece of dough into a tight ball (see page 24).

Resting: 30 minutes

7. Line up your dough balls on a tray, loosely cover with cling film dusted with flour and rest for 30 minutes to relax.

Shaping: 15–20 minutes

8. Dust your dough balls with flour and use a rolling pin to roll them out on the work surface to thin 15cm (6in) circles. If they resist and spring back when you try to roll them, roll each one out a little and then come back to the first, by which time it should have relaxed a bit and you will be able to roll it out a little further.

Spread them out, overlapping them on a couple of large trays, using plenty of flour, rather than stacking in a pile as they might stick together.

Baking: 10–20 minutes

9. When you are ready to 'bake' your tacos, preheat your griddle or heavy frying pan to high heat. They have to bake hot and quick, otherwise they will get too crispy, so take your time to bake them all in batches that you are comfortable with. If you prefer complete control, cook just a couple or even one at a time. Add your tacos to the hot griddle or pan and cook for 30 seconds on each side.
10. Let your tacos cool completely on a wire rack, overlapping each one slightly so that the steam between keeps them nice and soft.

TIPS

FREEZING YOUR TACOS

These are ideal for freezing because they are so THIN. Layer them up with a small baking parchment square in between each one to stop them sticking together and slide them into a reusable freezer bag. You can then take out however many you need and they will defrost really fast left on the work surface. Pop them into the oven preheated to 180°C fan/400°F/Gas Mark 6 on a foil-lined baking tray for a few minutes to warm them through.

BREAKFAST TACO WITH AVOCADO, CHILLI, LIME & A BUTTER-FRIED EGG

SERVES 2

A perfect spicy breakfast or brunch and all you need is two of your soft flour tacos! Here we fry them until CRISP and top with limey avocado; a well seasoned egg fried in BUTTER; toasted sesame; fragrant caraway and the world's most controversial herb: coriander (cilantro). Not bad for a ONE-pan wonder!

The real trick with an avocado is that it'll only be ready on its own terms so, just like with our bread, we need to employ a little patience here. Don't be tempted to use it when it's still a little hard. Give it time to soften properly, until that little stalky part is easily removed with minimum effort, and then you'll know it's good to go (plus, it makes it wickedly easy to get the stone out, see below). Peak too soon and this deliciously silky dish will be weirdly firm and kind of wet. Not great. Catch it at the right moment and all will be well and well worth the wait.

For the avocado
1 large ripe avocado
juice of ½ lime
1 teaspoon olive oil
a few slices of bird's eye
    chilli, to taste

For the eggs
40g (1½oz) butter
2 medium eggs
1 teaspoon sesame seeds
1 teaspoon caraway seeds
a few slices of bird's eye
    chilli, to taste

To serve
2 teaspoons olive oil
2 Soft Flour Tacos
    (see page 77)
fresh coriander (cilantro)
    leaves and stalks
sea salt and cracked
    black pepper

1. Halve your perfectly ripe avocado, squeeze the flesh into a large mixing bowl and then take out the stone. Add the lime juice.
2. Add the olive oil, a pinch of salt and your sliced chilli and mash everything together with a fork. Taste and adjust the seasoning if you need to and then set aside.
3. Bring a small non-stick frying pan (skillet), JUST big enough to hold your tacos, up to a medium heat on the stove. Drizzle in half the olive oil. Carefully place in a taco, move it around in the bottom of the pan to pick up some of the oil on the underside and then flip it over. Toast in the pan for 2 minutes or so until it is golden, then flip it over and toast the other side in the same way. Repeat with the other taco.
4. Season with salt, remove the taco from the pan and place it on a cooling rack so it doesn't go soggy while you're cooking the eggs.
5. Return the pan to the heat and add the butter. Let it melt and then foam gently before cracking in the eggs.
6. Season the eggs well straight away with a pinch of sea salt and cracked black pepper. When the underside is sealed and white, you can swish the eggs in the pan to encourage the butter up the sides. When the white is nearly cooked, tip the pan to the side so that the eggs slide to the side into a pool of butter. Use a dessert spoon to scoop the butter and baste the yolks to cook that wobbly white bit.
7. As the eggs finish, get your crisp tacos onto a plate and spread over your avocado. Remove the pan from the heat, lift the eggs from the butter and place on top of the avocado.
8. Lastly, toss your sesame seeds, caraway seeds and chilli slices into the remaining butter. Swish it around for 30 seconds or so to toast the seeds and infuse the butter and spoon it over the top of your eggs and round the edges of your dish.
9. Finish with a few picked coriander sprigs scattered over the top.

SLOW-COOKED PORK BELLY TACOS

SERVES 4

For me and my family, the joy of the taco is in the tabletop 'build' session. Picking your taco; filling it with the things you like in the order you like them in; eating it and doing it again. Here is enough for two to three tacos each. You don't need much inside each one and you'll be surprised how filling they are served alongside your choice of potatoes or rice.

   This pork belly is LOW maintenance. After marinating it in the rub, it's 'left' in the oven for five to six hours. You can pickle the veg in advance, slice the lettuce, make the sauce and then, come mealtime, just bring everything to the table. Try to choose a piece of pork belly with good visible layers of fat and meat to make sure the meat is MOIST and delicious after its LONG rest in the oven.

8–12 Soft Flour Tacos
   (see page 77)

For the pork
1 teaspoon chipotle flakes
½ teaspoon fennel seeds
½ teaspoon cumin seeds
½ teaspoon coriander seeds
1 teaspoon salt
½ teaspoon paprika
1 garlic clove
800g (1lb 12oz) pork belly
   (with nice layers)

For the pickled vegetables
1 carrot (about 100g/3½oz)
¼ white cabbage
   (about 100g/3½oz)
1 tablespoon white
   wine vinegar
1 tablespoon fresh mint
pinch of salt

For the garlic sauce
100g (3½oz) mayonnaise
100g (3½oz) thick
   plain yoghurt
½ garlic clove, crushed
pinch of salt

To finish
1 baby gem lettuce,
   thinly shredded
100g (3½oz) Manchego
   cheese, finely grated
Cooked rice
fresh coriander (cilantro)
   leaves, chopped
pickled green chillies

Marinating the pork: A day ahead
1. Using a large pestle and mortar, crush together the chipotle flakes, fennel, cumin and coriander seeds. Add the salt, paprika and garlic and crush again until you have a mixture the texture of damp sand.
2. Rub this all into the underside of your pork belly, the cut sides not the skin.
3. Chill your belly overnight.
4. Preheat the oven to 125°C fan/295°F/Gas Mark 2.
5. Place the belly into a snug dish or tray (properly snug as your belly will shrink as you cook it and choosing something really tight will allow it to cook in its own juices and fat once it renders out).
6. Cook for 5½ hours.

Pickling the vegetables
7. Peel and slice your carrot into the skinniest matchsticks you can. Slice the white cabbage super-thin too. Place them into a bowl, add the vinegar, mint and salt and scrunch everything together with your hands. Leave it to gently pickle for 15 minutes or so, giving it a toss and squeeze every once in a while.

Making the garlic sauce
8. Mix together your garlic sauce ingredients, taste and adjust the seasoning if you need to.

Putting it all together
9. When the pork is ready, turn up the heat on the oven to 180°C fan/400°F/Gas Mark 6. Stack your tacos on top of each other, wrap them in tin foil and put in the oven for 4–5 minutes to warm through while you peel the skin away from the pork and discard and shred the meat. Tip any fat away from the dish it was cooking in and add any juices or sticky stuff from the dish into your pork. Mix it through.
10. Serve DIY style on the table with some lettuce, Manchego, cooked rice scattered with chopped coriander leaf and pickled chillies.

BEEF SHIN CHILLI NACHOS

SERVES 3–4

These nachos are made by cutting and toasting up your leftover soft flour tacos, making for crispy tortilla chips, which are a base for another meal in itself. I've used beef shin here because its meat to fat ratio means it turns into the tastiest fall-apart beef chilli. You can buy diced, but if you can, try to get a large cut you can chunk up into big pieces. This dish is well worth it.

For the beef chilli
3 tablespoons olive oil
500g (1lb 2 oz) beef shin (shank), cut into 5cm (2in) chunks
2 onions, sliced
3 garlic cloves, finely grated
1 red chilli, sliced
1 teaspoon ground coriander
1 teaspoon ground cumin
1 teaspoon paprika
1 teaspoon chipotle flakes
1 teaspoon cocoa powder
1 tablespoon tomato purée (paste)
1 tablespoon chopped fresh thyme leaves
150ml (5fl oz) beef stock
100ml (3½fl oz) red wine
400g (14oz) tin chopped tomatoes
400g (14oz) tin borlotti beans
salt

For the nachos
5 Soft Flour Tacos (see page 77)
1 tablespoon olive oil
sea salt

For the salsa
200g (7oz) yellow and red tomatoes on the vine
1 tablespoon chopped shallot
1 tablespoon lime juice
1 tablespoon olive oil
1 tablespoon chopped fresh coriander (cilantro) leaves

To finish
100g (3½oz) Grated Cheddar
1 red chilli, sliced
1 tablespoon chopped fresh coriander (cilantro) leaves
100ml (3½fl oz) sour cream

Making the chilli

1. Preheat the oven to 125°C fan/295°F/Gas Mark 2.
2. Heat a large lidded ovenproof saucepan to a high heat, add the olive oil and brown your beef shin in batches on all sides for 2–3 minutes until properly golden. Set aside.
3. Turn down the heat and add your onions. Cook down with a large pinch of salt for 10 minutes until soft and sweet.
4. Add your garlic and chilli. Cook for a further 3 minutes.
5. Next, add all the spices, cocoa powder and tomato purée. Cook for a further 2–3 minutes.
6. Reintroduce the meat to the pan, add the thyme leaves, stock, wine and tinned tomatoes and bring up to the boil. Taste the cooking liquid at this point and adjust the seasoning if you need to before you pop the lid on and transfer the pan to the oven, where it will stay for the next 4 hours.
7. Remove the pan from the oven and check the meat pieces – they should easily fall apart with a fork. Drain and rinse the beans and stir them through the chilli. Return the pan to the oven for 30 minutes.

Making the nachos

8. Stack your flour tacos on top of each other and cut like a cake into 6 wedges. Place the wedges in a large mixing bowl, drizzle with the olive oil and season with salt. Toss everything together and spread the tacos out across 2 large parchment-lined baking trays in a single layer. Bake with the oven at 180°C fan/400°F/Gas Mark 6 for 8–12 minutes until golden and crisp.

Making the salsa

9. Chop your tomatoes into rustic cubes and place them in a mixing bowl. Add the shallot, lime juice, olive oil, coriander and a generous pinch of salt and toss everything together. Set aside.

Bringing it all together

10. Spread your nachos over a large plate, leaving a hole in the middle. Spoon your chilli into the gap and dress with grated Cheddar, sliced chilli and coriander.
11. Serve alongside your salsa and sour cream.

CHAPTER TWO

WET DOUGHS
& FLATBREADS

THIS IS WHERE WE CHANGE
THE GAME SLIGHTLY...

When we up the moisture content in a bread recipe, the dough gets ... wetter. More liquid. LOOSER. That makes it tricky to knead so we just ... don't.

Remember, in the principles section I mentioned that strength is made by the development of gluten, and that gluten development is a product of WORK (kneading) and REST (doing nothing). Well, here we do the latter and, FORTUNATELY, it's all the easier to make that happen BECAUSE the dough is wetter – in a more liquid environment the gluten develops even better. All we need to do is build some structure along the way.

And so let me introduce you to the classic 'stretch-and-fold' technique. A series of stretching the dough and folding it back over itself at intervals over TIME to build the structure in the dough and to tighten it up, giving it the ability to hold EVEN MORE GAS. We do this for the Ciabatta (see page 89) and Focaccia (see page 109) and Garlic Naan Bread (see page 101) in this section and the result is a SUPER-LIGHT bread with inconsistent bubbles inside – small ones and big ones and PLENTY of character.

From the Ciabatta we also learn the value of using a pre-ferment. A simple mix of flour, water and a teeny bit of yeast, mixed up ahead of time. When you do it, the reason WHY will become apparent as what begins as a thick and fragile batter-like mixture COMPLETELY TRANSFORMS into a stretchy, bubbly ALIVE pre-ferment when it's ready for your dough. There is no better illustration of the principle of TIME.

You'll see with your very own eyes the magic of the Pitta Bread (see page 124) puff, inflating itself and creating that POCKET inside. With the ability to toast STRAIGHT from the freezer, it is the ultimate convenience bread. And discover how simple it can be to create something impressive-looking for the dinner table in a Fougasse (see page 121).

This section also contains some Bake with Jack classic class dishes, which some of you will already know and love. The Minted Aubergine & Courgette with Lemon & Chilli (see page 94) and the Roasted Peppers with Capers & Basil (see page 95) have been well-loved standards for many years on the Mediterranean Bread Course. Following my love for principles in food as well as bread, we'll discover together the principle of crafting the perfect risotto too, topped with a slice of soft Brie and a garlic breadcrumb crust.

Take care when playing with wet doughs, use oil to stop them sticking where it is required and enjoy!

CIABATTA

MAKES 4 DECENT-SIZED CIABATTAS

Ah, the ciabatta … when I'm asked what my favourite bread to make is my go-to answer is the ciabatta. It's a true celebration of the characteristics of bread dough in its simplest form, an illustration of the principles at play throughout the process, a triumph of gluten development.

Bread dough happily does its own thing and we as home bakers are here to help coax it along its way to final glory, and that couldn't be more obvious than in the case of the ciabatta. And that's why I have so much love for it. It shouts from the rooftops that we are in this together, that alone we don't quite have all we need to achieve greatness, but together we can create something pretty special.

We'll be using a pre-ferment here – a mixture of flour, water and a little yeast given TIME to start gluten and flavour development in advance. The ciabatta's shape comes naturally, as the dough is so wet you couldn't do much else with it. And because it's wet, we build its strength through stretching and folding rather than traditional kneading to create those consistently inconstant bubbles inside, working firmly but not so much to lose the gas that's building inside. At each fold stage, your dough will become stronger and more pillow-like – it's magic!

TRICKY TO MAKE, EASY TO SHAPE AND BAKE / TOTAL TIME: 3–4 HOURS
FOR THE PRE-FERMENT 4–6 HOURS

You'll need: a lidded plastic container about 18 x 24cm (7 x 9½in), 9cm (3½in) deep for dough (it's so much easier to make rectangular loaves from a rectangular dough)

For the pre-ferment
250g (9oz) strong white bread flour
250g (9oz) room-temperature water
3g (½ teaspoon) fresh yeast, crumbled, or 1g (a pinch) fast-action dried yeast

For the dough
150g (5½oz) room-temperature water
8g (1 teaspoon) fresh yeast, crumbled, or 4g (1 teaspoon) fast-action dried yeast
250g (9oz) strong white bread flour, plus extra for dusting
8g (¼oz) salt
20g (¾oz) olive oil, plus extra for oiling

Making and resting the pre-ferment: 4–6 hours
1. In a large bowl, mix the pre-ferment ingredients together.
2. Cover the bowl with cling film and rest at room temperature for 4–6 hours.

Making the dough: 10–15 minutes
3. In a large mixing bowl, mix together the water and yeast until the yeast has dissolved.
4. Add the flour, salt and your pre-ferment, then mix with a dough scraper until the mixture starts to come together. Add the olive oil and mix again into a dough with no wet or dry patches or firm, lumpy areas.

Resting: 30 minutes
5. Well oil your rectangular plastic container, then pour in the dough, cover with the lid and rest at room temperature for 30 minutes.

First fold: 2 minutes
6. Oil the top of the dough and your hands, then dimple the top of the dough with your fingertips. Carefully slide your hands underneath one end of the dough, lift and then stretch and fold it all the way over the dough. Do the same with the other end of the dough, folding it over the top. Turn the container 90 degrees and repeat the dimpling and folding process.

Recipe continued overleaf

Resting: 30 minutes

7. Cover again and rest for another 30 minutes.

Second fold: 2 minutes

8. Repeat the dimpling and folding process exactly as before.

Resting: 30 minutes

9. Cover again and rest for 30 minutes.

Third fold: 2 minutes

10. Repeat the dimpling and folding process. By now you should notice a transformation in the structure of the dough into an alive and airy pillow, so you may need to dimple it a little more firmly, just enough to make it easier to fold up but without flattening it.

Resting: 30 minutes

11. Cover again and rest for 30 minutes.

Fourth fold: 2 minutes

12. Repeat the dimpling and folding process for a final time, then flip it over in the container smooth side up so that all the folds and seams are tucked underneath.

Resting: 30 minutes

13. Cover again and rest one more time for 30 minutes.

Shaping: 5–10 minutes

14. Line 2 large baking trays with some baking parchment.

15. Dust the work surface liberally with flour and use your dough scraper to turn the dough out upside down onto it, sticky side up, then dust that with flour really well too. Be gentle with your dough to keep as much air inside it as possible.

16. Divide the dough vertically into 4 long pieces with your dough scraper. Give the dough pieces another liberal dusting of flour and roll them over so that the top is back on the top. Get as much of your hands as possible underneath each end of one ciabatta at a time, then lift

and stretch it very slightly to make it a little longer and transfer 2 to each lined tray. Dimple the top of each ciabatta very slightly one last time.

Resting: 30 minutes

17. Let the loaves rest, uncovered, for 30 minutes.

18. Meanwhile, preheat your oven to 230°C fan/485°F/Gas Mark 9 with 2 shelves in the middle and a deep roasting tray on the oven floor. Half fill a kettle.

Baking: 20–25 minutes

19. Boil the kettle.

20. Place your baking trays on the oven shelves and carefully pour the hot water into the tray below. Bake your ciabattas for 20–25 minutes.

21. Let them cool completely on a wire rack.

TIPS

TIME TO DEVELOP

We know that TIME develops amazing flavour and strength in dough, leading to a better shape, better crumb texture and better moisture retention in the resulting bread, so a pre-ferment is just such a time opportunity to develop all that good stuff BEFORE making the dough. And all you have to do is mix up some flour, water and yeast and leave it to do its own work. After which it will have miraculously turned bubbly and SUPER stretchy, and just smell all the flavour that's developed!

THE EASY OPTION

I consider this to be a low-maintenance bread. Sure, it involves a certain amount of toing and froing, but if you're going about your day at home anyway, you can mix your dough, go off and do something else for a bit, then pop back to perform your folds from time to time. Once you've become accustomed to working with a wet dough like this, you'll be cracking out ciabattas easy peasy.

CURED MEATS, MARINATED VEGETABLE ANTIPASTI & OLIVES

SERVES 4–5 PEOPLE

Here's something nice for a faff-free evening with friends. Two marinated vegetable antipasti dishes you can make WAY ahead of time (and they are all the better for it), put together with some good-quality cured meats, marinated olives (homemade or shop-bought) and a couple of things to garnish. Make your own bread in the day and all you'll need to do is warm it through, plate everything nicely and open the wine …

If you wanted to go ALL OUT, try pairing this with the Well-dressed Tomato, Mozzarella, Basil & Fresh Chilli Salad (see page 96), a baked camembert with Onion & Rosemary (see page 168) or a Mint Ricotta, Green Bean Salad (see page 116).

CIABATTA

See page 89, to serve

CURED MEAT PLATE

10–12 slices of salami Napoli
    (coarse-cut with peppercorns)
10–12 slices of salami finocchio
    (fennel-seed salami)
6–8 slices of speck or prosciutto crudo
50g (1¾oz) caperberries
50g (1¾oz) sun-blushed tomatoes
olive oil
cracked black pepper

1. Delicately fold, place, bunch and drape your salamis and speck or prosciutto on a large flat plate. You can even do this part in advance if you like, just cover and refrigerate until you are ready.
2. When you are ready to serve, garnish by tucking in and around some caperberries and sun-blushed tomatoes. Drizzle with olive oil and season with black pepper.

MARINATED GARLIC, LEMON & HERB OLIVES

You can, of course, buy olives already marinated, but making your own is a really lovely touch for a home-prepared meal and literally takes a couple of minutes.

3 tablespoons olive oil
½ lemon
½ garlic clove, finely grated
2 tablespoons chopped fresh flat-leaf (Italian)
    parsley leaves and stalks
250g (9oz) stone-in olives, a mix of whichever
    ones you like the best

1. Pour the olive oil into a large bowl. Slice your lemon half into half-moons and add the pieces to the bowl with your garlic and parsley.
2. Next, add your olives to the bowl and mix everything together nicely. Told you it was easy.

MINTED AUBERGINE & COURGETTE WITH LEMON & CHILLI

Fresh mint is not just for lamb. In fact, I think it was made for courgettes. Your taste buds are in for a treat with these charred, minty, lemony, spicy slices of two highly underrated vegetables.

1 large or 2 small courgettes (zucchini)
1 aubergine (eggplant)
2 teaspoons sea salt
juice of 1 lemon
1 red chilli, sliced
4 tablespoons olive oil
3 tablespoons chopped fresh mint leaves

1. Top and tail your courgette and slice at an attractive angle into 1cm (½in) slices. Top and tail your aubergine and slice in half lengthways. Place each half cut side down onto your chopping board and cut at an angle into fancy 1cm (½in) half-moon slices.
2. Place your cut veg into a large mixing bowl. Sprinkle over the sea salt and toss together. Set aside for 1 hour for the salt to draw out some of the excess moisture.
3. While you are waiting, make your marinade. Squeeze the juice of your lemon into another large mixing bowl, add the sliced chilli and 3 tablespoons of olive oil, give it a mix and set aside.
4. Lift the vegetables from the bowl, leaving the water behind, tip the excess water down the sink and wipe out the bowl for later. Spread a clean fluff-free kitchen cloth on the side. Line up your courgette and aubergine slices in one layer and roll them up inside the cloth. Give them a squeeze to help dry them off, unroll the cloth and return your slices to the bowl.

5. Add the remaining tablespoon of olive oil to the bowl and toss the vegetable slices to coat them nicely and give them an even shine.
6. Heat a heavy non-stick frying pan (skillet) to a medium heat on the stove. Add your chopped mint to the marinade.
7. In batches, fry and char your courgette and aubergine slices. Place them in the pan in one layer and keep an eye on the heat. Your aim is for them to be evenly brown underneath and lightly charred before they are ready to turn. Try to avoid moving them around too much as they are cooking, aside from lifting a couple of slices along the way to peep underneath and make sure you're on the right track. The heat should be hot enough so that they take 2½–3 minutes to colour up on each side.
8. When each batch is done, slide them straight into the marinade. Return the pan to the heat and load up your next batch before returning to the bowl to give the cooked slices a mix.
9. When they are all done, give them a final mix and set aside to cool while inhaling the beautiful aromas.
10. These are best made a day ahead, but if you don't have time, an hour or so in the marinade will be plenty to infuse the flavours.

Shown on previous page

ROASTED PEPPERS WITH CAPERS & BASIL

The Mediterranean equivalent of Sweet & Sour. Charred sweet peppers marinated with red wine vinegar, fragrant basil and spiked with garlic.

4 (bell) peppers (yellow, orange and red)
3 tablespoons olive oil
1 tablespoon red wine vinegar
1 garlic clove
2 tablespoons capers
2 fresh basil sprigs
sea salt

1. Prick your peppers once each with a knife to make sure they don't explode in the oven (don't skip this part).
2. Place the peppers on a small parchment-lined baking tray and bake in the oven at 200°C fan/425°F/Gas Mark 7 for 40–45 minutes until soft with slightly charred skin. Set aside to cool.
3. In a large bowl, mix the olive oil with the red wine vinegar. Peel and slice the garlic thinly and add it to the bowl, then roughly chop the capers and add them to the bowl too.
4. Once baked, pull out the stalks from the peppers and discard, draining any liquid from inside. Pull them open with your fingers into segments, scrape the seeds away and peel the skin from the outside of each piece. Some parts of skin are easier to remove than others – if there are tricky patches don't stress, just leave them as they are.

5. Tear each pepper piece into thick strips and add them to the marinade. Pick the basil leaves from the stalks, tear them into pieces and add to the bowl. Season with a pinch of salt and toss everything together.
6. These are at their best when marinated overnight, but an hour will be fine if you are in a hurry.

WELL-DRESSED TOMATO, MOZZARELLA, BASIL & FRESH CHILLI SALAD

SERVES 2

Classic, classic, classic. The combination in this salad cannot be beaten and I won't pretend I invented it. But with something so traditional, something so harmonious, the real credit here goes to the ingredients.

Pick nice tomatoes, red ones, yellow ones, BIG ones, small ones, GOOD TASTY ones. Pick a decent mozzarella too and fresh basil, trimmed from a proud and healthy-looking plant set in the sun on your windowsill wherever you are.

I've spiked my salad with chilli and dressed it with PLENTY of olive oil and as you start to get down to the bottom of the plate, you'll realise … that spicy, salty, tomato juice, olive oil deliciousness hiding beneath is patiently waiting to be soaked up with homemade ciabatta.

350g (12½oz) of the tastiest colourful tomatoes you can find
1 red chilli
3 tablespoons olive oil
1 ball (150g/5½oz) of mozzarella
3 fresh basil sprigs
sea salt flakes and cracked black pepper
Ciabatta (see page 89), to serve

1. Cut your tomatoes thoughtfully into attractive shapes and place them in a large bowl. Slice some, wedge some, chop some, whatever you like, just take your time and make them nice.

2. Season well with a pinch of salt, gently toss them and set aside.

3. Top and tail your chilli and slice in half down the middle. Remove the seeds and discard them. Finely slice the chilli into 2mm (1/16in) strips and chop into teeny tiny squares. Place in a small bowl with the olive oil. Set aside.

4. Drain the liquid from the mozzarella, pat it gently on kitchen paper and tear it up into pieces.

5. Carefully lift your tomatoes from the bowl, leaving the excess salty juice behind, and arrange in an attractive layer on a large serving plate. Place your mozzarella in and around the tomatoes, pick the leaves from the basil sprigs and tuck them in, under and around. Season all over with a pinch of sea salt flakes and black pepper, paying close attention to the until now unseasoned mozzarella.

6. Spoon over the chilli and drizzle with the olive oil. Serve with homemade ciabatta.

LEEK & BRIE RISOTTO WITH CRISPY GARLIC BREADCRUMBS

SERVES 2

Risotto is the definition of humble. Isn't it incredible that there is so much love invested in a dish that it can make even a simple leek and a slice of cheese into an incredible dinner?

Here I've used an old bread offcut to create a tasty, crispy breadcrumb topping and hiding beneath, a molten slice of Brie. Don't feel like they need to be confined to this dish only, make extra crumbs and use them to top pasta dishes, soups and even salads.

For the breadcrumbs
100g (3½oz) stale bread
4 tablespoons olive oil
1 garlic clove
½ tablespoon chopped
   fresh thyme leaves
sea salt

For the stock
1 carrot, halved
1 celery stick, halved
1 medium white onion,
   peeled and halved
2 garlic cloves, peeled
   and halved
1 litre (34fl oz) water

For the leeks
1 leek
1 tablespoon olive oil
1 tablespoon butter
2 teaspoons chopped
   fresh thyme leaves

For the risotto
1 large banana shallot
35g (1¼oz) butter
150g (5½oz) Arborio rice
100ml (3½oz) white wine
800ml–1 litre (27–34fl oz) stock
20g (¾oz) Parmesan cheese,
   plus extra for grating
3 tablespoons single cream
2 thick slices (70g/2½oz)
   of Brie
olive oil
cracked black pepper

Making the crumbs

1. Whizz up your bread in a food processor until it resembles rustic crumbs.

2. Heat the oil in a large non-stick frying pan (skillet) to a medium heat. Add the crumbs and a pinch of salt and toss to coat them all in the oil. Toast them gently for 8 minutes or so until golden all over.

3. Finely grate the garlic and add to the pan with the chopped thyme leaves. Stir together and cook for a further minute or so. Tip the crumbs onto a kitchen paper-lined tray to cool and drain the excess oil.

Making the stock

4. Place your stock vegetables and water in a large saucepan. Bring to the boil and simmer gently for 20 minutes. Keep hot over the heat.

For the leeks

5. Remove any dodgy leaves from the outside of your leek. Top and tail it and split it down the middle. Slice each piece into 1cm (½in) thick slices and place them in a large mixing bowl. Fill the bowl to the top with water, mix around your leeks and leave them to settle so any dirt sinks to the bottom.

6. Lift out the leeks and place in a colander to drain.

7. Heat the olive oil in a large non-stick frying pan over a medium-high heat. Add the leeks and a pinch of salt, toss and cook on a fast sizzle for 2 minutes. Turn the heat down and cook for a further 4–5 minutes to intensify their flavour while taking on minimum colour.

8. Stir through the butter and thyme. Cook for a further 2 minutes, then spread the leeks out on a plate to cool and set aside.

Making the risotto

9. Chop your shallot finely, trying to match the size of the rice if you can. Place a large saucepan over a medium heat, add the butter, melt

Recipe continued overleaf

and let it sizzle, then add the shallot with a pinch of salt. Cook
for 2 minutes over a gentle heat and add the rice to the pan.

10. Toast the rice for 8–10 minutes. It will start going a little brown
in places and the butter will come out and start getting foamy again.
At this point, without any additional moisture, you are in no danger
of the rice sticking to the pan, so there's no need to stir it all the
time. The worst that can happen is that it can burn, so keep an
eye on the temperature and colour of the rice and shallot.

11. Crank up the heat a touch and add the wine. It will immediately
bubble and boil and simmer away. When the sound of the pan
goes from shhhhhhh back to sssssssssss, you know it's all gone.

12. Add a couple of ladles of your hot vegetable stock and stir the
pan while it is gently simmering and being absorbed by the rice.
As the rice takes on the stock and gets thick, add the next couple
of ladles. The more you stir, the more you are coaxing natural
starches from the rice and the creamier your final risotto will be.

13. Keep adding stock and stirring on and off for the next 18–20
minutes. Remember, there is no salt in your stock so, every once
in a while, taste the liquid surrounding the rice to see if it needs
a pinch and adjust it as you go along. Towards the end of cooking,
begin to taste the rice for 'doneness' too. When it still has a little
bite but no chalkiness in your teeth, it's done.

14. Remove the risotto from the heat. Add the leeks, Parmesan
and single cream and mix it all together.

15. Have a final check for seasoning and divide the risotto between
2 shallow bowls. Top each with a generous slice of Brie and leave
to warm through before finishing with a drizzle of olive oil and
a pinch of black pepper. Serve with your crispy crumbs.

TIP

AN IMPORTANT NOTE ON STOCK

In this recipe I've used vegetable stock that I've made. If you've never done
it, as you read the recipe you'll realise it's so easy it's silly.

I have seen vegetable stock dust used liberally in kitchens in soups and
risottos, but the idea of a powder made to TASTE LIKE vegetables in water is
crackers. REAL flavour is already here, in our leek, in our herbs, in our butter,
wine, rice and Parmesan. If we use it well, we can celebrate it. True vegetable
stock is not about embarking on a journey of simmering, skimming, passing,
straining, refining, clarifying … it's vegetables, imparting their subtle flavour
upon the water in which it sits for like, 20 minutes.

It's a LAYER of flavour. Not the ENTIRE flavour.

GARLIC NAAN BREAD

MAKES 6 LARGE NAAN BREADS

I have no Indian ancestry, so I don't have a family naan bread recipe passed down through the generations. BUT what I do have is an understanding of the PRINCIPLES of bread-making.

We know naan is ultra-light and soft, so it must be a pretty wet dough, and it has those little scorched bubbles on top. Traditionally, it's baked stuck to the side of a tandoor, a very hot barrel-shaped clay oven with burning hot coals at the bottom – SUPER-FAST to keep the softness and moisture in and encourage those large bubbles while toasting the bottom and scorching the top at the same time.

The aim is to create BIG, inconsistent BUBBLES in a super-wet dough, so we go for stretching and folding over kneading to achieve that. I've made these again and again, tweaking and adjusting, and through that process I've learnt a whole lot more. I hope you like them too!

=== EASY AND POSSIBLY A LITTLE STICKY TO MAKE, ===
TRICKY TO BAKE / TOTAL TIME: 3½–4 HOURS

You'll need: a large, heavy frying pan (skillet)

320g (11¼oz) room-temperature water
50g (1¾oz) natural yoghurt
15g (½oz) golden caster (superfine) sugar

12g (½oz) fresh yeast, crumbled, or 7g (¼oz) fast-action dried yeast
10g (½oz) olive or vegetable oil, plus extra for oiling
500g (1lb 2oz) strong white bread flour
8g (¼oz) salt
10g (½oz) nigella (black onion) seeds

For the garlic butter
125g (4½oz) room-temperature unsalted butter
1 garlic clove, finely grated
1 tablespoon chopped fresh coriander (cilantro)
pinch of salt

Making the dough: 15–20 minutes

1. In a large mixing bowl, mix together the water, yoghurt, sugar and yeast until the yeast has dissolved. Then add the oil.

2. Add the flour, salt and nigella seeds, then mix with a dough scraper until the mixture comes together into a cohesive dough with no obvious wet or dry patches.

Resting: 45 minutes

3. Cover the dough with an upturned bowl or plate and let the dough rest at room temperature for 45 minutes.

First fold: 5 minutes

4. Oil a small area of clean work surface with vegetable oil. Turn your dough out upside down onto the oily patch. Grasp a bit of the dough edge, stretch it out and then fold it over onto the dough. Repeat all the way round the dough edge, making about 10–12 folds, until you have a ball.

Resting: 30 minutes

5. Turn the dough over, smooth side up, and place it back in the bowl. Cover as before and rest for 30 minutes.

Recipe continued overleaf

Second fold: 5 minutes

6. Oil your work surface again, then turn the dough out upside down onto it. Repeat the first fold process BUT this time make only 4 to 6 folds.

Resting: 30 minutes

7. Turn the dough smooth side up and place it back in the bowl. Cover and rest as before.

Dividing and pre-shaping: 5–10 minutes

8. Oil your work surface again, then turn the dough out upside down onto it.

9. Use your fingertips to flatten the dough gently and cut it into 6 equal-sized pieces with your dough scraper. If you want them all to be exactly the same size, weigh them out at about 155g (5½oz) each.

10. Fold and roll each piece of dough into a loose ball (see page 24).

Resting and making the garlic butter: 45 minutes

11. Oil a large tray. Line up your 6 oily dough balls on the tray, cover loosely with cling film and let them rest for 45 minutes to relax and puff.

12. Meanwhile, mix the garlic butter ingredients together in a bowl until thoroughly combined. Set aside.

Final shaping and baking: 30–40 minutes

13. Preheat your large, heavy frying pan (skillet) over a medium-high heat and your grill (broiler) on hot (mine goes on full blast) with a shelf inside.

14. Oil another large tray for shaping. Place a dough ball on your new tray and press with your fingertips to dimple the dough slightly. Be delicate here, but make sure you press right down to the tray. Then pick the dough up and stretch it into that classic naan teardrop shape as best as you can.

15. Place your naan in the hot pan and cook the underside for 2 minutes, then transfer it to the grill and bake the top for 2 minutes. Let the first one be your tester! It should be dark golden underneath, and golden on the top with a few scorches on the biggest bubbles.

16. Repeat with the remaining dough balls.

17. If you are eating your naans straight away, spread with the butter while they are hot from baking and let it melt over the top. Otherwise, cool the naans completely on a wire rack.

TIP

MAKING AHEAD

Because these are thin, moist and lightly baked, they are perfect for freezing and bringing back to peak freshness straight from the freezer or stashing in the fridge. Once completely cool, spread with the garlic butter and layer them up with a sheet of baking parchment inbetween each one. Place them in a reusable plastic or freezer bag and keep them in the fridge for up to a week or the freezer until you're ready to use them. Then preheat your oven to 180°C fan/400°F/Gas Mark 6. Bake a buttered naan on a baking tray from the fridge for 4–5 minutes or from frozen for 10–12 minutes.

ONION BHAJI & MANGO NAAN WRAP

SERVES 2

Thin and crispy nests of spiced onion, all wrapped up in a warm garlic naan with a fresh mango salad and coconut yoghurt. Since they are so LIGHT, frozen naan bread comes back to full freshness in minutes under the grill and are perfect for making wraps. If you've never made onion bhajis before, erase all memory of those dense balls you can get in the supermarket. These are so different and so, so easy to make too.

For the mango salad
½ mango
10cm (4in) piece of cucumber
½ red chilli
½ tablespoon chopped fresh
   mint leaves
½ tablespoon chopped fresh
   coriander (cilantro) leaves
juice of ½ lime
pinch of salt

For the bhajis
1 medium white onion
   (roughly 150g/5½oz
   when peeled and sliced)
1 medium egg
1 teaspoon cumin seeds
1 teaspoon coriander seeds
½ teaspoon ground turmeric
60g (2¼oz) gram flour
   (or plain/all-purpose flour
   if you struggle to find it)
sunflower oil, for frying
salt

To finish
2 Garlic Naan Breads
   (see page 101)
½ baby gem lettuce
2 tablespoons coconut yoghurt
fresh coriander (cilantro) sprigs
a few slices of chilli
lime wedges, for squeezing

Making the salad

1. Peel your mango and slice off one half from the stone. Place it cut-side down on the chopping board and slice it lengthways into strips as thin as you can. Add to a large mixing bowl.
2. Halve your cucumber down the middle and use a peeler to slice it into long ribbons. Add them to the mango bowl.
3. Slice your chilli down the middle, remove the seeds, cut it into matchsticks and then the other way into teeny cubes. Add them to the bowl along with the chopped herbs, lime juice and pinch of salt. Mix it all together and set aside.

Making the bhajis

4. Top, tail and peel your onion. Cut it in half down the middle and slice it into half rings. Break them up, separating the layers.
5. Beat your egg in a large mixing bowl with a pinch of salt. Add your onion and toss to coat.
6. Crush your seeds lightly using a pestle and mortar just to crack them up, not to make them into a powder. Add them to another large bowl with the turmeric, flour and another pinch of salt and mix together.
7. Tip the spiced flour mixture into the onion mixture and mix around until there is no flour left. Divide the mixture into 4 round-ish piles using 2 spoons.
8. In a large heavy frying pan (skillet), heat 1cm (½in) of sunflower oil to a medium heat.
9. With your 2 spoons, lift the bhajis and pop them into the oil. Use the spoons to flatten and kind of separate the onion into an even-layered, quite sparse nest. There should be JUST ENOUGH of the flour and egg mixture to hold it together. Fry all 4 together if you can fit them in the pan, otherwise do them in batches of 2. They will take around 2½ minutes to get nice and golden on the

underside, then carefully flip them over in the oil to finish the other side for a further 2½ minutes.

10. Lift from the oil and drain on kitchen paper, seasoning with salt one more time while hot.

Bringing it all together

11. Warm your naan breads under the grill (broiler).

12. Place a couple of baby gem leaves on each one and a generous pile of your mango salad. Top with 2 bhajis per bread and a tablespoon of coconut yoghurt before garnishing with some coriander leaves on the stalk and chilli slices. Roll up your wraps and serve with lime wedges for squeezing.

SPICED SPLIT PEA BOWL WITH NAAN

SERVES 4

I feel like lentils, split peas and other such pulses often wrongly get a BAD WRAP, failing to cross the border from their possibly slightly boring reputation to something pretty cool and edgy! From dated to RETRO. From 'old hat' TO 'old school'! Well, to play my part in their resurrection and express my love for the humble split pea, here's a wholesome, warming bowl in which to dip your homemade naan. Spiked with chilli, spiced with fragrant fennel, cumin and coriander seed, this one is MOREISH. Feel free to make a massive batch and freeze before adding the fresh herbs at the end.

200g (7oz) yellow split peas
1½ teaspoons coriander seeds
1½ teaspoons cumin seeds
1 teaspoon fennel seeds
40g (1½oz) butter
1 tablespoon olive oil
1 medium white onion, sliced
1 carrot, peeled and
   coarsely grated
pinch of salt
½ red chilli, sliced
2 garlic cloves, finely grated
20g (¾oz) fresh ginger,
   finely grated
2 plum tomatoes, chopped
500ml (17fl oz) chicken stock
400ml (13½fl oz) tinned
   coconut milk
juice of ½ lime
2 tablespoons chopped
   fresh mint leaves
2 tablespoons chopped fresh
   coriander (cilantro) leaves

To finish
4 tablespoons thick
   plain yoghurt
fresh coriander
   (cilantro) leaves
lime wedges, for squeezing
a few slices of chilli
2–4 Garlic Naan Breads
   (see page 101), warmed

For the peas: A day ahead

1. Place your split peas into a container and cover with a couple of centimetres of water. Leave to soak overnight, in the fridge.

2. The next day, drain in a colander and rinse with clean water, then set aside.

3. Crush your spices together using a pestle and mortar and set aside.

4. Heat a large saucepan to a medium heat, add the butter and oil and let it foam before adding the onion and carrot. Cook with a pinch of salt for 10 minutes until soft and sweet with minimum colour.

5. Add the chilli, garlic and ginger and cook for a further 2 minutes.

6. Add the crushed spices and cook for a further 2 minutes before stirring in the peas and chopped tomatoes.

7. Cook for a minute or 2 just to get some heat into the peas, and then add the stock, coconut milk and lime juice.

8. Mix and bring to the boil. Boil well for 30 minutes. You may find in this time that the liquid will reduce too much, so top it up with some hot water from the kettle as you go if you need to.

9. Turn the heat down to a simmer and cook for a further 20–25 minutes until the peas are cooked through.

10. When your peas are cooked and the mixture has thickened, mash them a little with a masher and mix through your chopped fresh herbs.

11. Divide the peas among 4 bowls, top each with a tablespoon of yoghurt and garnish with more fresh coriander leaves, lime wedges and sliced chilli.

12. Serve alongside the warm naan breads.

--- TIP ---

AVOID STICKING

If the peas begin to stick to the base of the pan, remove it from the heat and let it sit for 2–3 minutes. This should loosen the stuck peas allowing you to mix them back into the rest with a spatula instead of leaving them there to burn!

ROSEMARY & SEA SALT FOCACCIA

MAKES 1 LARGE FOCACCIA OR 4 SMALL FOCACCIAS

A good focaccia is a dream bread – super-soft, super-light, a salty explosion of flavour on the top and PLENTY of olive oil. The key to this super lightness is its almost liquid dough, which isn't required to hold its shape, like a bloomer for example, as it's flat and contained in a pie tin or tray. This is the case where the often-quoted saying 'the wetter the dough, the better the bread' couldn't be more apt, and it's also why we can get away with skipping the kneading process.

We know that kneading dough develops its strength by making it strong and elastic so that when the yeast makes bubbles the dough can hold them all and PUFF UP, but there is something else that develops the strength too … TIME. That doesn't mean we can just sit back and do nothing, though. To build the all-important STRUCTURE, we need to pop back to our dough every once in a while when it's resting to give it a fold.

This beautiful, rustic bread makes a show-stopping centrepiece for a Mediterranean-inspired feast, ready to cut into rectangles or triangles or tear into chunks. It's at its best on the day you've made it, still soft on day two and after that, it will make an incredible toasted sandwich and the crispiest croutons you've ever experienced (see page 114).

═ EASY BUT PERHAPS A LITTLE STICKY TO MAKE, EASY TO BAKE / TOTAL TIME: 4–4¾ HOURS ═

You'll need: a high-sided baking tray about 30 x 40cm (12 x 16in) for making one large focaccia or 4 x 22cm (8½in) round enamel pie tins for 4 small focaccias (I prefer the latter because these are quicker to bake with less risk of toasting the toppings and losing their flavour, plus they look wicked!)

190g (6¾oz) room-temperature milk
190g (6¾oz) room-temperature water
12g (½oz) fresh yeast, crumbled, or 7g (¼oz) fast-action dried yeast
500g (1lb 2oz) strong white bread flour
8g (¼oz) salt

20g (¾oz) olive oil, plus extra for oiling

For the topping
3 fresh rosemary sprigs
olive oil
sea salt flakes

Making the dough: 5–10 minutes
1. In a large mixing bowl, mix together the milk, water and yeast until the yeast has dissolved.
2. Add the flour and salt, then mix with a dough scraper until the mixture starts to come together. Add the olive oil and mix again into a dough – as we are not kneading this one, it's really important that it comes together into a cohesive mass with no lumps or dry or oily patches.

Resting: 30 minutes
3. Cover the bowl with an upturned bowl and rest at room temperature for 30 minutes.

First fold: 5 minutes
4. Oil an area of clean work surface. Oil the surface of your dough and turn it out upside down onto the oily patch. For this first fold, we are the most thorough. Grasp a bit of the dough edge, stretch it out and then fold it over onto the dough. Repeat all the way round the dough, making about 10–12 folds, until you have a ball.

Resting: 45 minutes
5. Turn the dough over, smooth side up, and place it back in the bowl. Cover as before and rest for 45 minutes.

Recipe continued overleaf

Second fold: 2 minutes

6. Oil your work surface again, then turn the dough out upside down onto it. Repeat the first fold process BUT this time make only 6 to 8 folds.

Resting: 45 minutes

7. Turn the dough smooth side up and place it back in the bowl. Cover and rest as before.

Third fold: 2 minutes

8. Repeat the second fold process as before.

Resting: 30 minutes

9. Turn the dough smooth side up and place it back in the bowl. Cover as before BUT this time rest for 30 minutes.

10. Meanwhile, make your topping. Pick your rosemary leaves and place them in a bowl and add 4–5 tablespoons of olive oil. Mix together and set aside.

Dividing, shaping and topping: 5–10 minutes

11. If you're making one large focaccia, line your high-sided baking tray with baking parchment. Drizzle with a little olive oil and slide the whole dough pillow out of the bowl and into the tray.

12. If making 4 small focaccias, line and oil your pie tins as above. Slide the dough onto the work surface, smooth side up, cut it into 4 pieces with your dough scraper and carefully transfer each piece into a prepared tin. Be gentle with your dough to keep as much gas inside it as possible.

13. Press your puffy dough all over with your fingertips, right down to the tray, to create dimples and to spread the dough out naturally – don't try to stretch your dough sideways to make it fit the tray, as it will only ping back and go crinkly! And be careful not to flatten the dough and lose too much gas. Pour the rosemary oil over the top and dimple the dough again with your fingertips.

Resting: 45 minutes–1 hour

14. Let the focaccia rest, uncovered, for a final 45 minutes–1 hour until risen and delicate to the touch.

15. Towards the end of resting, preheat your oven to 200°C fan/425°F/Gas Mark 7 with a shelf in the middle, or 2 if using pie tins, and a deep roasting tray on the oven floor. Half fill a kettle.

Baking: 25–40 minutes

16. Boil the kettle.

17. Sprinkle a little sea salt evenly over the top of your focaccia. Place your baking tray or tins on the oven shelf or shelves and carefully pour the hot water into the tray below. Bake for 30–40 minutes for the large tray or 25–30 minutes for the pie tins. Slide a knife underneath the bread, lift it and take a peep. If it's golden all over the underside, it's ready, but if it's still a little pale in the centre, bake for another 5 minutes and check again.

18. Drizzle once again with olive oil, then remove the focaccia from the tray or tins as soon as it's cool enough to handle and let the focaccia cool completely on a wire rack.

—————— **TIP** ——————

TOPPING TIPS

A focaccia can be a blank canvas for so many good things as long as you follow a few simple rules:

＊ You need olive oil to stop the rosemary or other toppings from drying up and burning in the oven, and to allow its flavour to penetrate down into the bread. So, whatever topping you choose, mix it first with a generous amount of olive oil.

＊ Don't choose ingredients that will make the dough too wet. For example, halved cherry tomatoes with the juice squeezed out are great but chopped-up beef toms will make everything soggy!

＊ Woody herbs like rosemary, thyme, oregano and sage work better than fine soft herbs, like parsley, chervil and chives, which will dry out and lose their flavour if you bake them on the top of your bread, although feel free to add them AFTER baking.

A FEW TOPPINGS TO TRY

-1-
ONION & ROSEMARY

Slice a medium white onion and place it in a saucepan with a generous drizzle of olive oil and a pinch of salt. Bring the pan up to a medium heat and gently cook for 20–25 minutes until soft and sweet. Mix through 1 teaspoon of chopped fresh rosemary leaves and let it cool. TASTE to make sure you have the seasoning just right, then top your focaccia with this delicious mixture, and once it bakes you'll get that sweet and delicious onion flavour with little charred peaks. YUM.

-2-
GARLIC, OLIVE & WHOLE LEMON SLICES

This is a refined version of an idea somebody had in one of my classes. Whole lemon slices (peel and all) can be an acquired taste for some, but I love the bitterness that comes with it. Thinly slice half a lemon and place it in a bowl with 100g (3½oz) of torn pitted Kalamata olives, 2 finely grated garlic cloves, 2 tablespoons of mixed chopped fresh thyme and oregano (if you can find the latter fresh) and a generous drizzle of olive oil. Mix together and scrunch it all up with your hands to release the flavours. Pour over the top of your focaccia dough, spread it out and dimple it all over before the final resting.

-3-
TOMATO

Halve 150g (5½oz) of cherry tomatoes, squeeze out the juice of half of them and discard. Squeeze out the juice of the remaining tomatoes into a mixing bowl and add the tomato halves, some picked soft thyme sprigs and 2 cloves of finely grated garlic. Add a couple of good glugs of olive oil, a pinch of salt and scrunch everything up really well. Arrange the tomatoes over the top of your focaccia, push some of them right to the bottom and this will stop the dough ballooning up and your tomatoes sliding off the side! Finally, drizzle over the delicious juices from the bowl and leave for its final rest.

Focaccia toppings are limitless! Here are some more ideas:

Mushrooms – chestnut or wild, sautéed in a pan with garlic and herbs, combined with some nice cheese like taleggio and chopped hazelnuts (filberts).

Leftover Antipasti – charred (bell) peppers, sun-dried tomatoes, marinated courgettes (zucchini), aubergines (eggplants) and artichoke hearts; these oily and tasty antipasti items make ideal ready-made focaccia toppers.

Sunday Roast Veg – cold cooked broccoli, orange zest and pine nuts, cooked carrots with shallots, goat's cheese and pumpkin seeds; roasted parsnips with honey, thyme and feta cheese.

PROPER CAESAR SALAD WITH MASSIVE FOCACCIA CROUTONS & CRISPY CHICKEN

SERVES 2

Crisp lettuce, giant crunchy croutons and a punchy garlicky dressing under a blanket of shaved Parmesan – a good Caesar salad such as this can hold its own even without the chicken, though the addition of highly underrated crispy skin chicken thighs, if you so desire, makes it extra special.

   I use a Rosemary & Sea Salt Focaccia here for my croutons, which are simply the lightest and crunchiest on the planet, and best made when the focaccia is a couple of days old. You can of course use other breads – ciabatta would work well too (see page 89).

For the chicken (optional)
4 small chicken thighs, skin on
1 tablespoon olive oil,
   plus extra for cooking
1 tablespoon chopped
   fresh thyme leaves
finely grated zest of ½ lemon

For the croutons
200g (7oz) stale Rosemary
   & Sea Salt Focaccia
   (see page 109)
1½ tablespoons olive oil
pinch of sea salt flakes

For the dressing
½ garlic clove
1 anchovy fillet in oil, drained
50g (1¾oz) mayonnaise
50g (1¾oz) Greek yoghurt
20g (¾oz) Parmesan cheese,
   finely grated, plus extra
   for topping
1 teaspoon lemon juice
1 teaspoon olive oil, plus
   extra for drizzling

1 baby red cos (romaine)
   lettuce, for the salad
salt and cracked black pepper

Marinating the chicken (if using): A day ahead
1. Remove the bone from your chicken thighs, losing the minimum amount of meat as possible, and trim off any nobbly bits.
2. In a large mixing bowl, mix together the olive oil, thyme and lemon zest. Toss the chicken in the mixture, then transfer it and the marinade to a smaller container, cover and refrigerate overnight.

Making the croutons
3. Preheat your oven to 180°C fan/400°F/Gas Mark 6. Line a large baking tray with baking parchment.
4. Tear your focaccia into BIG chunks, 4–5cm (1½–2in) wide. Place in a large mixing bowl, add the olive oil and sea salt and toss together. Wipe the bread around the bowl to mop up the remaining oil like a sponge before spreading in a single layer on your lined tray.
5. Bake for 15–20 minutes until golden. Turn the oven off, open the door a crack and let the croutons cool and dry out.

Making the dressing
6. Using a large pestle and mortar, crush the garlic with the anchovy and pound to a paste. Add all the other ingredients and mix together. Taste and season with salt if you feel you need to.

Cooking the chicken
7. Season the chicken thighs with a pinch of salt all over. Add 1 tablespoon of olive oil to a heavy frying pan (skillet) large enough to hold them quite snugly (they will shrink as they cook). Place the thighs, skin side down, in the cold pan and bring it up to a steady sizzle over a medium heat. Give them 12–15 minutes on the skin side, lifting to peep under every once in a while – the skin should get really golden like crackling and you should see the heat creep halfway up the sides of the chicken. Then turn up the heat, turn

the thighs and cook for another 2–3 minutes to finish off. Remove from the pan and rest on a plate for 5–10 minutes.

Putting it all together

8. Pick and wash your lettuce leaves, then dry them in a spinner or on kitchen paper.

9. Place leaves in a bowl with 12–16 croutons, reserving 2 big ones for later. Add your dressing and toss everything together until well coated. Using tongs, divide the lettuce leaves and croutons between 2 bowls, alternating between the 2 and building your salad nice and high.

10. If using, slice the chicken at a shallow angle and tuck the slices in and around the salad, or serve on a separate board.

11. Shave over a fine blanket of Parmesan and season with cracked blacked pepper.

12. Finally, scrunch up the reserved croutons in your hands, sprinkle the crumbs over the top and drizzle with a little olive oil.

MINT RICOTTA, GREEN BEAN SALAD

SERVES 3–4

This salad has been a Bake with Jack class standard forever – fresh greens with a silky lemon dressing, layered with minty ricotta and finished with salty, nutty pumpkin seeds. It's perfectly complemented by grilled or toasted focaccia slices for spreading the ricotta over, but equally delicious stuffed into a pitta pocket (see page 124).

100g (3½oz) frozen broad
    (fava) beans
250g (9oz) fine green beans
50g (1¾oz) pumpkin seeds
60g (2¼oz) rocket
    (arugula) leaves
salt and cracked black pepper

For the ricotta
250g (9oz) pot of ricotta cheese
2 tablespoons chopped
    fresh mint leaves
finely grated zest of 1 lemon
1 tablespoon olive oil

For the dressing
juice of ½ lemon (20ml/½fl oz)
2 teaspoons Dijon mustard
1 teaspoon caster
    (superfine) sugar
3 tablespoons olive oil,
    plus extra for drizzling

grilled (broiled) or toasted
    slices of focaccia
    (see page 109), to serve

Making the ricotta

1. In a large mixing bowl, mix all the ricotta ingredients together, adding a pinch of salt. Taste and adjust the seasoning if you need to, then place it back in its pot and refrigerate for an hour or so to allow the flavours to come together.

Preparing the beans

2. Place your broad beans in a bowl, cover with cold water and set aside to defrost gently, refreshing the water if it freezes up. Drain, then pop each bean from its shell and lay on kitchen paper to dry.
3. Trim the tops from your green beans. Blanch in a large pan of salted, boiling water for 2 minutes, drain and set aside to dry.

Toasting the seeds

4. Toast the pumpkin seeds in a small, dry frying pan (skillet) over a medium heat until they start popping. Keep toasting for 30 seconds, add a pinch of salt, then sprinkle with just enough water to dissolve the salt so that it sticks to the seeds – too much water and your seeds will become chewy. Cook away the water, dry out the seeds, then continue to toast until golden. Cool on a plate.

Making the dressing

5. Place the lemon juice, mustard, sugar and a pinch of salt in a jam jar, add the lid, shake to combine and dissolve the sugar.
6. Add the olive oil and shake like crazy to emulsify as best you can. With an eggless dressing made this way, it can split back into its 2 constituent parts if it's left to stand, so keep it in the jar and shake one more time just before dressing your salad.

Putting it all together

7. Put the beans and rocket in a large bowl. Pour over 2–3 tablespoons of your lemon dressing and toss everything together.
8. Build the salad up on a plate, alternating the dressed beans and rocket with spoonfuls of the ricotta, finishing with ricotta on the top. Sprinkle over the pumpkin seeds, drizzle with olive oil and sprinkle with some cracked black pepper.
9. Serve with grilled or toasted slices of focaccia.

FOUR-CHEESE FOCACCIA TOASTIE WITH TOMATO DIPPING SAUCE

SERVES 2 HUNGRY PEOPLE OR 1 REALLY HUNGRY PERSON

Sometimes things just happen. One day I had a sorry-looking stale pie-tin focaccia left over. It just so happens that it was the EXACT SAME SIZE as my smallest frying pan. And in the fridge I had some random cheese offcuts, the last remaining knob of garlic and parsley butter, some cold pasta sauce ... and the rest is history. Enjoy!

1 small (pie-tin) Rosemary
& Sea Salt Focaccia
(see page 109)
2 tablespoons Garlic & Parsley
Butter (see page 60)
100g (3½oz) cheese – I had
Cheddar, mozzarella and
taleggio in equal parts
leftover tomato sauce from
Stale Bread Meatballs with
Pappardelle (see page 41)
salt and cracked black pepper

1. Slice your focaccia in half horizontally. Butter the bottom half with 1 tablespoon of the butter and arrange your cheese on top. Season with salt, then replace the lid.

2. Carefully transfer the focaccia to a small frying pan (skillet) where it will fit snugly.

3. Cut a circle of baking parchment exactly the size of the bread and place on top, followed by a small saucepan with a can of beans or something similar inside. This will press your toastie nicely.

4. Cook your toastie SLOWLY over a low heat for 5–6 minutes, then remove the paper, pan and can and flip your toastie. Replace the paper, pan and can and toast for another 5–6 minutes until the cheese is melty inside.

5. Cut in half and serve alongside your sauce, hot or cold!

TIP

CONTINGENCY PLAN

If you're making this on a gas stove, you'll be able to keep the temperature of the pan really steady. Still have a peep underneath every once in a while, though, to make sure nothing is burning. On electric or induction stoves, it's a little trickier, as they will click on and off as they try to adjust the temperature and will probably end up scorching the underside. If this is you, then have the oven on at 180°C fan/400°F/Gas Mark 6 just in case. Give the toastie a minute or 2 on each side in the frying pan before removing the paper, pan and beans from the top and transferring it to the oven (if your pan is ovenproof or move your toastie onto a baking tray) for 10–12 minutes to heat through to the middle.

FOUGASSE

MAKES 4 DECENT-SIZED FOUGASSE

These look lovely, don't they? The amazing thing about fougasse is that they are SO EASY to make and look so impressive in your bread basket that your dinner guests may not believe you didn't just pop out to an artisan bakery to buy them.

A simple dough like this can be completely transformed in terms of flavour and texture just by giving it more TIME. Once we have kneaded the dough in the traditional way, all we have to do is … nothing! You simply stash it in the fridge for tomorrow where it slowly ticks over making an amazing flavour all by itself. There is no second rest before it bakes, so we can just take the dough straight from the fridge, cut it into designs that we like and BAKE them! Fougasse is traditionally a leaf shape, but don't feel you have to recreate the shapes I have made here EXACTLY. In fact, I'd love it if you applied your own creative flair and made something never before seen.

=========== EASY TO MAKE, EASY TO BAKE / TOTAL TIME: 7–9 HOURS ===========

320g (11¼oz) room-temperature water 12g (½oz) fresh yeast, crumbled, or 7g (¼oz) fast-action yeast	450g (1lb) strong white bread flour, plus extra for dusting	50g (1¾oz) strong wholemeal flour 10g (½oz) salt

Making the dough: 15–20 minutes

1. In a large mixing bowl, mix together the water and yeast until the yeast has dissolved.
2. Add the flours and salt. Mix with a dough scraper until the mixture comes together.
3. Turn your dough out onto a clean work surface and knead without any additional flour for 8 minutes.

Resting: 6–8 hours

4. Shape the dough into a ball and place it back in the bowl. Cover the bowl with cling film and place it in the fridge for 6–8 hours.

Dividing and shaping: 10–15 minutes

5. Preheat your oven to 230°C fan/485°F/Gas Mark 9 with a shelf in the middle and a deep roasting tray on the oven floor. Half fill a kettle.
6. Line a baking tray with baking parchment.
7. Remove your dough from the fridge – you should notice that it now smells amazing.
8. Dust the work surface lightly with flour and turn the dough out upside down onto it, then dust the sticky side with flour too.

9. Using your fingertips, gently dimple your dough into a circle and cut it into 4 triangles with your dough scraper. Liberally dust them with flour.
10. For a leaf shape, working with one piece of dough at a time, make a long cut down the middle (see page122) with the long flat side of your dough scraper, then make shorter cuts down each side. Stretch the dough to open all the cuts then add very small cuts around the outside edge to give your fougasse little spikes. Place it on your lined tray.
11. If you can't fit ALL your fougasse onto one baking tray, the shaped-up fougasse will happily sit and wait their turn to be baked on a sheet of baking parchment.

Baking: 15–30 minutes

12. Boil the kettle.
13. Place your baking tray on the oven shelf and carefully pour the hot water into the tray below. Bake the fougasse for 12–15 minutes.
14. Let them cool completely on a wire rack.

A FEW FLAVOURS TO TRY

-1-
BLACK OLIVE
& ROSEMARY

This is my favourite fougasse flavour by miles
– I just can't help but love the olive/bread
combo. Pat 100g (3½oz) of torn pitted Kalamata
olives dry in between a few sheets of kitchen
paper. When you have finished kneading your
dough, give it 5–10 minutes to relax a little.
Then press down with your fingertips and
knuckles to spread the dough into a circle,
sprinkle half your olives and ½ a tablespoon
of chopped fresh rosemary leaves over the
top and fold them up inside. Press the dough
out flat again and repeat with the remaining
olives and another ½ tablespoon of rosemary.
Shape the dough into a ball and continue with
the resting stage through to baking as in the
main method (see page 121).

-2-
SESAME & CARAWAY

Spread a mixture of sesame and caraway seeds
out over a tray. Spray the top of your shaped-up,
ready-to-bake fougasse with water and flip the
fougasse upside down into your tray of seeds so
that they stick. Give the fougasse a little shake
before placing it on your lined tray for baking.

-3-
FRESH HERBS

Add 1 tablespoon of finely chopped woody
herb leaves, such as rosemary, thyme, sage
or oregano, to the flour at the beginning
of the method for fresh, fragrant fougasse.

TIP

CUTTING KNOW-HOW

When making cuts in your fougasse, use the 2 straight
sides of your dough scraper, the long side for long cuts
and a short side for small cuts, but avoid the curved
edge, as I find it's all too easy to make a mess
of things that way. Push the scraper straight down
into the dough to cut, as opposed to using a sawing
motion. Be sure to stretch the cuts open to really
exaggerate them, otherwise they may close up as
the fougasse dough puffs up slightly during baking.

PITTA BREAD

MAKES 12 PITTA BREADS

Ever wondered how to get that pocket in the middle of a pitta bread? Like there is some special folding tactic to create layers inside for you to fill with your own personal choice of deliciousness? Well, let me tell you the secret ... there is no secret. The hole just arrives as if by magic, and watching it happen with your own eyes is very pleasing indeed.

Here I've added yoghurt to the yeasted dough mix for that characteristic pitta TWANG. It rests just once to develop strength and flavour, then thinly rolled balls of the dough inflate in the oven into light, soft cushions, creating a big pocket inside that opens wide naturally, rather than having to be prised apart, for your imagination to run wild with flavours and fillings. It's a beautiful thing. AND not only are they freezable (just like the tacos on page 77 but no need for the baking parchment), they're toastable in the toaster or under the grill STRAIGHT FROM the freezer.

While the recipe makes twelve, you can of course halve the ingredient quantities to make six, or double them up if you're stocking up for the freezer.

=== EASY TO MAKE, EASY TO BAKE / TOTAL TIME: 2–3 HOURS ===

170g (6oz) room-temperature water
200g (7oz) natural set Greek yoghurt

12g (½oz) fresh yeast, crumbled, or 7g (¼oz) fast-action dried yeast
450g (1lb) strong white bread flour, plus extra for dusting

50g (1¾oz) strong wholemeal bread flour
8g (¼oz) salt
10g (½oz) olive oil

Making the dough 15–20 minutes
1. In a large mixing bowl, mix together the water, yoghurt and yeast until the yeast has dissolved.
2. Add the flours and salt, then mix with a dough scraper until the mixture starts to come together. Add the olive oil and mix again into a rough dough.
3. Turn your dough out onto a clean work surface and knead without any additional flour for 8 minutes.

Resting 1–1½ hours
4. Shape the dough into a ball and place it back in the bowl. Sprinkle the top with a little flour, cover with a clean cloth and rest at room temperature for 1–1½ hours.

Dividing and pre-shaping 5–10 minutes
5. Dust the top of the dough lightly with flour and use your dough scraper to turn it out upside down onto the work surface, sticky side up.

6. Use your fingertips to flatten the dough gently and cut it into 12 equal-sized pieces with your dough scraper. If you want them all to be exactly the same size, weigh them out at about 75g (2½oz) each. Fold and roll each piece of dough into a tight ball (see page 24).

Resting 20–30 minutes
7. Line up your dough balls on the work surface or on a tray. Dust only the tops with flour, cover them with the cloth and rest for 20–30 minutes to relax and spread slightly.
8. Towards the end of resting, preheat your oven to 200°C fan/425°F/Gas Mark 7 with a baking tray on the middle shelf.

Shaping and baking: 20–30 minutes
9. Using a rolling pin and plenty of flour for dusting, roll out 3 dough balls into oval shapes, about 20cm (8in) long and 12cm (4½in) wide.

Recipe continued overleaf

10. Place the pittas on the hot baking tray and bake for 4 minutes until puffed up like glorious bread pillows.

11. Using a heavy cloth, oven glove or a wooden peel, remove the pittas very carefully from the oven and place them on a wire rack to cool completely and deflate. They will be full of steam and very, very hot, and the steam often escapes somewhere on the pitta, so beware of little jets of steam that will burn.

12. Repeat with the remaining dough balls until all your pittas are baked.

─── TIP ───
COLOURLESS BAKING

The idea here is to bake your pitta breads with little to no colour at all. The reason is that, whether you are freezing them or not, you'll be toasting them in the toaster or under the grill (broiler) before filling. If your pitta is already golden after baking, it will toast to a crisp!

CRISPY HALLOUMI PITTA POCKETS WITH TZATZIKI & POMEGRANATE

SERVES 2

Your homemade pitta breads will have a PROPER POCKET inside, and this hot and crispy halloumi cooked in a 'southern-fried' style is the perfect filling, alongside fresh and minty tzatziki, a crisp salad and juicy pomegranate pearls that pop in the mouth.

For these, have your pittas poised in the toaster slot before you fry your cheese to get them to the table as fresh as possible. And do be careful when cutting a hot pitta, it will be super-steamy inside!

For the tzatziki
125g (4½oz) cucumber
a generous pinch of sea salt
80g (2¾oz) plain yoghurt
½ garlic clove, finely grated
2 teaspoons finely chopped
  fresh mint leaves

For the halloumi
½ pack (115g/4oz)
  of halloumi cheese
100g (3½oz) plain
  (all-purpose) flour
1 teaspoon paprika
1 teaspoon fennel seeds
1 teaspoon dried oregano
½ teaspoon garlic powder
½ teaspoon onion powder
½ teaspoon dried chilli
  (hot pepper) flakes
½ teaspoon salt
½ teaspoon cracked
  black pepper
100g (3½oz) plain yoghurt
sunflower oil

To finish
2 Pitta Breads (see page 124)
some crispy lettuce leaves
a few juicy pomegranate seeds

For the tzatziki

1. Grate your cucumber on the coarse side of a box grater. Place in a mixing bowl and mix together with a generous pinch of salt. Place the cucumber in a colander set over a bowl to allow the salt to draw out the moisture, and the moisture to drip away. Leave it for 15–20 minutes.

2. Squeeze out the cucumber and place it in a clean bowl. Add the yoghurt, garlic and mint leaves and mix together. You may not need to season with salt but have a taste and see what you think. Sometimes there is enough left in the cucumber to not need to add any more. Set aside for later.

For the halloumi

3. Drain the water from your halloumi and cut it lengthways into 2 large slices, probably just less than 1cm (½in) thick. Line up your slices on some kitchen paper to drain off nicely.

4. Measure and mix your flour, spices, salt and pepper together in a large bowl.

5. In another bowl, place the yoghurt and add the halloumi slices, tossing them to coat.

6. Now that the halloumi is coated, lift a tablespoon of yoghurt from the bowl and add it to your spiced flour. Mix it in and squeeze the mixture with your hands, pressing it between your fingers to create a kind of flaky texture to your flour mix. This will help make your halloumi super-crispy.

7. Lift your halloumi from the bowl and coat your slices in the flour mix, burying it in the flour and pressing the flour into the cheese to stick. Lift it out, give it a little shake and transfer it to a plate. Continue with the other slice.

Recipe continued overleaf

8. Heat 5mm (¼in) of sunflower oil in a large heavy frying pan (skillet) to a medium heat. Gently lower your halloumi into the pan and fry for 2½ minutes on each side, until golden.
9. Remove them from the oil, drain the excess on kitchen paper, then straight away place the cheese on a cooling rack to stop them getting soggy. Season with a pinch of sea salt.

Bringing it all together
10. Toast your pitta breads in the toaster. Carefully cut them down the long side and open up the pocket, remembering that they will likely be full of steam so go carefully. Fill your pittas with some crisp lettuce leaves, a slice each of halloumi, a good spoon of tzatziki and a sprinkling of pomegranate seeds.

BAKED FETA CHEESE WITH TOMATOES, OLIVES & OREGANO

SERVES 2

In tavernas all over Greece, you'll find feta cheese. In salads, stuffed inside steak, deep-fried and … baked. Sometimes simply with olive oil and some sliced chilli, sometimes under a blanket of rich tomato sauce (try half a batch of the meatball pasta sauce on page 41) and ALWAYS with dried oregano.

When feta bakes, you see, it doesn't melt. Instead, it softens and holds its shape but becomes beautifully spreadable. Serve it with some homemade pitta breads (see page 127) for a delicious way to start a meal with friends.

250g (9oz) yellow and
  red cherry tomatoes
  on the vine
75g (2½oz) Kalamata and
  queen green olives
1 garlic clove
4 tablespoons olive oil
200g (7oz) pack of feta
a pinch of dried oregano
Pitta Breads (see page 127)

1. Halve, quarter and slice your tomatoes. Pop them in a large mixing bowl with the olives and grate in the garlic.

2. Add the olive oil and mix everything together.

3. Place your feta in a snug baking dish that will look nice on your table. Bury it beneath a pile of your olive and tomato mix. Sprinkle a pinch of oregano over the top.

4. Bake your feta in an oven preheated to 180°C fan/400°F/ Gas Mark 6 for 15–20 minutes until the tomatoes are roasty and the cheese is soft to the middle. Serve in the middle of the table with plenty of pitta bread.

CHAPTER THREE

FLAVOURED BREADS

THERE ARE MANY WAYS TO INCORPORATE FLAVOUR INTO OUR DOUGH AND EVEN MORE FLAVOURS PERFECT FOR INCORPORATING

With a classic Fruit-and-Nut Loaf (see page 149), we'll be incorporating the fruit THROUGHOUT the dough, doing our best to get a little bit in every slice. For the Garlic Bread (see page 143), we'll be FOLDING IN flavour in layers for a beautiful pull-apart texture. For the Cheddar Cheese Bread (see right!), I've given you two options and the freedom to make your own choice. This is just an illustration of where you can go with bread, depending on how YOU'D like it to come out in the end.

Olive Parmesan & Sesame Breadsticks (see page 155) are a MASSIVE winner as a pre-dinner nibble. By removing the need for a final rise before baking, we make them crispy on the outside, chewy rather than fluffy and also … quick to make. That means you'll have plenty of time to knock up a couple of tasty dips to serve them with.

Pasta is another passion of mine. It's something I have been cooking for years and yet another thing I could talk all day long about. I'm not necessarily talking about fresh pasta made from flour and eggs either, dried pasta is a triumph in itself. By no means inferior to the fresh stuff, dried pasta is a different thing entirely, and here I've created a quick-and-easy spaghetti dish that is the kind of thing my family and I eat regularly. You don't need a lot of stuff to make great pasta – just a hunk of good cheese, some green veg and homemade bread on the side and dinner is done.

With the breads in this chapter, I've tried to really illustrate the principle of combining flavours with bread dough in the different ways that we can. As you start to get to grips with the breads in chapters one and two, you can begin to combine those doughs with the techniques here too, making Cheddar cheese bagels, for example, or olive rolls!

CHEDDAR CHEESE BREAD

MAKES 2 SMALL LOAVES

Let this be a lesson in your power to make your own decisions in bread-making.

You can put cheese in bread and it's delicious, but the WAY you choose to do it will change how your bread comes out. In this recipe I have gone for two alternative approaches: I've cubed the cheese and added it after the kneading, incorporating it INTO the dough, and then I've grated the cheese and added it at the pre-shaping stage. The first method results in molten pockets of cheese throughout the entire loaf, while with the second you get a subtle layer of melted cheese spiralled inside the bread. Both are delicious in their own right. I use mature Cheddar because it packs a punch, but feel free to substitute a milder cheese if you prefer. Any cheese you can grate will work nicely – experiment!

So, by applying the principles here according to your own taste, you can truly make something to be proud of. Just. For. You.

EASY TO MAKE, EASY TO BAKE / TOTAL TIME: 2–4 HOURS

You'll need: a grignette

230g (8oz) room-temperature water

8g (¼oz) fresh yeast, crumbled, or 4g (1 teaspoon) fast-action dried yeast

350g (12½oz) strong white bread flour, plus extra for dusting

25g (1 teaspoon) strong wholemeal bread flour

6g (⅛oz) salt

15g (½oz) room-temperature butter, broken up into small pieces

100g (3½oz) Cheddar cheese, cubed or coarsely grated (see method)

Making the dough: 15–20 minutes

1. In a large mixing bowl, mix together the water and yeast until the yeast has dissolved.
2. Add the flours and salt, then mix with a dough scraper until the mixture starts to come together into a rough dough. Add the butter and dimple it into the dough with your fingertips.
3. Turn your dough out onto a clean work surface and knead without any additional flour for 8 minutes.

METHOD ONE:

For molten cheese pockets: 10 minutes

* Dust the dough lightly with flour and press with your fingertips and knuckles to flatten and spread it into a 35cm (14in) circle.
* Sprinkle over half the cheese cubes evenly and pat them gently onto the surface of the dough. Fold the bottom third of your dough circle up and then the top third down over it. Press all over with your fingertips to stick the layers together.
* Turn the dough 90 degrees, then repeat the process with the remaining cheese, BUT this time, instead of folding the dough, roll it up into a short sausage.

Resting: 1–1½ hours

4. Shape the dough into a ball and place it back in the bowl. Sprinkle the top with a little flour, cover with a clean cloth and rest at room temperature for 1–1½ hours.

Dividing: 5–10 minutes

5. Dust the top of the dough lightly with flour and use your dough scraper to turn it out upside down onto the work surface, sticky side up.

Recipe continued overleaf

6. Use your fingertips to flatten the dough gently as far as you can and cut it in half with your dough scraper.

METHOD TWO:
For a subtle cheese layer: 5 minutes
✳ Sprinkle each piece of dough with half your grated cheese.

Pre-shaping
7. Fold and roll each piece into a ball, then cup slightly to tighten (see page 24).

Resting: 15 minutes
8. Line up the dough balls on the work surface. Dust only the tops lightly with flour, cover with the cloth and rest for 15 minutes to relax and spread slightly.

Final shaping: 5–10 minutes
9. Line a baking tray with baking parchment.
10. Dust the work surface lightly with flour. Working with one at a time, slide your dough scraper underneath a dough ball to release it and flip it sticky side up onto the dusted surface.

11. Press with your fingertips and knuckles to flatten and spread the dough into a 15–20cm (6–8in) circle. Fold the bottom third of your dough circle up and then the top third down over it. Press the seam to stick it together, then turn seam side down and place on your lined tray.

Resting: 45 minutes–1 hour
12. Cover your loaves with the cloth and rest for 45 minutes–1 hour.
13. Towards the end of resting, preheat your oven to 220°C fan/475°F/Gas Mark 9 with a shelf in the middle and a deep roasting tray on the oven floor. Half fill a kettle.

Slashing: 5 minutes
14. Boil the kettle.
15. Use the grignette to make a swift slash at a shallow diagonal on the top of the loaf from one end to the other.

Baking: 30–35 minutes
16. Place your baking tray on the oven shelf and carefully pour the hot water into the tray below. Bake your loaves for 30–35 minutes until golden.
17. Let them cool completely on a wire rack.

TIPS

OTHER WAYS TO ADD CHEESE

Adding grated cheese to the flour at the dough-mixing stage will mean it completely disappears into the dough as you are kneading it, turning it into CHEESE DOUGH. The result is a chewy bread with a subtle flavour of cheese throughout.

Grated cheese sprinkled on top of a loaf just before baking will often slide off the top of your bread as it bakes, but brushing the dough with BEATEN EGG first will help it to stay put for toasty, melty, crispy cheese bubbles to complement your crust.

THE CRUST BUST TRICK

How do you get a loaf to burst open when baked on a tray like mine? The trick is to bake your loaves when they are very slightly underproved – that is, still a little bouncy to the touch, a little firmer than you would normally prove a tin loaf. Then when baked with steam, there will be the PRESSURE you need left inside the loaf to JUMP in the oven, and the increase in volume will bust the crust.

GREAT BRITISH HAM HOCK SANDWICH WITH PICKLED CAULIFLOWER & MUSTARD MAYO

SERVES 2 VERY HUNGRY PEOPLE OR 4 AS PART OF A PICNIC

Some things in the food world never age and ham hock is one of those. It's literally UNIVERSAL, used all over the globe in all different ways, such as with sauerkraut, mash and mustard, pinto beans and rice and soy sauce and five-spice. But for me, it's OLD SCHOOL, bringing back memories of college years making stocks with bay leaves, carrots, celery and a few floating peppercorns.

Here I've made a HUGE sandwich with a whole Cheese Bread (see page 133), spiked with fresh peppery watercress and mustard mayo and some humble cauliflower, into which I've breathed new life with a sweet pickling.

Ham hocks are so cheap to buy from the butcher. Cured like ham, you may need to soak yours overnight in water to remove some of the saltiness, but I think the days of packing them in salt have largely passed. Check with your butcher, but either way, give it a good wash in the sink.

Your ham hock is a slow-cook job, so if you prefer you can buy it ready-cooked, but if you are doing it my way, keep hold of the stock and use it for something equally old school and equally delicious, like chicken and ham pie or pea and ham soup.

---

1 Cheddar Cheese Bread loaf
(see page 133)
a handful of watercress
(about 60g/2¼oz)

For the cauliflower
1 cauliflower (you will only
use half, about 150g/5½oz
when sliced – see method)
80ml (2¾fl oz) white
wine vinegar
50g (1¾oz) golden caster
(superfine) sugar
1 teaspoon wholegrain mustard
pinch of salt

For the ham hock
1 ham hock (mine
weighed 1.4kg/3lb)
2 celery sticks, halved
1 medium carrot,
halved lengthways
1 small white onion, halved
3 garlic cloves, halved

Pickling the cauliflower: A day ahead

1. Remove the leaves and end of the stalk from your cauliflower. Cut your cauliflower lengthways down the middle into 2 halves, and put one half back in the fridge for the next time. Slice the remaining half from the root to the edge into thin slices – I find this is the best way to get whole intact slices, but don't stress too much about it.

2. For the pickling liquid, mix the other ingredients together in a small bowl.

3. Put the cauliflower into a reusable freezer bag, pour over the liquid and do your best to squeeze out as much air as you can. Seal the bag and gently shake it, squeeze it and scrunch it to get all the cauliflower into some of the liquid.

4. Place the bag in a bowl or plastic container in case of any leaks and refrigerate overnight.

Cooking the ham hock

5. Wash your ham hock well or soak it overnight (see above). Place it in a large saucepan with all the other ingredients except the thyme and cover with fresh water. Bring to the boil and skim the foam from the surface, then continue boiling for 2–4 hours, depending on the size of your ham hock – mine was LARGE and took the full 4 hours.

Recipe continued overleaf

a few fresh rosemary
  and thyme sprigs
1 small bay leaf
3–4 black peppercorns
1 teaspoon chopped fresh
  thyme leaves

For the mustard mayo
100g (3½oz) mayonnaise
1 teaspoon Dijon mustard
1 teaspoon wholegrain mustard
1 tablespoon olive oil
2 tablespoons chopped fresh
  parsley leaves and stalks
pinch of salt

You'll know when it is done because you'll EASILY be able to slide the 2 bones out of the middle with a pair of tongs.

6. Ideally, you would leave your ham hock to cool completely in the cooking liquid before removing, but this can take AGES, so allowing it an hour or 2 before removing it is a nice gesture towards keeping the meat moist when it does come out. Peel off and discard the skin, then work your way through separating the meat from the sinew and dodgy bits.

7. Shred some of the ham with a fork, keep some chunky and put it all into a mixing bowl. Add 2 tablespoons of the cooking liquid, sprinkle over the thyme and toss it all together.

8. Any leftover ham can be kept covered with the cooking liquid in an airtight container in the fridge for up to 4–5 days. The liquid will turn to jelly and keep the ham juicy, plus the jelly is wicked delicious if you are into that.

Building the sandwich

9. If you need to bring the fresh 'n' crispy quality back to your cheese bread loaf, preheat your oven to 180°C fan/400°F/Gas Mark 6 and warm it through for 10–12 minutes.

10. Mix all the mustard mayo ingredients together in a bowl.

11. Cut the loaf in half horizontally and spread the cut sides generously with the mustard mayo.

12. Lay a bed of watercress on the bottom half, followed by a layer of drained cauliflower. Next pile on the ham hock and finally top with a little more cauliflower and watercress. Replace the sandwich lid.

13. Slice, share (if you want) and enjoy!

TORTANO BREAD

MAKES 2 TORTANO RINGS

Originally an Italian Easter bread, the tortano is classically shaped into a ring with chopped salami, boiled egg and cheese inside, and it's wicked delicious.

I started making these breads in my Easter class years ago and they have evolved over time into something I feel so proud of. They really come into their own with the use of lard, which brings them crispiness and an incredible savoury flavour, but if it's not for you, replace it with butter. Initially my slightly younger, slightly more naive self considered it a little weird to bake chopped boiled eggs into bread dough, but I quickly learnt as soon as I tried it that it's perfectly normal and oh so tasty. Without it, it just wouldn't be the same!

This is one of those breads that my family and I can't stop eating, hot from the oven, until they're all gone. Almost a meal in themselves, they'll play a lovely part at a picnic too.

EASY TO MAKE, EASY TO BAKE / TOTAL TIME: 3–4 HOURS

225g (8oz) room-temperature water
10g (½oz) fresh yeast, crumbled, or 5g (½ tablespoon) fast-action dried yeast
375g (13oz) strong white bread flour, plus extra for dusting

5g (1 teaspoon) salt
10g (½oz) olive oil

For the filling
40g (1½oz) lard
100g (3½oz) salami, cut into 1cm (½in) cubes

2 hard-boiled eggs, shelled and cut into 1cm (½in) cubes
40g (1½oz) pecorino cheese, grated
1 tablespoon chopped fresh thyme leaves
sea salt and cracked black pepper

Making the dough: 15–20 minutes

1. In a large mixing bowl, mix together the water and yeast until the yeast has dissolved.

2. Add the flour and salt, then mix with a dough scraper until the mixture starts to come together. Add the olive oil and mix again into a rough dough.

3. Turn your dough out onto a clean work surface and knead without any additional flour for 8 minutes.

Resting: 1–1½ hours

4. Shape the dough into a ball and place it back in the bowl. Sprinkle the top with a little flour, cover with a clean cloth and rest at room temperature for 1–1½ hours.

Dividing, filling and shaping: 15–20 minutes

5. Line a baking tray with baking parchment.

6. Dust the top of the dough lightly with flour and use your dough scraper to turn it out upside down onto the work surface, sticky side up.

7. Use your fingertips to flatten the dough gently and it cut in half with your dough scraper.

8. Dust with flour, then use a rolling pin to roll each piece of dough into a landscape rectangle about 15 x 30cm (6 x 12in).

9. Spread half the lard over the top of one of the dough rectangles, then sprinkle half the salami, egg, pecorino and thyme over the top. Season with black pepper and a pinch of salt. Roll up the dough into a sausage and press the seam to stick it together.

10. Cut your dough sausage in 2 and roll out each half with your palms on the work surface until they are about 45cm (17¾in) long. Dust them really well with flour, then twist them around one another, bring the ends together

Recipe continued overleaf

to form a ring and press together to stick. Place on your lined tray.

11. Repeat with the other dough rectangle and the remaining filling ingredients.

Resting: 1–1½ hours

12. Cover your rings with the cloth and rest for 1–1½ hours.

13. Towards the end of resting, preheat your oven to 230°C fan/485°F/Gas Mark 9 with a shelf in the middle and a deep roasting tray on the oven floor. Half fill the kettle.

Baking: 25–30 minutes

14. Boil the kettle.

15. Place your baking tray on the oven shelf and carefully pour the hot water into the tray below. Bake your rings for 25–30 minutes until golden.

16. Let them cool on a wire rack slightly and eat while still warm and crispy.

GARLIC BREAD

MAKES 1 DECENT-SIZED GARLIC BREAD

Garlic butter is the perfect vehicle for FLAVOUR in your bread dough – or any Flavoured Butter that you like (see page 60 for other options). Here we layer the butter through the bread dough with a little Cheddar cheese to make a tearable, shareable centrepiece for a meal around the table.

=== EASY TO MAKE, EASY TO BAKE / TOTAL TIME: 3–4½ HOURS ===

You'll need: a baking dish – I used one about 28 x 18cm (11 x 7in), but you can use whatever you have and like the look of, though make sure it's shallow so that the bread bakes evenly

160g (5½oz) room-temperature water
6g (1 teaspoon) fresh yeast, crumbled, or 3g (1 teaspoon) fast-action dried yeast
250g (9oz) strong white bread flour, plus extra for dusting
4g (1 teaspoon) salt

For the garlic butter
50g (1¾oz) room-temperature butter
½ garlic clove, finely grated
1 teaspoon chopped fresh thyme leaves
pinch of salt

50g (1¾oz) Cheddar, Parmesan or pecorino cheese, or a mixture, grated, for the filling
sea salt flakes, for sprinkling

Making the dough: 15–20 minutes
1. In a large mixing bowl, mix together the water and yeast until the yeast has dissolved.
2. Add the flour and salt, then mix with a dough scraper until the mixture starts to come together into a rough dough.
3. Turn your dough out onto a clean work surface and knead without any additional flour for 8 minutes.

Resting: 1–1½ hours
4. Shape the dough into a ball and place it back in the bowl. Sprinkle the top with a little flour, cover with a clean cloth and rest at room temperature for 1–1½ hours.

Dividing and pre-shaping: 2–5 minutes
5. Lightly dust the top of the dough with flour and use your dough scraper to turn it out upside down onto the work surface, sticky side up.
6. Use your fingertips to flatten the dough gently and cut it in half with your dough scraper. Fold and roll each piece of dough into a ball, then cup slightly to tighten (see page 24).

Resting and making the garlic butter: 15–30 minutes
7. Line up your dough balls on the work surface. Dust only the tops lightly with flour, cover with the cloth and rest for 15–30 minutes to relax and spread slightly.
8. Meanwhile, mix the garlic butter ingredients together in a bowl until thoroughly combined.

Final shaping and filling: 5–10 minutes
9. Using a rolling pin, roll out each dough ball into a 25cm (10in) square.
10. Use your dough scraper to spread each piece evenly with half the garlic butter, leaving a 3cm (1in) strip along the bottom edge free of butter. Sprinkle half the grated cheese over each buttered area and pat it down lightly with your palms to stick it to the dough.
11. Starting from the buttered edge, roll up each dough square into a tight sausage until you reach the bare strip, then use that to seal the seam. Roll each sausage with your palms on the work surface so that it is an even thickness and about 30cm (12in) long.

Recipe continued overleaf

12. Transfer your dough sausages to a chopping board and use a long serrated knife to cut them both in half lengthways, all the way from one end to the other.

13. Turn them cut side up and, working in pairs, fold one strand over the other all the way down to create a twisted rope design, while all the time keeping the cut sides facing up. Repeat for the other strands.

Resting: 1–1½ hours
14. Place the garlic bread inside your baking dish, cover with cling film dusted with flour and rest for 1–1½ hours.

15. Towards the end of resting, preheat your oven to 200°C fan/425°F/Gas Mark 7 with a shelf in the middle and a deep roasting tray on the oven floor. Half fill a kettle.

Baking: 20–25 minutes
16. Boil the kettle.

17. Sprinkle a pinch of sea salt evenly over the top of your bread and place the dish on the oven shelf, then carefully pour the hot water into the tray below. Bake your garlic bread for 15 minutes. Remove from the oven and you'll see some butter pooled in the base of the dish. Spoon it back over the top of the bread and return the dish to the oven for another 5–10 minutes.

18. Let the bread cool very slightly and serve in the baking dish straight to the table.

TIP

GET CREATIVE

Once you've layered the dough with butter and cut your strands, you can weave them into any shape you like – a four-strand plait works really well here and looks beautiful (see page 236). I quite often find inspiration in the various dishes, trays and pie tins I have in my kitchen cupboard, so have a dig around in yours and choose something that will look lovely on the table.

GREEN VEGETABLE SPAGHETTI WITH PARMESAN

SERVES 2

Pasta was a big part of my life for a while when I was working in a Sardinian restaurant and then bistro. Every day we would have a bowl of pasta and we would actually SIT DOWN to eat it before the start of service. That was completely unheard of in my career up until that point. Normally we'd be eating on the go, stood up in the kitchen, or out by the bins (nice!) and if we were to sit down, it certainly wouldn't be on a chair, it would be on an upturned bucket AT BEST. That's the irony of being a chef.

I enjoyed our pasta ritual so much that after the Sardinian restaurant, I returned to where I was working before and brought the 11:30am pasta tradition with me. It was about making something out of nothing – we'd find something kicking around in the fridge and use that. Cooked well, pasta needs only a few ingredients, sometimes even just one: olive oil, a bit of cheese or the water the pasta is cooked in to make something special.

I could fill a whole book with pasta dishes, but since this is (mostly) a bread book, I have chosen this dish to really and truly illustrate the pasta principle. I hope you like it. Serve it with a homemade Garlic Bread (see page 143). The crispy breadcrumbs in the Leek & Brie Risotto on page 98 would go well too.

80g (2¾oz) purple sprouting broccoli
80g (2¾oz) spring greens, savoy cabbage or cavolo nero
50g (1¾oz) frozen petits pois or peas
200g (7oz) good-quality dried spaghetti
40g (1½oz) butter
1 tablespoon chopped fresh mint leaves
50g (1¾oz) finely grated Parmesan cheese, plus extra for the top
olive oil
sea salt and cracked black pepper
Garlic Bread (see page 143), to serve

1. Bring a large pan of water seasoned well with salt to the boil. Taste the water – it should be salty like the sea and when you are adding salt, don't worry too much about the amount going in, you won't be eating it all!
2. Trim the dodgy ends from your broccoli and slice each piece down the middle into 4 pieces, nice and thin. Shred your greens thinly too and have your peas ready. Put all the veg in a bowl for later.
3. Cook your spaghetti in the water until al dente. Crank up the heat and lift the spaghetti from the water. Place it in a large bowl with the butter on top. Don't stress about any spaghetti stragglers in the water – they'll only be in there for a minute more while the veg cooks.
4. Tip all the vegetables into the water and simmer for 1 minute while you toss the spaghetti in the butter and get a colander ready in the sink.
5. Drain the vegetables in the colander, lifting the colander quickly and placing the saucepan underneath it to catch the pasta water – you'll need it!
6. Tip all the drained veg into the spaghetti bowl, add the mint, Parmesan and 6 tablespoons of the reserved pasta water.
7. Toss everything together really well. The action of tossing will encourage the starch in the pasta to thicken the surrounding sauce.
8. Pile your pasta high in 2 shallow bowls and finish with some more Parmesan, a drizzle of olive oil and a pinch of black pepper. Serve with garlic bread.

WHOLEMEAL FRUIT-AND-NUT LOAF

MAKES 2 MEDIUM FREE-STANDING BLOOMERS

This loaf is 50:50 – 50 per cent white flour and 50 per cent wholemeal flour, which means it has TONS of wholemeal-y flavour without the hearty heaviness of a full-on 100 per cent wholemeal loaf. It's essentially a savoury bread dough, with the sweetness coming from the fruit only, which makes these loaves a perfect picturesque accompaniment to a carefully curated board of cheeses.

We are incorporating dried fruit here, and although you don't HAVE to, I like to soak my dried fruit in water to plump it up before I add it in for two reasons. One, it makes them SUPER-JUICY in the final bread, and two, it stops the fruit soaking up moisture from the dough itself and making the whole thing quite dry and tight. It CAN, however, make things a little slippery and the fruit a little delicate when it comes to incorporating them into the dough. So, make sure you pat (not squeeze) them all dry on kitchen paper really well before you add them gently in the two-stage process revealed below.

=== EASY TO MAKE, EASY TO BAKE / TOTAL TIME: 3–4 HOURS, ===
PLUS OVERNIGHT SOAKING OF THE DRIED FRUIT

330g (11½oz) room-temperature water
12g (½oz) fresh yeast, crumbled, or 7g (¼oz) fast-action dried yeast
250g (9oz) strong white bread flour, plus extra for dusting

250g (9oz) strong wholemeal bread flour
8g (¼oz) salt
15g (½oz) olive oil

For the filling
100g (3½oz) raisins
50g (1¾oz) walnuts, chopped
OR
100g (3½oz) dried apricots, halved
50g (1¾oz) whole almonds
OR
100g (3½oz) dried figs, quartered
50g (1¾oz) blanched hazelnuts

Pre-soaking the dried fruit: Overnight
1. Place your chosen dried fruit in a bowl and pour over just enough water to come halfway up the sides of the fruit. Cover and leave to soak at room temperature overnight to plump up the fruit.
2. Drain the soaked fruit and pat dry really well with kitchen paper. Mix together with your chosen nuts.

Making the dough: 15–20 minutes
3. In a large mixing bowl, mix together the water and yeast until the yeast has dissolved.
4. Add the flours and salt, then mix with a dough scraper until the mixture starts to come together. Add the olive oil and mix again into a rough dough.

5. Turn your dough out onto a clean work surface and knead without any additional flour for 8 minutes.

Adding the filling: 5–10 minutes
6. Lightly dust your dough and press with your fingertips and knuckles to flatten and spread it into a 35cm (14in) circle. Sprinkle over half your fruit and nuts evenly and dimple them into the dough with your fingertips. Fold the bottom third of your dough circle up and then the top third down over it. Press all over with your fingertips to stick the layers together.
7. Turn the dough 90 degrees, then repeat the process with the remaining fruit and nuts, BUT this time instead of folding the dough, roll it up into a short sausage.

Recipe continued overleaf

Resting: 1–1½ hours
8. Shape the dough into a ball and place it back in the bowl. Sprinkle the top with a little flour, cover with the cloth and rest at room temperature for 1–1½ hours.

Dividing and pre-shaping: 2–5 minutes
9. Dust the top of the dough lightly with flour and use your dough scraper to turn it out upside down onto the work surface, sticky side up.
10. Use your fingertips to flatten the dough gently and cut it in half with your dough scraper. Fold and roll each piece of dough into a ball, then cup slightly to tighten (see page 24).

Resting: 15 minutes
11. Line up the dough balls on the work surface. Dust only the tops lightly with flour, cover with the cloth and rest for 15 minutes to relax and spread slightly.

Final shaping: 5–10 minutes
12. Line a baking tray with baking parchment.
13. Lightly dust the work surface with flour. Working with one at a time, slide your dough scraper underneath a dough ball to release it and flip sticky side up onto the dusted surface.
14. Press with your fingertips and knuckles to flatten and spread the dough into a circle. Slide your fingers, palms up, underneath each side of the dough. Grip the dough and pull to stretch it sideways. At an angle, fold one side two-thirds of the way over the dough and the other side in the same way so that it overlaps the first fold and you have a kind of 'A' shape. Roll up the dough from the point towards you into a tight sausage and press the seam to stick it together, then turn seam side down (see page 34).
15. Spray or brush the top of each loaf with water and dust really well with flour, then, using a small serrated knife, make 3 shallow diagonal cuts, closer to lengthways than crossways.

Resting: 45 minutes–1 hour
16. Place your loaves on the lined tray, cover with the cloth and rest for 45 minutes–1 hour.
17. Towards the end of resting, preheat your oven to 200°C fan/425°F/Gas Mark 7 with a shelf in the middle and a deep roasting tray on the oven floor. Half fill a kettle.

Baking: 30–35 minutes
18. Boil the kettle.
19. Place your baking tray on the oven shelf and carefully pour the hot water into the tray below. Bake your loaves for 30–35 minutes.
20. Let them cool completely on a wire rack.

TIP

TIME TO RELAX

When you are kneading bread dough, you are developing the gluten inside and bringing elasticity and bounciness to it, which is great for when it rises BUT might make things tricky when we are trying to press the dough flat and incorporate our fruit. Fortunately, the fix is an easy one – just wait. All your dough needs is 10–15 minutes to RELAX and then it will be much more willing to allows us to flatten it.

BLUE CHEESE WITH WALNUTS & A CHICORY & FENNEL SALAD

SERVES 2

Your Wholemeal Fruit-and-Nut Loaf (see page 149) is essentially a savoury bread, only sweetened by the addition of the fruit. This, combined with the nuttiness, makes it a perfect match for cheese.

Everybody has their own cheese threshold, their cheese limit, where the strength of the cheese becomes too much. For me, I love blue cheese but there is a tipping point where things just get too … blue. Fortunately, there is a MASSIVE variety of blue cheese to choose from, a whole scale ranging from a mild to OH MY … So, if you're not a fan, try not to write things off just yet, there may be one there that tickles your fancy.

200g (7oz) blue cheese
  of your choice
a handful of walnuts
olive oil
a few slices of Wholemeal
  Fruit-and-Nut Loaf
  (see page 149)

For the salad
1 red chicory (endive)
1 white chicory (endive)
½ fennel bulb
1 carrot
2 tablespoons lemon juice
1 tablespoon olive oil
1 tablespoon fresh flat-leaf
  (Italian) parsley leaves
sea salt

1. Bring your cheese out of the fridge nice and early to bring it up to room temperature.

2. Toast your walnuts in the oven at 180°C fan/400°F/Gas Mark 6 for 12–15 minutes, cool and chop roughly.

3. Place the cheese on a board or plate, scatter with the walnuts and drizzle with olive oil.

4. Trim the brown root from the chicory, remove any dodgy leaves and discard, then halve each of them down the middle. Put them cut-side down on the chopping board and slice lengthways as thinly as possible. Place in a large mixing bowl.

5. Trim the root from the fennel, halve it down the middle and set half aside. Turn it cut-side down onto the chopping board and slice lengthways as thinly as possible. Add it to the bowl with the chicory.

6. Peel your carrot. Push a fork into the top part so that you are able to hold it in place horizontally on the chopping board, using the fork. Use the peeler to peel it into thin ribbons. Add the ribbons to the bowl.

7. Next add the lemon juice, olive oil and parsley together with a pinch of salt. Toss everything together. Serve the salad alongside your bread and blue cheese.

OLIVE, PARMESAN & SESAME BREADSTICKS

MAKES 16 BREADSTICKS

The perfect pre-dinner nibble alongside a cold beer or glass of good wine, these breadsticks are quick to make since there is no second resting before baking, which also helps to keep them crunchy on the outside and chewy on the inside.

This flavour combination was inspired by one of my very first private classes many years ago where I was introduced to a Middle Eastern spice mix called za'atar, a blend of woody herbs like thyme, marjoram and oregano, sumac and toasted sesame seeds. I was blown away by the flavour – it just worked!

Here I've used the principle of za'atar to breathe new life into a classic olive breadstick, and it's a great example of creating flavour combinations by bridging the gap between two flavours that you may not think typically go together. Olives work really well with herbs, and za'atar illustrates that they work well with sesame, so they also act as a link between olives and sesame, making them a great pairing too! It's an interesting rule to play with, and although it may not work in EVERY context, it certainly does here.

EASY TO MAKE, FUN TO SHAPE, EASY TO BAKE / TOTAL TIME: 2–2½ HOURS

165g (6oz) room-temperature water	25g (1oz) strong wholemeal bread flour	25g (1oz) Parmesan cheese, grated
6g (1 teaspoon) fresh yeast, crumbled, or 3g (1 teaspoon) fast-action dried yeast	4g (1 teaspoon) salt	1 tablespoon mixed chopped fresh thyme and oregano leaves
225g (8oz) strong white bread flour, plus extra for dusting	*For the filling* 100g (3½oz) mixed pitted olives, finely chopped	20g (¾oz) sesame seeds

Making the dough: 15–20 minutes

1. In a large mixing bowl, mix together the water and yeast until the yeast has dissolved.

2. Add the flours and salt, then mix with a dough scraper until the mixture starts to come together into a rough dough.

3. Turn your dough out onto a clean work surface and without any additional flour for 8 minutes.

Resting and making the filling: 1–1½ hours

4. Shape the dough into a ball and place it back in the bowl. Sprinkle the top with a little flour, cover with a clean cloth and rest at room temperature for 1–1½ hours.

5. Mix the filling ingredients together in a bowl.

Filling and shaping: 10–15 minutes

6. Preheat your oven to 220°C fan/475°F/Gas Mark 9 with 2 oven shelves in the middle

and a deep roasting tray on the oven floor. Half fill a kettle.

7. Line 2 baking trays with baking parchment.

8. Dust the top of the dough lightly with flour and use your dough scraper to turn it out upside down onto the work surface, sticky side up.

9. Press with your fingertips and knuckles to flatten the dough, then grasp and pull the corners into a landscape rectangle about 25 x 30cm (10 x 12in).

10. Tip all your filling mixture onto the top of the dough and spread it evenly all over, right to the edges, then press down with your palms to stick it to the dough.

11. Pick up the long side nearest to you and fold it one-third of the way over the dough away from you. Then pick up the third furthest from you and fold it over the top all the way to the

Recipe continued overleaf

edge towards you. Use your fingertips to press firmly all over and stick the dough in place. You should now have a rectangle about 12 x 35cm (4½ x 14in). Dust the top really well with flour.

12. Use a dough scraper to cut the dough rectangle vertically into 16 strips about as wide as your finger.

13. Working with one at a time, hold a strip of dough at each end and stretch it lengthways to about 25cm (10in) long, then twist it. Line the strips up on your lined trays, giving them a little room either side, as they will puff up slightly in the oven.

14. Your sticks may try to untwist themselves when left on the tray. Twist them all up and let them do their thing, then when they're all done, return to the first one you did. Now that it has relaxed a little, you should find it more receptive to the idea.

Baking: 12–15 minutes

15. Boil the kettle.

16. Place your baking trays on the oven shelves and carefully pour the hot water into the tray below. Bake your breadsticks for 12–15 minutes until golden.

17. Let them cool completely on a wire rack.

—————— **TIP** ——————

FROM FREEZER TO OVEN

These tasty breadsticks are ideal for baking straight from the freezer. Bake them initially for about 8 minutes only, just enough to hold their shape but not take on any colour. Then let them cool completely, place them in a reusable freezer bag and freeze. When you want to serve them, preheat your oven to the same temperature as before. Place however many breadsticks you need on a baking parchment-lined tray and bake for 6–8 minutes until golden.

OLIVE, PARMESAN & SESAME BREADSTICKS DIPS

The breadsticks are delicious as they are, but if you want to take it to the NEXT LEVEL, pair with one of these dips for a tasty predinner snack or starter.

PISTACHIO PESTO DIP

The flavours here in the breadsticks are pretty full on. This dip has a lovely toasty nuttiness brought about by the pistachios and I've freshened it up and made the flavours slightly more subtle with Greek yoghurt.

40g (1½oz) fresh basil, leaves and stalks
30g (1oz) roasted salted pistachios, shells off
15g (½oz) Parmesan cheese, finely grated
2 tablespoons olive oil
10 teaspoons set Greek yoghurt
sea salt

1. Before you begin, put a few teeny-tiny basil leaves to one side, and a couple of pistachios for garnish. Roughly chop the pistachios.
2. Place all the basil into a mini food processor. It might be a squeeze to start with, but you'll soon see it whizz down to not much at all. Give it a whizz to start things off.
3. Add the pistachios and whizz it all up again nice and fine, this time scraping any leaves or chunks from the sides as you go.
4. Finally, add the Parmesan, olive oil and a pinch of salt and whizz again until you have a thick but quite fine paste.
5. Spoon it out into a large mixing bowl and mix in the yoghurt. Taste and adjust the seasoning if you need to before spooning it into a dip bowl or spreading it thickly on a plate. Garnish with the reserved basil leaves and a sprinkling of chopped pistachios.

WHIPPED FETA CHEESE WITH LEMON

You can make this straight from the fridge, but if you're thinking ahead, get the cheese out a couple of hours early to come up to room temperature and it'll make your dip super-smooth.

200g (7oz) feta cheese
100g (3½oz) cream cheese
olive oil
1 lemon
dried oregano

1. Break up the feta into a food processor. Whizz it up with the blade on medium speed, past the crumbled stage all the way until it is spreadable. Scrape down the sides with a spatula a few times along the way to make sure you get it all.
2. Add the cream cheese and whizz it up again on medium speed until smooth.
3. Spoon the cheese into a large dipping pot or spread it on a plate. Drizzle with olive oil and finely grate some lemon zest over the top before scattering over a pinch or dried oregano.

SUN-DRIED TOMATO AIOLI

Slowly, slowly, slowly. That's how you make aioli. Get your whisking hand ready and summon your powers of patience because this will likely take 15–20 minutes to make. Possibly more … Add the oil a little bit at a time and whisk well before the next addition. I use sun-dried tomatoes from a jar here. Drained of their oil, they are blended into a purée and I use the oil in the dip. You can, if you prefer, buy sun-dried tomato purée and use rapeseed oil instead.

1 medium egg yolk
½ garlic clove, finely grated
juice of ½ lemon, plus extra if needed
100ml (3½fl oz) rapeseed (canola) oil or
    tasty oil from a jar of sun-dried tomatoes
50ml (1¾fl oz) extra-virgin olive oil
2 tablespoons sun-dried tomato paste,
    shop-bought or made by whizzing
    sun-dried tomatoes in a food processor
sea salt

1. In a large bowl, whisk together the egg yolk, garlic and lemon juice with a pinch of salt.
2. Add a teeny bit of both oils and whisk it till they're gone, then add a little more and repeat. The sauce should get thicker and thicker as you go. Add some extra lemon juice along the way to loosen it if it's getting too thick to whisk, otherwise save it to the end and add to taste.
3. When both oils are in you should have a glossy, thick aioli.
4. Add the sun-dried tomato paste and mix it in. Taste it and adjust with additional salt or lemon juice as required.

—— TIP ——
MAKE IT EASY FOR YOURSELF

If you are serving these as a starter before a meal with friends, you'll likely be spending most of your attention on the main course, and possibly pudding. With your olive breadsticks frozen and ready to go WAY in advance (see page 156) you can also get working on your dip(s) ahead of time too. Aioli will keep nicely in the fridge for 3–4 days, as will the whipped feta (see page 157). Just be sure to get that one out to come up to room temperature an hour or so before serving, or else it will be ROCK SOLID. Just after blending, Pistachio pesto (see page 157) will keep happily in the fridge for two days. Mix it with the yoghurt just before serving.

CHAPTER FOUR

STONE
BAKING

LET'S TAKE HOMEMADE BREAD TO THE NEXT LEVEL

Stone baking is arguably the best way to bake bread – the raw, puffed-up dough is slid directly onto a HOT stone in the oven on its naked bottom. It's the immediate heat of the stone in contact with the dough base that makes the dough JUMP UP and increase in volume. The yeast goes crackers making gas in the warmth AND the gas expands in the heat. It's that 'burst' that makes a baguette rise to its FULL potential, creating the decorative and delicious tear as the increase in volume BUSTS open the crust on the top where you've scored it. And it's also the contact with that heat that makes a crispy base for pizzas.

Here, we upgrade our scoring with the use of a super-sharp razor blade, the grignette just like we did with the Cheddar Cheese Bread on page 133. Reason being, this time round we are scoring AFTER the final rest, just before we bake. Up until now, we have been, for the most part, proving up and baking on trays. In these cases, the dough rises to its FULL POTENTIAL on the tray, puffing up until it's delicate, then we bake, get a LITTLE jump in the oven but not much, then the crust sets its shape.

Here we WANT the BIG increase in volume to happen INSIDE the oven. When dough meets stone. So, when the dough is left to prove for the final time in the case of the Baguette (see page 165), Olive, Lemon & Thyme Rye Ring or Pavé (see page 181), for example, we don't let it go until it's really fragile. We puff up PART of the way, saving the rest of the puff for when it goes in the oven. That's how we get that BURST on top.

We use a couple of key pieces of kit to be able to make this happen: a stone for the oven, a couple of peels for sliding things off and, since we are baking with zero support, we'll need to provide some support while the dough proves using a couche or a basket. PLENTY of steam is important for a good rise here and crusty crust too and so, after you've made the dough and rested it well, with the exception of pizzas, the process of stone baking becomes:

Shape the dough > rest with support > transfer to peel > score >
slide onto stone > bake with STEAM.

In the past we've been able to get away with a little error in shaping our
bread, especially for loaves baked in a tin, but in stone baking there is much
less room for inconsistencies. Although your bread will still be delicious,
use these to practise and refine your shaping techniques. You'll likely get
a couple of hook-nosed baguettes and funny-shaped batards but that's all
part of the fun. At least they won't look like you bought them from a shop!

BAGUETTES

MAKES 4 BAGUETTES

Baguettes are a real craft, one of those classic pedestal breads, and that's code for the following message. These baguettes probably won't come out perfect the first time, so please expect and be okay with that because with each batch you make, you'll be rewarded with a little more knowledge and begin to get more of a feel for the process until you are cracking out incredible baguettes time after time.

It's for that reason that I have made this recipe as simple as possible so that it's repeatable with minimum faff factor. There is no kneading involved, no pre-ferment, no overnight rest, just a straight-up white dough handled nicely to make crispy baguettes with the classic tear on top. Amazing baguettes are completely achievable in your oven at home. Trust me, trust the process, practise, practise, practise and you'll crack it.

One word of caution, though. In class we often get carried away rolling our baguettes super-long so we can carry them over our shoulder down a Parisian high street but remember … roll them too long and they won't fit in your oven!

══════ EASY TO MAKE BUT TRICKY TO MASTER / TOTAL TIME: 3–4 HOURS ══════

You'll need: a baking or pizza stone; 4 narrow wooden peels, preferably, or 1 large; grignette

350g (12½oz) room-temperature water
12g (½oz) fresh yeast, crumbled, or 7g (¼oz) fast-action dried yeast

500g (1lb 2oz) strong white bread flour, plus extra for dusting
10g (½oz) salt

Making the dough: 10–15 minutes
1. In a large mixing bowl, mix together the water and yeast until the yeast has dissolved.
2. Add the flour and salt, then mix with a dough scraper until the mixture starts to come together into a cohesive dough. Continue mixing for a minute or 2 to make sure the dough has come together really well.

Resting: 30 minutes
3. Shape the dough into a ball and place it back in the bowl. Sprinkle the top with a little flour, cover the bowl with a clean cloth and rest at room temperature for 30 minutes.

First fold: 2 minutes
4. Dust your work surface lightly with flour and use your dough scraper to turn the dough out upside down onto it, sticky side up.
5. Use your fingertips to flatten the dough slightly. Grasp a bit of the dough edge, stretch it out and then fold it over onto the dough.

Repeat all the way round the dough, making about 12–15 folds, until you have a ball.

Resting: 30 minutes
6. Turn the dough over, smooth side up, and place it back in the bowl. Cover with the cloth and rest for 30 minutes.

Second fold: 2 minutes
7. Dust the work surface again, then turn the dough out as before. Repeat the first fold process BUT this time make only 10 folds.

Resting: 30 minutes
8. Return the dough to the bowl smooth side up, cover and rest as before.

Dividing and pre-shaping: 5 minutes
9. Turn your dough out, upside down, and press it very gently with your fingertips and knuckles. Cut into 4 equal-sized pieces with your dough scraper. If you want them all to be exactly

Recipe continued overleaf

the same size, weigh them out at about 215g
(7½oz) each.

10. Roll up each piece of dough into a rough,
loose sausage, then turn seam side down.

Resting: 15 minutes
11. Line up your dough sausages on the
work surface, cover with a cloth and rest
for 15 minutes to relax.

Final shaping: 15–20 minutes
12. Place a clean cloth on a large baking tray
and dust it well with flour, to create a 'couche'
to support your baguettes during their final rest.
13. Working with one at a time, turn a dough
sausage over and press gently with your
fingertips on the half closest to you to flatten
very lightly. We'll be rolling the dough down to

the bottom edge, not in one go like a Swiss roll but carefully in stages. Starting at one end and finishing at the other, fold that top plump edge about half way down and press with a thumb to stick. Now you should have a slightly plumper top half that's beginning to look like a baguette and a kind of flap hanging off the bottom.

14. Repeat exactly the same as before, bringing the top edge down even closer to the bottom and sealing again with your thumb. Repeating the action one last time should bring the 2 edges together, completing the baguette shape. Pinch the seam to seal it up.

15. Roll out the baguette with your palms to about 30cm (12in) long, making the ends pointy by applying a little extra pressure.

Resting: 30–40 minutes

16. Line up your baguettes, seam side up, on the floured cloth and make a pleat in between each one so that they don't stick. Dust really well with flour and rest for 30–40 minutes.

17. Meanwhile, preheat your oven to 230°C fan/485°F/Gas Mark 9 with your baking or pizza stone on a middle or top shelf and a deep roasting tray on the oven floor. Half fill a kettle.

Slashing and baking: 20–25 minutes

18. Boil the kettle.

19. Carefully transfer your baguettes onto their individual wooden peels or the large one, seam side down. Use the grignette to make a few very shallow diagonal cuts, almost lengthways, down the centre of each baguette (see my tip right), then slide them onto the hot baking stone in the oven. Carefully pour the hot water into the tray below. Bake your baguettes for 15–20 minutes (see my tip right).

20. Remove the baguettes from the oven with your peel and let them cool on a wire rack.

TIPS

THE RIGHT TOUCH

For some breads we let the dough puff, then we take it back down to shape and let it puff again before we bake it. But when we bake a baguette, we want it to burst open to achieve that signature crispy crunchy rip on the top. So here we create a dough that is in a constant state of puff from the point we make it until we bake it, and instead of knocking the air out we give the structure tension as the pressure builds inside. Your aim is to approach the folds, pre-shape and final shape with a touch gentle enough not to push all the air out but firm enough to tighten the structure nicely. It's a tricky balance I know, and it comes with practise.

SLASHING FOR SUCCESS

It's logical to assume that to get those diagonal openings on the top of your baguette you need to make cuts at around 45 degrees, but that's not the case! Think about the way we rolled the dough up, like a Swiss roll but in stages, with the tension going across the WIDTH of the baguette. In theory, it wants to open up sideways along the entire length, but if we cut it at a 45-degree angle or, even worse, across the width, it just doesn't want to open up that way. So yes, we make diagonal cuts, but as close to lengthways as possible. Imagine a central strip running down the middle of your baguette and try to place all your cuts along it for the best chance of them opening up nicely.

THE SECRET TO A GREAT CRUST

For a good crust, you need to bake the baguettes with as high a heat as possible for as long as possible to make sure they are done without burning, so aim to keep the heat high for the full baking time, but depending on your oven, turn it down to 180°C fan/400°F/Gas Mark 6 if you need to. Much of the success of your crust lies in how well your oven keeps the steam in. If you find you lose the crust as the bread cools, spritz your baguettes all over with water to make them really wet and return them to the oven for 8–10 minutes for a crust that stays put!

BAKED CAMEMBERT

Here's one to complement tasty salads and homemade bread. Choose a Camembert in a wooden box and it already has its baking vessel built-in. Remove and unwrap the cheese and place it back in its box, then upturn the lid and put it underneath. Score the top with a sharp knife almost up to the edges. Take care not to pierce the base or you'll get molten cheese escaping when it bakes. To make doubly sure you don't get any leaks, place the box on tin foil and crunch it up around the edges. Bake the Camembert for 15–20 minutes in the oven at 180°C fan/400°F/Gas Mark 6. This will be enough to roast the top of these Camemberts while making the middle molten and gloriously gooey.

   Here are just a few of the almost INFINITE ideas to top a baked Camembert...

HERBS

Simple and delicious. Top with 1 teaspoon of chopped woody herbs (rosemary, thyme, oregano), and a tablespoon of olive oil. Squeeze the Camembert a little by the edges for the oil to work its way into the cuts. Season with black pepper and bake.

ONION & ROSEMARY

Cook a peeled and sliced onion in a medium saucepan in a generous amount of olive oil for 10 minutes or so until soft and sweet but with no colour. Mix in a teaspoon of chopped fresh rosemary. Top your Camembert and BAKE.

GARLIC & HERB CRUST

Cheese on cheese? Why not! Whizz up 20g (¾oz) of stale-but-not-dry breadcrumbs. Mix with 10g (½oz) grated Parmesan cheese, a pinch of salt, pepper and thyme leaves, and a teaspoon of olive oil. Pile and press on the top and BAKE for a crunchy crust.

PESTO POOL

This time bake your Camembert first. While it's in the oven, whizz up 30g (1oz) fresh basil leaves and stalks, 15g (½oz) pine nuts, 10g (½oz) finely grated Parmesan cheese and 4 tablespoons of olive oil in a mini food processor with a pinch of salt. Dent the centre of your baked Camembert with the back of a spoon and spoon the pesto on top.

CARAWAY & SESAME CRUST

In a bowl, mix 2 tablespoons of sesame seeds, ½ a teaspoon of caraway seeds and 1½ tablespoons of honey. Spread it on the top of your cheese, season with flaky salt and BAKE.

CHUTNEY

Take 2–3 tablespoons of your favourite shop-bought chutney (GASP!) and spread atop your mighty cheese. BAKE!

TOMATO & BASIL

Mix 3 tablespoons of sun-blushed tomatoes with some of the oil they came in and some fresh basil leaves. Pile upon your cheese and bake.

GRAPES & THYME

Mix a handful of seedless grapes with a teaspoon of olive oil and a pinch of fresh thyme leaves. Pile on top of your cheese, add a pinch of sea salt and bake.

SULTANAS & FENNEL SYRUP

Spoon over 2–3 tablespoons of your sultanas (golden raisins) steeped in Fennel Syrup (see page 276).

COURGETTE ANTIPASTI

Leftover antipasti from pages 92–95? No problem, spoon it over the Camembert and bake!

HOT CHOCOLATE, BAGUETTE, COLD BUTTER & SEA SALT

SERVES 2

One time at school I went on a French exchange trip. It was a LEARNING experience, a time for great GROWTH for us all …

I stayed with a French family. I didn't speak French, I shared a freezing loft room with a fat cat that slept ON TOP of me, and there was a toilet in the corner.

It was the first and probably only time I understood what homesick felt like. In the daytime we hung out with our school pals having a great time on day trips, but the rest of the time I was with the family by myself trying not to cry. Among all the memories I have of that trip is one about bread …

One morning we all came to have breakfast in the French students' school. We sat on a LONG table and ate cereal (I think), and then after we finished the teachers came around with jugs of hot chocolate, baskets of sliced baguettes and cold butter. They filled our empty bowls with steaming chocolate and left.

I'm not sure exactly how it came about, but through some miracle of the collective intelligence of thirty non-French-speaking 13-year-old kids, cogs began turning and we started to figure it out … One by one, we buttered our bread, dipped it into the chocolate, and fell into complete silence as we realised the deliciousness our friends from across the channel had been experiencing without us all this time. For the first time, our eyes were open.

60g (2oz) dark
  chocolate chips
20g (¾oz) milk
  chocolate chips
400ml (13½fl oz) whole milk
2 freshly baked or refreshed
  Baguettes (see page 165)
cold salted butter
sea salt flakes

1. Place your chocolate chips into a large mixing bowl.
2. Warm your milk on the stove top until very nearly bubbling.
3. Pour the milk over the chocolate and whisk until it has all melted.
4. Divide between 2 mugs and serve with buttered baguettes, sprinkled with sea salt flakes.

PIZZA MARGHERITA

MAKES 5 PIZZAS

Pizza is a pretty straightforward dough and yet a slow-moving one, as here we are after just enough puff so that the base isn't dense and doughy and to inflate the crust around the edge. But the dough needs TIME to fully hydrate the flour for a crispy underside, to develop flavour and to let it relax enough to be pushed out big and thin rather than being too springy and resistant to our efforts. Then it's crowned with a raw tomato sauce, thinly sliced toppings of your choice and mozzarella before being baked as hot as your oven will go and fast. I always recommend baking your pizza on a hot stone, as there really is no other way to get the right result.

Properly delicious homemade pizzas are completely achievable at home. It's those finer details that really make it sing and they come with practise – after all, pizza making is a craft evolved over countless years of repetition. But we don't have to be professional pizzaiolos to make something amazing. As long as we follow the pizza principles, we can make something EXCEPTIONAL that fits into our everyday schedules at home.

Perfect pizza toppings and combinations are INFINITE, and I could literally fill this whole book with them all, but I've limited myself to a few of my all-time favourites, starting with this classic.

=== EASY TO MAKE, TRICKY TO SHAPE, EASY TO BAKE / ===
TOTAL TIME: DAY ONE 2¼–3½ HOURS; DAY TWO 1–1¼ HOURS

You'll need: a baking or pizza stone; wooden peel

For the pizza dough base
310g (11oz) room-temperature water
4g (1 teaspoon) fresh yeast, crumbled, or 2g (½ teaspoon) fast-action dried yeast

500g (1lb 2oz) strong white bread flour, plus extra for dusting
8g (¼oz) salt

For the pizza sauce
350g (12oz) jar passata (puréed tomatoes)
pinch of sugar, if needed
pinch of dried oregano
1 tablespoon olive oil, plus extra for drizzling

For the topping
375g (13oz – 2½ x 150g/5½oz balls) mozzarella cheese (drained weight), for topping
a large handful of fresh basil leaves
salt and cracked black pepper

DAY ONE

Making the dough: 10–15 minutes
1. In a large mixing bowl, mix together the water and yeast until the yeast has dissolved.
2. Add the flour and salt, then mix with a dough scraper until the mixture comes together into a cohesive dough with no obvious wet or dry patches.

Resting: 1–1½ hours
3. Shape the dough into a ball and place it back in the bowl. Sprinkle the top with a little flour, cover with a clean cloth and rest for 1–1½ hours.

Folding: 5 minutes
4. Dust the work surface lightly with flour and turn the dough out upside down onto it, sticky side up.
5. Use your fingertips to flatten the dough slightly. Grasp a bit of the dough edge, stretch it out and then fold it over onto the dough. Repeat all the way round the dough, making about 12–15 folds, until you have a ball.

Recipe continued overleaf

Resting: 1–1½ hours

6. Turn the dough over, smooth side up, and place it back in the bowl. Cover with the cloth and rest for 1–1½ hours.

Dividing and pre-shaping: 5–10 minutes

7. Dust the work surface and the top of the dough lightly with flour and use your dough scraper to turn it out onto the dusted surface. Cut it into 5 equal-sized pieces with your dough scraper. If you want them all to be exactly the same size, weigh them out at about 165g (6oz) each. Fold and roll each piece of dough into a tight ball (see page 24).

Resting: Overnight

8. Line up your dough balls on a tray, dust with flour and cover loosely with cling film or another upturned tray. Place the tray in the fridge and rest overnight.

DAY TWO

Preparing the sauce and topping: 5–10 minutes

9. Pour the passata into a bowl and season with salt to taste. Some passata is quite acidic, so you may need a little sugar just to take the edge off. Then stir in the oregano and olive oil and set aside.

10. Drain the mozzarella of its water, tear into pieces and place on a plate lined with kitchen paper. Cover with another sheet of kitchen paper and place in the fridge to dry slightly.

Making your pizza base: 30–45 minutes

11. When you are ready to make your pizzas, preheat your oven to 230°C fan/485°F/Gas Mark 9 with a baking or pizza stone on the middle shelf for 30–45 minutes to get that stone nice and hot. Traditional pizza ovens are ridiculously hot, so if your oven goes higher than mine and you're confident it has an even heat throughout, crank it up!

12. Meanwhile, stretch out your pizza dough, which should be slightly puffy and should have spread a little.

13. Dust the work surface lightly with flour. Working with one at a time, dust a dough ball well with flour and use a dough scraper to lift it from the tray onto the dusted surface.

14. Using your thumbs, press the dough down all round the edge, dimpling it just inside where you imagine the crust to be. Then using your fingertips, push down on the domed middle to flatten it. Pass the dough from hand to hand, stretching it out evenly into a circle about 25cm (10in) wide. You might find it easier to grasp the dough by the edge just inside the crust and work your grasp all the way round the edge, letting the weight of the dough hanging down to do the stretching for you.

Or spin it in the air, catching it on your knuckles in between! Place your pizza base on a piece of baking parchment.

Adding the sauce and topping: 5 minutes

15. Place 2 tablespoons of the sauce in the centre of the pizza base. Using the back of the spoon, spread it round in a circle, working your way out to the inside edge of the crust. Top with a few pieces of mozzarella (75g/2½oz per pizza) and season with a little salt and cracked black pepper. Add a drizzle of olive oil.

Baking: 5–10 minutes each

16. Slide your dough on the paper onto your wooden peel and slide it onto the hot stone in the oven, paper and all. Depending on the temperature of your oven, the pizza will take around 5–10 minutes to bake until browned on the top and crisp on the base. If you can, slide out the paper halfway through baking, but if not, it will quite happily stay there until the end of baking.

17. Remove your pizza from the oven with your peel and slide it onto a wire rack. Remove the paper if you haven't already.

18. I like to let my pizza rest for 5 minutes or so before cutting, just to keep the base nice and crisp – you won't be able to eat it straight away without burning your mouth anyway! Scatter over a few basil leaves before serving.

TIPS

ALLOWING FOR MISTAKES

Pushing out your pizza dough into a perfect thin circle will take practise, but if you mess it up, all is not lost. Just reshape it into a ball and have another go. The only problem is, it will take a good hour or two to relax enough for that. So if you're worried about making a mistake and not having enough pizza to go around, make extra and you can always freeze any left over for another time …

FAIL-SAFE BAKING PARCHMENT

I ALWAYS bake on baking parchment, as there is zero risk of spoiling your perfect pizza trying to get it onto the peel or sauce leaking onto your hot stone and gluing your pizza to it.

FREEZING LEFTOVER DOUGH

If you have dough left over at the end of pizza night, shape it back into balls, place it on a baking parchment-lined tray and rest for an hour or so, then place the tray in the freezer for about 4 hours until solid. Transfer the dough to a reusable freezer bag, label and return your frozen pizza 'pucks' to the freezer. When ready to use, tray up however many you need, cover and defrost in the fridge overnight OR leave at room temperature for 4 hours or so to defrost and relax enough to stretch them as in the method.

ROSEMARY, SPECK, DRESSED ROCKET, CAPERS & PECORINO

MAKES 1 PIZZA/6 SLICES

There is a lot to be said for adding freshness to a pizza AFTER it has been baked. Speck is basically a smoked version of prosciutto spiced with black pepper, juniper and garlic. It's delicious, and if it were to be cooked on top of our pizza, we would lose all its nuances of flavour. Whereas draped over some dressed fresh rocket leaves and complemented by capers, we can truly celebrate its finer qualities.

1 pizza dough base
   (see pages 173–175)
2 tablespoons pizza sauce
   (see pages 173–174)
75g (2½oz – ½ x 150g/5½oz
   ball) mozzarella cheese
   (drained weight)
1 fresh rosemary sprig
25g (1oz) rocket (arugula) leaves
½ teaspoon olive oil,
   plus extra for drizzling
½ teaspoon balsamic vinegar
2 slices of speck
½ tablespoon baby capers
pecorino cheese, for shaving
salt and cracked black pepper

1. Follow the method on pages 173–175 to prepare your pizza base and add the sauce and mozzarella.
2. Pick the leaves from the rosemary sprig and scatter over, then continue with the method to season, drizzle with olive oil and then bake your pizza (see page 175).
3. In a large mixing bowl, toss your rocket leaves with the olive oil and balsamic vinegar, and season with a pinch of salt.
4. Fresh from the oven, top your pizza with the dressed rocket. Tear and drape over your speck. Sprinkle over the capers and finely shave over a blanket of pecorino.
5. Finally, drizzle over some olive oil and sprinkle with a pinch of cracked black pepper.

GARLIC BREAD PIZZA

MAKES 1 PIZZA/6 SLICES

On pizza night at our house, we all take it in turns pushing, topping and baking our own pizzas exactly how we like them, and while we do that, we share a garlic pizza bread, ALWAYS. That's just house rules.

1 ball of pizza dough, after
   resting overnight
   (see pages 173–174)
1 tablespoon Garlic and
   Parsley Butter (see page 60)
pecorino cheese, for grating

Pictured overleaf

1. We want to make a light and fluffy garlic bread, so here we use our fingertips to dimple down into the dough and spread it into a 15–20cm (6–8in) circle while keeping as much air in as possible. Place on a piece of baking parchment.
2. Spread over the butter.
3. Follow the method on page 175 to bake your garlic bread just as you would a pizza until puffy and golden.
4. Remove from the oven and grate a fine, generous blanket of pecorino over the top while it is still hot.
5. Cut into 6 slices and tuck in while you're topping your pizzas.

SALAMI FINOCCHIONA, GORGONZOLA, FRESH CHILLI & BLACK OLIVE

MAKES 1 PIZZA/6 SLICES

In one of my many lives, I somehow wound up as head chef of an Italian restaurant for a while. Although we weren't able to communicate very well, the Italian-only-speaking pizzaiolo working there opened my eyes to the simplicity of the pizza – the joy in the dough. This pizza is an evolution of an Italian fennel sausage and blue cheese combo he made me for lunch one time that blew my mind.

1 pizza dough base
(see pages 173–175)
2 tablespoons pizza sauce
(see pages 173–174)
75g (2½oz – ½ x 150g/5½oz
ball) mozzarella cheese
(drained weight)
6–7 slices of salami finocchiona
(about 40g/1½oz)
50g (1¾oz) Gorgonzola cheese
1 red chilli, sliced (I used
a bird's eye for the HEAT,
but feel free to use
something milder)
7–8 pitted Kalamata olives
olive oil, for drizzling
salt and cracked black pepper

Pictured overleaf

1. Follow the method on pages 173–175 to prepare your pizza base and add the sauce and mozzarella.
2. Fold and tear your salami, then distribute evenly around the pizza. Break the Gorgonzola into 5 or 6 pieces and deliberately tuck a piece in, around and on the salami. Sprinkle over your sliced chilli and olives.
3. Drizzle with a little olive oil and season with salt and cracked black pepper, then continue with the method to bake (see page175).

OLIVE, LEMON & THYME RYE RING

MAKES 1 RYE RING

This tasty ring has been a favourite of mine for a long time, yet another bread refined over practise running classes and courses in other people's homes over the years.

Just a little rye flour here is enough to make a massive contribution in flavour – a layer of rustic heartiness that other flours don't have. It may only be a little, but you will find it certainly makes the dough stickier. Stay strong and knead as usual without any additional flour dusted onto the work surface until you shape the dough at the very end.

Here I've used a mixture of black Kalamata and green queen olives for maximum flavour interest, then we get a little fragrance from the lemon zest and a lot from the thyme. It's an all-time great-tasting combo, and it works so well with the rye.

The crust on this bread is at its best on day one, but after that you can bring the crispiness back by refreshing it in the oven at 180°C fan/400°F/Gas Mark 6 for 5–10 minutes.

=== EASY TO MAKE, MORE ADVANCED TO PERFECT AND BAKE / TOTAL TIME: 3–4 HOURS ===

You'll need: a 23cm (9in) round banneton proving basket with liner or a clean cloth; small ramekin, dariole mould or espresso cup; baking or pizza stone, wooden peel; grignette

250g (9oz) room-temperature water
9g (¼oz) fresh yeast, crumbled, or 5g (½ tablespoon) fast-action dried yeast
300g (10½oz) strong white bread flour, plus extra for dusting
75g (2½oz) wholemeal rye flour
6g (1 teaspoon) salt

For the filling
120g (4¼oz) mixed pitted Kalamata and queen olives, torn
2 teaspoons chopped fresh thyme leaves
grated zest of 1 lemon

Making the dough: 15–20 minutes

1. In a large mixing bowl, mix together the water and yeast until the yeast has dissolved.
2. Add the flours and salt, then mix with a dough scraper until the mixture starts to come together into a rough dough.
3. Turn your dough out onto a clean work surface and knead without any additional flour for 8 minutes.

Resting: 5–10 minutes

4. Cover the dough with a clean cloth and rest on the work surface for 5–10 minutes to make the next stage easier.

Adding the filling: 10 minutes

5. While the dough is initially resting, mix the filling ingredients together in a bowl.

6. Dust the work surface lightly with flour and press the dough with your fingertips and knuckles to flatten and spread it into a circle. Sprinkle half your filling evenly all over the dough right to the edge. Pat it down with your palms to stick it to the dough.
7. Roll up your dough into a loose sausage.
8. Turn the dough 90 degrees and repeat the process with the remaining filling.

Resting: 1–1½ hours

9. Shape the dough into a ball and place it back in the bowl. Sprinkle the top with a little flour, cover with the cloth and rest at room temperature for 1–1½ hours.

Recipe continued overleaf

Pre-shaping: 5 minutes

10. Dust the top of the dough lightly with flour and use your dough scraper to turn it out upside down onto the work surface, sticky side up.

11. Use your fingertips to flatten the dough slightly, then roll it up into a rough sausage.

Resting: 10 minutes

12. Turn seam side down and dust only the top lightly with flour. Cover with the cloth and rest on the work surface for 10 minutes to relax and spread slightly.

Final shaping: 10 minutes

13. Slide your dough scraper underneath the dough and flip it, then press with your fingertips to flatten it and roll it up into a tight sausage. Then roll it with your palms on the work surface to make it longer, about 50cm (20in) if you can. You might need a little flour at this point so that the dough doesn't get sticky, but try not to use too much otherwise the dough will be too dusty and tricky to roll. Bring the 2 ends together into a ring and press together to stick.

14. Place your ramekin, dariole mould or espresso cup upturned in the centre of the banneton basket, then line the basket with the liner or a cloth over the top – this will help your ring stay as a ring while it proves. Dust the lined basket well with flour and place the ring upside down, seam side up, over the mould.

Resting: 45 minutes–1 hour

15. Cover your ring with another cloth and leave to rest for 45 minutes–1 hour.

16. Towards the end of resting, preheat your oven to 230°C fan/485°F/Gas Mark 9 with a baking or pizza stone on the middle shelf and a deep roasting tray on the oven floor. Half fill a kettle.

Slashing: 5 minutes

17. Boil the kettle.

18. Carefully upturn your basket onto your wooden peel to turn out the ring seam side down.

19. Use the grignette to slash 4 straight lines round the ring to form a square on the top.

Baking: 25–30 minutes

20. Slide the ring onto the hot stone in the oven. Carefully pour the hot water into the tray below. Bake your ring for 25–30 minutes, but keep an eye on it, and if it's colouring up too much, turn the oven down to 180°C fan/400°F/Gas Mark 6 after the first 15 minutes.

21. Remove the ring from the oven with your peel and let it cool completely on a wire rack.

BALSAMIC AUBERGINE, PUY LENTIL & ROASTED GARLIC SALAD

SERVES 3–4

This salad is almost a meal in itself and a great one to make in advance as the flavour only gets better. Take in a packed lunch or serve alongside the Cured Meats and Marinated Vegetable Antipasti (see page 92) with a fresh bread, such as the Olive, Lemon & Thyme Rye Ring, of course (see page 181).

Be sure to roast the vegetables really well to intensify the flavour and lose any of that spongy, undercooked aubergine texture.

---

2 aubergines (eggplants)
2 red (bell) peppers
olive oil
1 bulb of garlic
100g (3½oz) puy lentils
1 teaspoon finely chopped
   fresh rosemary leaves
2 tablespoons
   balsamic vinegar
a small pot (100g/3½oz)
   of Greek yoghurt
sea salt and cracked
   black pepper
Olive, Lemon & Thyme Rye
   Ring (see page 181)

1. Cut your aubergines and peppers into chunks, toss them in 3 tablespoons of olive oil and season with salt.

2. Spread out on a parchment-lined baking tray and roast them in the oven at 180°C fan/400°F/Gas Mark 6 for 40–45 minutes until soft and slightly charred. At the same time, wrap up your garlic bulb in tin foil and roast that until soft. It'll take around the same amount of time.

3. While you are waiting, cook your lentils in water following the instructions on the packet. Drain, season with salt and set aside.

4. When the garlic is cool enough, squeeze the cloves out of their skins into a large mixing bowl. Add the rosemary, balsamic vinegar, 2 tablespoons of olive oil and mix everything together. Take the vegetables out of the oven and tip them straight into the dressing, tossing it together. Add the lentils and mix again. Taste and adjust the seasoning if you need to.

5. Build up your salad onto a plate, spooning the yoghurt in between the layers and finally on top. Drizzle with a little extra olive oil and a pinch of black pepper. Serve with the fresh bread.

PANCETTA, GARLIC & HERB PAVÉ

MAKES 2 PAVÉS

In this bread I've combined smoky, salty pancetta with punchy garlic and robust herbs to make two rustic pavés PACKED with flavour. It just shows how simple combinations treated with care can produce something so delicious.

I always say that anything added into bread dough is effectively 'steamed' inside during the baking process, and so the filling here requires a little preparation to make sure the flavour really is at its best. We brown the pancetta, and ever so slightly cook the garlic and herbs in the fat it releases – more like INFUSING their flavour, to use a cheffy term. Then that smoky, garlicky, fragrant fat can be used in the actual dough in place of any additional butter or oil to really double up the flavour and make sure we don't waste anything.

Best on day one, this bread will keep for a couple of days before it needs refreshing in the oven at 180°C fan/400°F/Gas Mark 6 for a few minutes or toasting.

=== EASY TO MAKE, EASY TO SHAPE AND BAKE / TOTAL TIME: 3–4 HOURS ===

You'll need: a baking or pizza stone; large wooden peel; grignette

245g (8½oz) room-temperature water
8g (¼oz) fresh yeast, crumbled, or 4g (1 teaspoon) fast-action dried yeast

275g (9¾oz) strong white bread flour, plus extra for dusting
100g (3½oz) strong wholemeal bread flour
6g (1 teaspoon) salt
fat reserved from cooking the pancetta for the filling (I got 25g/1oz out of mine)

For the filling
320g (11¼oz) cubed pancetta
2 garlic cloves, sliced
1 tablespoon chopped fresh rosemary leaves
1 tablespoon chopped fresh sage leaves

Preparing the filling: 10–15 minutes
1. Place your pancetta cubes in a cold frying pan (skillet) and bring up to a medium heat. Let them cook on a gentle sizzle for 5–6 minutes until they are just golden all over. Remove from the heat and add your garlic and herbs. Let them cook in the residual heat for 30 seconds, then tip the mixture into a sieve set over a bowl to catch the fat underneath. Leave to cool.

Making the dough: 15–20 minutes
2. In a large mixing bowl, mix together the water and yeast until the yeast has dissolved.
3. Add the flours and salt, then mix with a dough scraper until the mixture starts to come together into a rough dough. Add the reserved pancetta fat and dimple it into the dough with your fingertips.

4. Turn your dough out onto a clean work surface and knead without any additional flour for 8 minutes.
5. Cover the dough with a clean cloth and rest on the work surface for 5–10 minutes to make the next stage easier.

Adding the filling: 2 minutes
6. Dust the dough and the work surface lightly with flour, then roll out the dough with a rolling pin into a 30cm (12in) circle. Sprinkle your filling mixture evenly all over the dough right to the edge, then press down with your palms to stick it to the dough.
7. Roll up your dough into a loose sausage. Then turn it 90 degrees, press it flat with your fingertips and roll up again into a short sausage.

Recipe continued overleaf

Resting: 1–1½ hours

8. Shape the dough into a ball and place it back in the bowl. Sprinkle the top with a little flour, cover with the cloth and rest at room temperature for 1–1½ hours.

Dividing and pre-shaping: 5–10 minutes

9. Dust the top of the dough lightly with flour and use your dough scraper to turn it out upside down onto the work surface, sticky side up.

10. Use your fingertips to flatten the dough gently and cut it in half with your dough scraper. Fold and roll each piece of dough into a ball, then cup slightly to tighten (see page 24).

Resting: 10 minutes

11. Line up your dough balls on the work surface. Dust only the tops lightly with flour, cover with the cloth and rest for 10 minutes to relax and spread slightly.

Final shaping: 5–10 minutes

12. Dust the work surface lightly with flour. Working with one at a time, slide your dough scraper underneath a dough ball to release it and flip it sticky side up onto the dusted surface.

13. Press with your fingertips and knuckles to flatten and spread the dough into a 15cm (6in) circle. Use a rolling pin to roll 4 flaps – top, bottom, left and right – leaving the middle a plump square. Fold each flap over the middle and press to stick them down, then press the dough out into a 15cm (6in) square.

14. Line a tray with a clean cloth and dust it well with flour. Place your 2 pavés on the tray, seam side up, and make a pleat in the cloth between them to stop them from sticking together as they rise.

Resting: 45 minutes–1 hour

15. Cover your pavés with another cloth and rest for 45 minutes–1 hour.

16. Towards the end of resting, preheat your oven to 230°C fan/485°F/Gas Mark 9 with a baking or pizza stone on the middle shelf and a deep roasting tray on the oven floor. Half fill a kettle.

Slashing and baking: 25–30 minutes

17. Boil the kettle.

18. Carefully lift the side of the cloth and gently roll the pavés onto your large wooden peel, seam side down.

19. Use the grignette to make a swift slash diagonally on the top of each pavé, then slide them onto the hot stone in the oven. Carefully pour the hot water into the tray below. Bake your pavés for 25–30 minutes, but keep an eye on them, and if they are colouring up too much, turn the oven down to 180°C fan/400°F/Gas Mark 6 after the first 15 minutes.

20. Remove them from the oven with your peel and let them cool completely on a wire rack.

BURRATA WITH DRESSED CHARD & ASPARAGUS

SERVES 2

With the Pancetta, Garlic & Herb Pavé (see page 187) so packed with flavour, it makes sense to pair it with this dish. Simple lemon-dressed greens, fresh asparagus and milky burrata to accompany a salty, smoky, robust bread. It doesn't take much to make nice greens sing in this tasty fresh springtime dish.

200g (7oz) rainbow chard (swiss chard)
6–8 asparagus spears
1 lemon
olive oil
1 burrata
pinch of chopped fresh thyme leaves
sea salt and cracked black pepper
1 Pancetta, Garlic & Herb Pavé (see page 187)

1. Bring a large pan of salted water to the boil. Trim the dodgy ends from your chard and asparagus and discard.

2. Plunge your asparagus and chard into the boiling water and cook for 1 minute, then remove from the water into a colander and let them steam dry a little before transferring them to a large mixing bowl.

3. Squeeze over the juice of half your lemon, drizzle in 2 tablespoons of olive oil and toss everything together with some tongs. Divide between 2 plates.

4. Halve your burrata and tear over the top of your cooked greens. Drizzle with olive oil, season with sea salt flakes and cracked black pepper and sprinkle over some chopped thyme leaves. Serve with torn chunks of the bread.

BEETROOT, ROSEMARY & RAISIN BATARD

MAKES 2 MEDIUM BATARDS

This one's a stunner. Essentially a savoury dough, the earthy depth of the beetroot combined with sweet raisins and fragrant rosemary make this pink-tinged beauty perfect for your end-of-evening cheeseboard, and what a talking point for you and your guests!

For this, we use the juice from the beetroot along with the coarsely grated flesh for stunning visual effect, incredible flavour as well as a bouncy and moreishly moist crumb texture. Make it with love and promise me one thing – do not, under any circumstances, use pre-cooked beetroot, vacuum-packed or pickled, otherwise instead of a beautiful pinkish purple hue your loaves will be a disappointing dull grey. As always, effort is rewarded, and it couldn't be illustrated any better than with this bread.

Thanks to the moisture in the beetroot, you'll most likely get an extra day's keeping quality out of this bread, so best on the day of baking but still good on day three. Then it's toast time.

=== EASY TO MAKE, TRICKY TO MASTER / TOTAL TIME: 3–4 HOURS, PLUS OVERNIGHT ===
FRUIT SOAK AND 1½ HOURS TO BAKE THE BEETROOT, PLUS COOLING

You'll need: a baking or pizza stone; large wooden peel; grignette

room-temperature water, to top up (see method)
12g (½oz) fresh yeast, crumbled, or 7g (¼oz) fast-action dried yeast
500g (1lb 2oz) strong white bread flour, plus extra for dusting
10g (½oz) salt

For the filling
50g (1¾oz) raisins
2 medium fresh beetroots (beets)
1 tablespoon chopped fresh rosemary leaves

Pre-soaking the raisins: Overnight

1. Place your raisins in a bowl and pour over just enough water to cover. Soak overnight at room temperature.

2. Drain the soaked fruit and pat dry really well with kitchen paper.

Cooking the beetroot: 1–1½ hours

3. Preheat your oven to 180°C fan/400°F/ Gas Mark 6. Wrap your beetroots individually in foil and bake for 1–1½ hours until they can be easily pierced to the centre with a sharp knife. Let them cool in the foil, then slide off the skin with your fingers and grate the beetroots on the coarse side of a box grater.

Making the dough: 15–20 minutes

4. Squeeze the juice from your grated beetroot into a jug and set the gratings aside. Depending on your beetroot, you might get a decent amount or nothing at all, but make use of whatever you can squeeze out. Top up the juice to 325g (11½oz) with room-temperature water.

5. In a large mixing bowl, mix together the beetroot water and yeast until the yeast has dissolved.

6. Add the flour and salt, then mix with a dough scraper until the mixture starts to come together into a rough dough.

7. Turn your dough out onto a clean work surface and knead without any additional flour for 8 minutes.

Recipe continued overleaf

8. Place the dough on a large baking tray, high-sided if you have one. Sprinkle over half the grated beetroot, raisins and rosemary and dimple it into the dough with your fingertips. Work the beetroot through the dough in the tray by lifting each bit of the dough edge, folding it over and pushing it into the middle. It will get messy, but keep kneading like this, scooping up anything that falls out with your dough scraper and placing it back on the top, and the dough will take everything in. When the beetroot seems to be evenly incorporated, repeat with the remaining filling ingredients. They may not all be contained within the dough, but at least there will be some throughout.

Resting: 1–1½ hours
9. Shape the dough into a ball and place it back in the bowl. Sprinkle the top with a little flour, cover with a clean cloth and rest at room temperature for 1–1½ hours.

Dividing and pre-shaping: 2–5 minutes
10. Dust the top of the dough lightly with flour and use your dough scraper to turn it out upside down onto the work surface, sticky side up.
11. Use your fingertips to flatten the dough gently and cut it in half with your dough scraper. Fold and roll each piece of dough into a ball, then cup slightly to tighten (see page 24).

Resting: 10 minutes
12. Line up your dough balls on the work surface. Dust only the tops lightly with flour, cover with the cloth and rest for 10 minutes to relax and spread slightly.

Final shaping: 5–10 minutes
13. Lightly dust the work surface with flour. Working with one at a time, slide your dough scraper underneath a dough ball to release it and flip it sticky side up onto the dusted surface.
14. Press with your fingertips and knuckles to flatten and spread the dough into a circle. Then imagine that your circle is a square and grasp each imaginary top corner, stretch them out and then fold into the middle of the dough. Fold down the point at the top. Roll up the dough from the top to the bottom into a tight sausage, building tension as you go, then press the seam to stick it together. Roll the sausage a little with your palms on the work surface to lengthen and make the ends pointy.
15. Line a tray with a clean cloth and dust it really well with flour. Place your loaves on the tray, seam side up, and make a large pleat in the cloth inbetween them to stop them from sticking together as they rise.

Resting: 45 minutes–1 hour
16. Cover your loaves with another cloth and rest for 45 minutes–1 hour. Towards the end of resting, preheat your oven to 230°C fan/485°F/Gas Mark 9 with a baking or pizza stone on the middle shelf and a deep roasting tray on the oven floor. Half fill a kettle.

Slashing: 5 minutes
17. Boil the kettle.
18. Carefully lift the side of your cloth and gently roll the batards onto your wooden peel so that they are seam side down.
19. Use the grignette to make a long cut down one side of each loaf from one end to the other. Then to make a wheat pattern, make a line of short diagonal cuts the length of the other side, and another line of short cuts next to it to mirror the first.

Baking: 30–35 minutes
20. Slide your batards onto the hot stone in the oven. Carefully pour the hot water into the tray below. Bake your batards for 30–35 minutes, but keep an eye on them, and if they are colouring up too much, turn the oven down to 180°C fan/400°F/Gas Mark 6 after the first 15 minutes.
21. Remove the batards from the oven with your peel and let them cool completely on a wire rack.

THE PERFECT CHEESEBOARD
SERVES 4–6 PEOPLE

For me, creating the perfect cheeseboard is about creating VARIETY and ABUNDANCE. When it comes to cheese selection, you will have your own ideas, but it's nice to cover all the bases. I'm talking about something creamy, sliceable and ideally ripe and runny, like Chaource, Brie or Reblochon. Something blue, like a Stilton, or go local – here in the UK we have Norbury Blue, which is delish. Something a little crowd-pleasing is always a good idea, like Cheddar or even a smoked one; you know, non-offensive. Then something niche and goaty or we can even go outside the box, perhaps with the Pecorino Chunks, Sultanas, Fennel Syrup & Toasted Walnuts recipe (see page 276).

   Cheese selection decided, it's time to get HEAVY with accompaniments ... Lace your board with all the classics: grapes, nuts, celery, apple, chutney in a pretty jar like you made it, pears, figs, quince paste? YES PLEASE. If it's Christmas time, how about a couple of satsumas, cracked open and looking inviting.

   And finally, the bread ... a Beetroot, Rosemary & Raisin Batard (see page 191) will be a nice talking point. With its stunning colour and being dotted with sweet raisins, it's the perfect accompaniment. Or the Wholemeal Fruit-and-Nut Loaf (see page 149) would work really well. Something simple, like a crusty baguette or sourdough, would sing and, for crunch, some crispbreads. Perhaps to add a little faff-free variety, crackers for their crispiness to complement the bread that you've made.

   For a special occasion, you COULD really go to town or you could keep things simple for a low-key evening and put some care and attention into selecting just a few of these things that match up nicely. Whatever you do, take some time over the deliberate placing of your choices, tucking a little pile of nuts here or some fig wedges there. To take the edge off being the first in a crowd to touch an immaculately presented cheeseboard, the subtly enticing crumble of a blue cheese wedge should be just enough to get people started. When it comes to presentation, effort is always rewarded.

YOUR CHEESE OF CHOICE

The Creamy
The Blue
The Crowd-Pleaser
The Goaty One

OTHER CLASSICS

Nuts
Celery sticks
Chutney
Quince paste

FRUIT

Grapes
Apples
Pears
Plums
Blackberries
Figs

YOUR BREAD OF CHOICE

Beetroot, Rosemary & Raisin Batard
(see page 191)
Wholemeal Fruit-and-Nut Loaf (see page 149)
Baguette (see page 165)
Sourdough Loaf (see page 264)
Sourdough Crispbreads (see page 273)
Crackers
Butter or Homemade Butter (see page 59)

CHAPTER FIVE

ENRICHED
DOUGHS

ENRICHED MEANS EGGS, BUTTER, MILK AND SUGAR

Here you'll find sweet buns, doughnuts, stollen, brioche – all those luxurious bakes – the additional ingredients make them soft, light and buttery.

There are a couple of things to note here. One is that enriched doughs ALWAYS take longer to rise up. You'll notice these recipes have more yeast than previous ones because all those extra bits and bobs weigh heavy on the dough and it'll need a little extra booster.

Also, we have started off here with slightly warmer liquid to get a head start and, YES, I know I am breaking my own rules here! But we can compensate for that slightly warmer start if we make sure we cover the dough with an upturned bowl, or cling film in some cases, instead of a simple cloth, just to make sure nothing dries out. Check the liquid temperature in the recipe, use eggs at room temperature and soft butter too, but don't be tempted to warm things further still. If the butter melts inside the dough, it will become greasy and difficult to handle instead of silky and buttery as it should be.

One more thing to note is the slightly longer kneading time: 10 minutes where before we've been doing 8. It's a small adjustment but helps us to make sure the strength is built in the dough enough to create a super-light bread. In the case of the Brioche (see page 200), we take things even FURTHER by first working the dough, and THEN incorporating the butter in stages afterwards.

The dishes that follow on from these breads have to be some of my favourites – transforming a leftover hot cross bun into a breakfast pancake stack was a good day in the test kitchen.

When we bake enriched breads, they tend to take on colour pretty quickly thanks to their sweetness. And so, we bake them at a slightly lower temperature than anything else in this book. Fortunately, the lighter a dough is, the less time it takes to bake, so that principle works in our favour here since these are the lightest of them all. Also, the classic 'tap on the bottom and if it sounds hollow it's done' rule doesn't really apply. The best practice for breads in this section is to slide a knife underneath and have a peep. If it's golden on the base, it'll be done to the inside.

CHOCOLATE BRIOCHE
MAKES 2 ROUND LOAVES

Brioche is the ultimate enriched dough. It pushes the quantity of eggs and butter to its limits and the result is a dough that rises FAR beyond what you ever thought was possible and is the softest, lightest bread you can imagine.

Because there is so much butter here, we need to incorporate it into the dough bit by bit so that it's able to absorb it without becoming a slippery mess. And with all that butter and the eggs, the dough can take AGES to rise. But don't be tempted to make it too warm to speed it up, otherwise the butter will melt and your dough will get super-greasy. You may think the amount of butter is a little excessive, but the dough puffs up SO BIG that you only need a little bit of dough to make a big loaf. Think about it – a single sandwich tin loaf uses 500g (1lb 2oz) flour, yet for two loaves of brioche we use only 375g (13oz). So, when you're eating it, it's really not that much as it's mostly just air. Compared to a slice of cake, for example, I would say this is the relatively 'healthy' option!

=== TRICKY TO MAKE, EASY TO BAKE / TOTAL TIME: 3¼–4½ HOURS ===

You'll need: 2 x 18cm (7in) round, 5cm (2in) deep Panibois wooden moulds, but similar-sized cake or pie tins will work equally well

95g (3¼oz) warm milk, 25–30°C (77–86°F)
3 medium eggs (150g/5½oz egg without the shells), plus 1 egg, beaten, for glazing
20g (¾oz) fresh yeast, crumbled, or 10g (½oz) fast-action dried yeast
375g (13oz) strong white bread flour, plus extra for dusting

40g (1½oz) golden caster (superfine) sugar
5g (1 teaspoon) salt
150g (5½oz) room-temperature unsalted butter, broken into pieces
150g (5½oz) dark chocolate chips

Making the dough: 20–30 minutes

1. In a large mixing bowl, whisk together the milk, eggs and yeast with a balloon whisk until the yeast has softened.

2. Add the flour, sugar and salt along with about a quarter (35g/1¼oz) of the butter (to help our dough be a little more manageable and a little less sticky when we knead). Mix with a dough scraper until the mixture starts to come together into a rough dough.

3. Turn your dough out onto a clean work surface and knead gently without any additional flour for 6 minutes. Things are going to get a little messy here, so relax into it and use your scraper to release the dough from the table and your hands every once in a while and have a little tidy. (You can opt for working the dough in the bowl to feel more comfortable.)

4. Place the dough in the bowl and put one-third of the remaining butter on top. Dimple it in all over with your fingertips, pushing the butter into the dough. The first time you do it, keep folding it over itself, pushing the dough into the middle, rotating the bowl and repeating. At first it will look as if the butter will never be incorporated but keep going and the slippery dough will take on the butter and become silky.

5. When it does, do exactly the same thing with the other two-thirds of butter. As you add more and more butter, the dough will become looser and silkier. At this point I change tactic, scooping my hand underneath towards my body, stretching the dough UP and FORWARDS before going back in for another scoop.

Recipe continued overleaf

6. When the last bit of butter has been fully incorporated, sprinkle over your chocolate chips and work them into the dough in exactly the same way.

7. Turn the dough out onto the work surface and rest for 3 minutes.

Resting: 1½–2 hours
8. Shape the dough into a smooth ball with the help of a little dusting of flour and place it back in the bowl. Sprinkle the top with a little flour on the top, cover with an upturned bowl and rest at room temperature for 1½–2 hours.

Dividing and shaping: 5–10 minutes
9. Dust the work surface lightly with flour and use your dough scraper to turn the dough out upside down onto it, sticky side up.
10. Use your fingertips to flatten the dough slightly and cut it into 12 equal-sized pieces. If you want them all to be exactly the same size, weigh them out at about 75g (2½oz) each.
11. Fold and roll each piece into a tight ball (see page 24) – use a light touch here so that the dough doesn't get too sticky, dust sparingly if you need to and try to be swift, as the longer you handle the dough, the stickier it will become!
12. In each of your baking moulds or tins, arrange 5 dough balls around the edge and one in the middle.

Resting and glazing: 1–1½ hours
13. Cover your brioche loosely with cling film dusted with flour and rest for 1–1½ hours or so.
14. Towards the end of resting, preheat your oven to 180°C fan/400°F/Gas Mark 6 with a shelf in the middle and a deep roasting tray on the oven floor. Half fill a kettle.
15. Check the brioche after 45 minutes to see how they are getting on. If they are rising nicely, egg wash them at this point before they get too delicate. Using a soft brush, paint the tops with a thin layer of beaten egg. Then let them rest for the remaining time.

Baking: 20–25 minutes
16. Boil the kettle.
17. Place your moulds or tins on the oven shelf and carefully pour the hot water into the tray below. Bake your brioche for 20–25 minutes until golden.
18. Carefully slide a knife underneath one and lift it slightly to peep at the underside. If the base is as golden as the top, they are done, but if not, return them to the oven for 3–5 minutes at a time until they are.
19. Let them cool completely on a wire rack.

TIPS

THE SOFT APPROACH

If you want to improve the flavour and texture of your brioche, making them SUPER-soft, refrigerate your dough overnight. Once you have incorporated the chocolate, return the dough to its bowl, cover with cling film and pop it into the fridge. The following day, remove it from the fridge and rest at room temperature for 30 minutes, then shape, rest and bake as per the method. You'll find the shaping so much easier, as your dough will be firmer, although it might take a little longer to rise – expect it to take at least 2 hours in total depending on your kitchen temperature on the day.

MAKING THE BEST OF YOUR BRIOCHE

I'm quite an easy-going chap when it comes to rules, but when we make brioche in class, there is one very important rule we must stick to: always, always eat some of your brioche when it's still warm from the oven, at its freshest best. Then if any should make it past day two, show any leftovers a little love in the oven, preheated to the same temperature as before for 5–8 minutes, depending on size. Or you can reheat a slice or two in the toaster, keeping your eyes peeled as it toasts up quick and being careful of those chocolate pieces, which will turn to magma. Let it cool slightly inside the toaster before removing.

CHOCOLATE BRIOCHE TIRAMISU

SERVES 8

As if leftover brioche was ever a thing … Just in case it ever is though, this is a great way to use it all up.

Aside from swapping out the classic savoiardi biscuits for brioche slices and adding a little extra chocolate to the party, I haven't messed around too much with this recipe. It's straight up no-nonsense tiramisu. Make it in advance to give the mascarpone time to set and other than that, most of its success lies in the quality of its few ingredients: good coffee, good eggs and good mascarpone. Have fun.

125ml (4fl oz) strong
    black coffee
2 tablespoons coffee liqueur
350g (12½oz) Chocolate
    Brioche (see page 200)
3 medium eggs
75g (2½oz) icing
    (confectioners') sugar
250g (9oz) mascarpone
½ teaspoon vanilla
    bean paste
150g (5½oz) block or bar
    of dark chocolate

1. Brew your coffee and add the coffee liqueur. Set aside.
2. Slice your brioche and use your dish (about 18 x 28cm/7 x 11in) to make sure you have the right amount – you'll need enough for 2 layers.
3. Separate your eggs into 2 large mixing bowls: yolks in one, whites in the other.
4. Whisk up the yolks with a balloon whisk or electric hand whisk until thick, foamy and light in colour – 3 minutes brisk whisk should be enough. Add the icing sugar and whisk again for a minute or so, just to make sure you've made your best efforts to aerate it. Add the mascarpone and vanilla paste and whisk it in until just smooth.
5. Clean your whisk and now whip up your egg whites in the other bowl until fluffy and stiff. Fold a third of the whites into the mascarpone and mix with a large metal spoon to loosen it. Then add the next third and fold it in, finally followed by the rest. Fold it all together and you should have a sweet, delicious, moussey mascarpone mix.
6. Layer half your brioche on the bottom of your dish. Use a pastry brush to liberally douse the brioche with half your coffee mix.
7. Generously grate over a fine layer of chocolate and add half the mascarpone on top. Spread it nice and evenly, flattening it on top with the flat side of a dough scraper.
8. Next, layer in your remaining brioche, brush with the rest of the coffee exactly as before and grate another layer of chocolate over the top.
9. Spread over the rest of the mascarpone, making it nice and flat with your dough scraper, then go to town with the chocolate, grating a thick blanket over the top.
10. Use the corner of a piece of kitchen paper wrapped round a finger to clean up the edges of your dish. Refrigerate your tiramisu for 6 hours or overnight to set nicely.
11. When you are ready to serve, cut your portions with a knife and scoop out with a large spoon.

BRIOCHE HOT DOG ROLLS & BURGER BUNS

MAKES 8 BURGER BUNS OR 12 HOT DOG ROLLS

Imagine that you've just crafted the perfect burger, grilled it to perfection – juicy on the inside, crispy and slightly charred on the outside – then topped it with whatever you fancied before popping it in a chewy and dense roll with a thick crust. Now imagine biting into it and everything inside squeezing out all over your clothes.

There are several reasons why brioche is used a lot for burgers and hot dogs. It's super-soft so that everything DOESN'T slide out when you bite into it. It's slightly sweet to contrast nicely with the saltiness inside, and buttery but not overly flavourful to take the shine away from the filling. And it's LIGHT, so you don't get full up on the bread and have no room for your fries (and milkshake!) It just makes perfect sense.

So why not up your game in barbecue season and make your own buns to toast up over the coals. You can prepare these a couple of days ahead to make life easy for yourself on barbecue day if you like and keep them in a reusable plastic or freezer bag ready to toast or freeze them if you're preparing them even further in advance.

=== EASY TO MAKE, EASY TO BAKE / TOTAL TIME: 3–4½ HOURS ===

You'll need: 2 x small high-sided baking trays for hot dog rolls – mine are 18 x 28cm (7 x 11in), 3cm (1¼in) deep, and fit 6 perfectly

225g (8oz) room-temperature water
2 medium eggs (100g/3½oz egg without the shell), plus 1 egg, beaten, for glazing
20g (¾oz) fresh yeast, crumbled, or 10g (½oz) fast-action dried yeast
500g (1lb 2oz) strong white bread flour, plus extra for dusting

8g (¼oz) salt
20g (¾oz) golden caster (superfine) sugar
150g (5½oz) room-temperature unsalted butter, broken into pieces
sesame seeds and sea salt flakes, for sprinkling the burger buns

Making the dough: 15–20 minutes

1. In a large mixing bowl, mix together the water, eggs and yeast until the yeast has dissolved.
2. Add the flour, salt, sugar and one-third of your butter, then mix with a dough scraper into a rough dough.
3. Turn your dough out onto a clean work surface and knead without any additional flour for 6 minutes.
4. Place the dough back in the bowl. Put half the remaining butter on top and dimple it in all over with your fingertips. Then lift a bit of the dough edge, fold it over and push it into the middle. Keep rotating the bowl and repeating. At first it will look as if the butter will never be incorporated, but keep going and the slippery dough will take on the butter and become silky.
5. Repeat the process with the remaining butter.
6. Knead the dough for another minute on the work surface to make sure everything is nicely incorporated.

Resting: 1–1½ hours

7. Shape the dough into a smooth ball and place it back in the bowl. Sprinkle the top with a little flour, cover with an upturned bowl and rest at room temperature for 1–1½ hours.

Burger buns: 5–10 minutes

8. Line a baking tray with baking parchment.

9. Dust the work surface lightly with flour and use your dough scraper to turn the dough out upside down onto it, sticky side up.

10. Use your fingertips to flatten the dough slightly and cut it into 8 equal-sized pieces with your dough scraper. If you want them all to be exactly the same size, weigh them out at about 115g (4oz) each.

11. Fold and roll each piece of dough into a tight ball (see page 24) – use a light touch here, as the dough can get quite sticky quite quickly, and dust sparingly if you need to (see my tip below).

12. Place the dough balls on your lined tray, making sure there is plenty of room around each one for them to rise without touching one another.

Hot dog rolls: 20–30 minutes

13. Line your 2 high-sided baking trays with baking parchment.

14. Turn the dough out on a lightly floured work surface as above.

15. Use your fingertips to gently flatten the dough slightly and cut it into 12 equal-sized pieces. If you want them all to be exactly the same size, weigh them out at around 80g (2¾oz) each.

16. Fold and roll each piece into a tight ball (see page 24).

17. Line up your dough balls on the work surface. Dust only the tops with flour, cover with a clean cloth and rest for 10–15 minutes to relax.

18. Working with one at a time, flip a dough ball over, press it flat into a circle and, starting with the side furthest from you, roll it up into a sausage. Roll with your palms on the work surface until it is about 15cm (6in) long.

19. Line up your dough sausages on your lined trays keeping them evenly spaced so that they will join up as they rise.

Resting and glazing: 1–1½ hours

20. Cover your buns or rolls loosely with cling film dusted with flour and rest for 1–1½ hours.

21. Towards the end of resting, preheat your oven to 180°C fan/400°F/Gas Mark 6 with a shelf in the middle and a deep roasting tray on the oven floor. Half fill a kettle.

22. Check the buns after 45 minutes to see how they are getting on. If they are rising nicely, egg wash them at this point before they get too delicate. Using a soft brush, paint the tops with a thin layer of beaten egg. If you have made burger buns, sprinkle over some sesame seeds and a little sea salt. Then let them rest for the remaining time.

Baking: 20 minutes

23. Boil the kettle.

24. Place your baking tray or trays on the oven shelf and carefully pour the hot water into the tray below. Bake your buns or rolls for 20 minutes until golden. Remove a tray of buns from the oven, slide a knife underneath one and lift it slightly to peep at the underside. If the base is golden as well as the top, then they are done. If not, return them to the oven for 3–5 minutes at a time until they are.

25. Let them cool completely on a wire rack.

─────────── **TIP** ───────────

IF THINGS GET REALLY STICKY...

Brioche dough is so soft and delicate that it can often get sticky at the shaping stage. Try to work quickly, dusting with a minimum of flour when you need to, and don't let the dough get too warm in your hands. If a piece of dough becomes too tricky to handle, give it a dust and set it aside while you shape up the rest, then come back to it. The surface should have dried out a little and the dough relaxed ready to give it another go.

BARBECUE HOT DOG WITH CHARRED CORN & PEPPER SALSA

SERVES 4

I am a closet hot dog fan. There, I said it. When I am demonstrating at a food festival, I normally get in early, make my doughs, set up my stuff and then BAIL to hunt out the hot dog stall before I go on stage. For this recipe, we're using your Brioche Hot Dog Rolls (see page 206) and I wanted to make something simple to load them with. Since you have the coals a burnin', and it really doesn't take much to heat a hot dog, you can use that heat to char some sweetcorn and red pepper to make a tasty salsa to top your dogs with later.

---

4 good hot dogs
4 Brioche Hot Dog Rolls
   (see page 206)
sliced pickles
yellow mustard (optional)

For the salsa
1 corn on the cob
1 red (bell) pepper
1 tablespoon chopped fresh
   coriander (cilantro) leaves
1 tablespoon olive oil
1 tablespoon lime juice
good pinch of salt

1. Get your coals on nice and hot and burn the flames down until they are at an even heat. Char your corn on the cob and pepper until blackened for a couple of minutes on each side. Set aside to cool slightly.
2. Slice the corn from the sides of your cob and place it in a large bowl. Peel the blackened skin away from the pepper, tear it open and discard the seeds and stalk. Chop into pieces the same size as your corn and add it to the bowl. Mix well with the coriander, olive oil, lime juice and a good pinch of salt, then set aside.
3. Place your hot dogs on the grill (broiler) and while they are cooking up, split and toast your buns too. Leave them somewhere to keep warm.
4. Nestle your dog in its bun, tuck a few sliced gherkins down one side and pile your salsa on top. Finish with an (optional) drizzle of yellow mustard.

SMASH BURGERS

SERVES 2

Remember I said I've had a LOT of jobs? That was true. And in that time, I've made a TON of burgers: burgers with raw onions in, burgers with cooked onions, burgers with mustard inside, chilli and garlic, breadcrumbs to bulk and egg to bind, but in a smash burger there is … nothing. It's meat and technique. THIS is the way we've adopted burgers at Bake with Jack Towers, just 20 per cent fat beef, a little salt and pepper, and that's it.

A true smash is pressed minced beef cooked FAST, making the inside JUICY and the outside CRISPY and salty, and it's very important to put two in a bun because … er … double the crispiness I suppose. You'll need a flat griddle and open your windows … it's about to get smoky in here.

340g (12oz) 20% fat
   minced beef
4 baby gem leaves
1 beef (beefsteak)
   tomato, sliced
4 slices of gherkin
4 slices of Gouda
2 Brioche Burger Buns
   (see page 206)
6 slices of smoked streaky
   bacon (optional)
sea salt and cracked
   black pepper

For the burger sauce (optional)
1 tablespoon tomato ketchup
1 tablespoon mayo
½ teaspoon Dijon mustard
½ teaspoon pickle juice
6–10 shakes of Tabasco,
   to taste
1 tablespoon finely
   chopped fresh parsley
   leaves and stalks

1. Divide your mince into 4 equal pieces (weigh them if you like to 85g/3oz each). Squeeze each piece just enough to be able to roll it into a ball without it cracking.

2. Before you start cooking, get EVERYTHING ready so you can give your burgers 100 per cent of the attention they deserve.

3. Have a small saucepan ready (you'll use this to smash the burgers) and a square of parchment paper big enough to cover a burger.

4. Pick your lettuce leaves, slice your tomato and gherkins, slice your cheese, cut your buns, have your salt and pepper at the ready.

5. If you're making the burger sauce, mix all the ingredients together.

6. Get your grill (broiler) on and toast up your buns ahead of time. Crisp up your bacon here too and set aside, then leave the grill on for cheese melting later.

7. Heat up your flat griddle pan on the stove until smoking hot. Take a ball of beef and place it on the griddle. Pop the parchment paper on top and SQUASH really flat with the underneath of the saucepan. Your burgers will likely shrink up as they cook, so go BIGGER than the size of your bun. Remove the paper.

8. Place the next burger with some controlled urgency and zero panic and do exactly the same and continue until all burgers are on the griddle. Season them all with a pinch of sea salt and cracked black pepper.

9. Your burgers should only cook for a couple of minutes on each side and it might be that the first one is ready to flip by the time you've finished seasoning them all. Get a palette knife or fish slice and shimmy it underneath a burger. It should pretty much release itself when it has become crispy enough underneath. Flip each burger and season the other side with salt and pepper. Cook for a further 1–2 minutes and begin to apply a slice of cheese to the top of each and the bacon to 2 of them. Stack the burgers on the griddle in

twos to make bacon sandwiches and transfer to the grill to melt the cheese while you faff around with plates and buns. Turn of the griddle.
10. Spread some burger sauce on the burger base, if using, add a couple of gherkin slices and top with the burger stack. Add another dose of sauce here, if using, before topping with a big slice of beef tomato, your lettuce, more burger sauce if you want, and finally the bun lid. Enjoy.

— TIP —

STRESS-FREE GRILLING

Cooking four burgers in this way from the get-go might be a little stressful at first, so if you like, do a tester one before you do the rest, just to get the technique down and know what to expect. If your burgers are sticking, try not to panic and smash them up getting them off. It's a 'smash' burger, not a 'smashed-up' burger. Be patient – let it cook a little longer and it should loosen itself.

WILD MUSHROOM & REBLOCHON BRIOCHE ROLL

SERVES 2

NOW you're talkin'. This is what it's about: a touch of CLASS, something a little bit FANCY, like me … Don't stress too much about wild mushrooms. You can get those mixed packs in the supermarket, and mine came with shiitake, oyster mushrooms and a couple of chestnut mushrooms, just to make sure I don't get too carried away. So long as you follow the mushroom principle below, you'll get cracking flavour out of even the most … uninspiring.

Mushrooms need to be cooked hot. They have a lot of water inside so try not to move them around too much in the pan, otherwise they'll take out the heat, the water will come out, and they will end up simmering in their own juices instead of frying nicely. And it's in that fry, that golden surface, where the best flavour lies. When you come to add them to the pan, season them with salt and give them a good two to three minutes cooking before you flip them for the first time. Peep underneath to see how the colour is coming, and only flip when golden.

Be SURE to toast up your brioche and while your mushroom choice is not essential, Reblochon is, in my humble opinion, the tastiest of all soft cheeses.

---

4 slices of Reblochon cheese
200g (7oz) mixed wild
   mushrooms (see above)
2 tablespoons olive oil
pinch of salt
20g (¾oz) butter
1 teaspoon chopped fresh
   thyme leaves
½ garlic clove, finely grated
2 tablespoons white wine
1 tablespoon chopped fresh
   flat-leaf (Italian) parsley
   leaves and stalks
2 Brioche Hot Dog Rolls
   (see page 206)

1. Remove your cheese from the fridge to come up to room temperature while you are getting on with the mushrooms.
2. Brush any dirt from your mushrooms and trim off any dodgy bits. Tear your oysters into large pieces, quarter any large shiitakes and halve the smaller ones. Halve your chestnut mushrooms too.
3. Heat the olive oil in a large non-stick frying pan (skillet) to a medium-high heat. Add the mushrooms with a pinch of salt and let them sizzle for 2–3 minutes until golden underneath before flipping them over. They should probably take 7–8 minutes in total to get a lovely golden brown all over. Turn the heat down, let the pan cool a little and push the mushrooms to one side of the pan.
4. In the empty side of the pan, place the butter, chopped thyme and garlic. Let the butter melt and sizzle a little before tossing the mushrooms in it for 2 minutes or so.
5. Splash in the white wine and simmer it all away until it's gone. Add the parsley and toss together. Transfer the mushrooms to a plate while you split and toast 2 two brioche rolls, hot-dog style.
6. Slide a couple of slices of cheese down one side and pile your mushrooms into the middle. Serve hot.

MALTED CINNAMON BUNS WITH CREAM CHEESE FROSTING & PECANS

MAKES 12–15 CINNAMON BUNS

Cinnamon buns are one of those bakes best made at home. Even if you got them from a proper bakery, you would never be able to buy them straight from the oven.

In all the years I have hosted classes, the cinnamon bun moments are the best. When we've all baked our breads and we're eating supper together to finish our evening, it just so happens that the cinnamon buns are ready, still a little warm from the oven, just in time for us to pass them around the table and conduct a taste test before we go home. What are the chances?!

I've used a proportion of malthouse bread flour here – a mixture of white flour, malted wheat flakes and malted barley flour – and it really does bring a new, fuller dimension of flavour to these cinnamon buns. If you don't have it or can't find it, please don't stress – just replace it with strong white bread flour, but keep an eye out for it for next time round.

Cream cheese frosting here is a must, and this one is just sweet enough while holding onto its natural cool freshness to contrast with the warm, sticky bun beneath and the toasty crunchy pecans on top.

Eat these on day one. Seriously. And if any make it to day two, warm them through in the oven at 180°C fan/400°F/Gas Mark 6 for 8 minutes or so to revive them.

═══ EASY TO MAKE, FUN TO SHAPE, EASY TO BAKE / TOTAL TIME: 3¼–4¼ HOURS ═══

You'll need: 2 x high-sided baking trays (it's tricky to bake all the buns on 1 large tray through to the middle without catching the outer ones) or 2 x 25cm (10in) round pie tins (as I often use); length of cotton thread; stand mixer or handheld electric mixer

20g (¾oz) fresh yeast, crumbled, or 10g (½oz) fast-action dried yeast
175g (6oz) warm milk, 25–30°C (77–86°F)
1 medium egg (50g/1¾oz egg without the shell)
275g (9¾oz) strong white bread flour, plus extra for dusting
100g (3½oz) malthouse bread flour (or strong white bread flour)
50g (1¾oz) golden caster (superfine) sugar
5g (1 teaspoon) salt
35g (1¼oz) room-temperature unsalted butter, broken up into pieces

For the filling
100g (3½oz) soft light brown sugar
5–8g (1–1½ tablespoons) ground cinnamon, to taste
75g (2½oz) room-temperature unsalted butter

For the frosting
100g (3½oz) room-temperature unsalted butter
100g (3½oz) icing (confectioners') sugar
180g (6½oz) full-fat cream cheese

a few toasted and chopped pecans, for sprinkling

Making the dough: 15–20 minutes

1. In a large mixing bowl, whisk together the yeast, milk and egg with a balloon whisk until the yeast has softened.

2. Add the flours, sugar and salt, then mix with a dough scraper until the mixture starts to come together into a rough dough. Add the butter and dimple it into the dough with your fingertips.

Recipe continued overleaf

3. Turn your dough out onto a clean work surface and knead without any additional flour for 10 minutes. It will get sticky, but be patient, using your scraper to tidy up every once in a while, and the dough will come together.

Resting and making the cinnamon sugar: 1½–2 hours

4. Shape the dough into a ball and place it back in the bowl. Sprinkle the top with a little flour, cover with another upturned bowl and rest at room temperature for 1½–2 hours.

5. Meanwhile, mix together the sugar and cinnamon in a small bowl.

Filling and shaping: 10–20 minutes

6. Dust the top of the dough with flour and use your dough scraper to turn it out upside down onto the work surface, sticky side up.

7. Use your fingertips and knuckles to flatten the dough slightly into a circle and lightly dust the sticky side. Roll out the dough with a rolling pin into a rectangle about 30 x 45cm (12 x 17¾ in) – you may need to dust it along the way so that it doesn't get sticky.

8. Use your dough scraper to spread your soft butter all over the dough, leaving a 2cm (¾in) strip along the edge closest to you free of butter. Sprinkle the cinnamon sugar all over the buttered area and pat it down with your palms to stick it to the butter.

9. Starting from the side furthest from you, roll up the dough into a sausage until you reach the bare strip, then use that to seal the seam.

10. Use your thread to divide and mark your sausage into 12–15 slices for cutting. Slide a length of cotton thread underneath the dough at the first cutting mark, then bring it up around the sides, cross the ends over and pull to 'snip' the dough. Repeat to cut your dough sausage into rounds.

11. Arrange your buns, cut side up, in your baking trays or pie tins with a little room inbetween so that they will join up as they rise.

Resting and preparing the frosting: 1–1½ hours

12. Cover your buns loosely with cling film dusted with flour or with upturned bowls if in pie tins and rest for 1–1½ hours until risen and delicate to the touch.

13. Towards the end of resting, preheat your oven to 180°C fan/400°F/Gas Mark 6 with a shelf (or 2 if your baking trays won't fit on one) in the middle and a deep roasting tray on the oven floor. Half fill a kettle.

14. Place the butter and icing sugar for the frosting in the bowl of your stand mixer, or in a large mixing bowl if using a handheld mixer, and beat on a slow speed until mixed, then beat on a high speed for 2 minutes. Add the cream cheese and beat just enough to incorporate it. Set aside at room temperature until you need it.

Baking and topping: 20–25 minutes

15. Boil the kettle.

16. Place your trays or tins on the oven shelf or shelves and carefully pour the hot water into the tray below. Bake your buns for 20–25 minutes.

17. Let them cool slightly on a wire rack.

Finishing: 5 minutes

18. Spread the cream cheese frosting over your buns and sprinkle over the toasted pecans.

TIP

THE BEAUTY OF THE TEAR

These buns look great baked individually in a Yorkshire pudding tray or similar, BUT you are missing the point there. It's the part in between two joined-up cinnamon buns which when torn apart leaves the softest, yummiest exposed edge that is the most delicious!

DOUGHNUTS

MAKES 12 DOUGHNUTS

Some things you make at home are head and shoulders over any shop-bought version, CERTAINLY from a supermarket. Doughnuts are one of those for a couple of very good reasons. Firstly, homemade doughnuts contain only REAL ingredients – nothing artificial, no funny business, no nonsense. And secondly, because you're able to eat them at their very best rather than from a bag that's been sat on a shelf for a couple of days. When you enjoy a warm doughnut for the first time at the perfect moment after you've just made them, you'll suddenly realize: 'Oh, THIS is a doughnut!' and then begin to wonder what all the other weird things posing as doughnuts out there are.

A doughnut in its simplest form is a light enriched dough, briefly deep-fried, dusted in sugar and filled with whatever you fancy. They are best enjoyed after they have cooled enough to eat them, and you can even give them a couple of minutes in the oven at 180°C fan/400°F/Gas Mark 6 the following day to bring them back to fresh. BUT I would be more inclined to make a batch, keep some for me and share the rest with the neighbours so that they can enjoy them at their best too.

EASY TO MAKE, EASY TO FRY / TOTAL TIME: 3¼–4½ HOURS

You'll need: a proper deep-fat fryer, preferably, but you CAN use a deep pan with a thermometer, although it's a little tricky to control and keep a steady temperature

180g (6½oz) warm milk, 25–30°C (77–86°F)
1 medium egg (50g/1¾oz egg without the shell)
20g (¾oz) fresh yeast, crumbled, or 10g (½oz) fast-action dried yeast
375g (13oz) strong white bread flour, plus extra for dusting

45g (1½oz) golden caster (superfine) sugar, plus 75g (2½oz) for coating
5g (1 teaspoon) salt
35g (1¼oz) room-temperature unsalted butter, broken up into pieces
sunflower oil, for oiling and deep-frying

Making the dough: 15–20 minutes

1. In a large mixing bowl, whisk together the milk, egg and yeast with a balloon whisk until the yeast has softened.

2. Add the flour, sugar and salt, then mix with a dough scraper until the mixture starts to come together into a rough dough. Add the butter and dimple it into the dough with your fingertips.

3. Turn your dough out onto a clean work surface and knead without any additional flour for 10 minutes. It has the potential to be slippery and buttery here, but keep your scraper handy to tidy up every once in a while and the dough will come together nicely.

Resting: 1½–2 hours

4. Shape the dough into a ball and place it back in the bowl. Sprinkle the top with a little flour, cover with an upturned bowl and rest at room temperature for 1½–2 hours.

Dividing and shaping: 5–10 minutes

5. Oil 2 baking trays lightly.

6. Dust the work surface lightly with flour and use your dough scraper to turn the dough out upside down onto it, sticky side up.

7. Use your fingertips and knuckles to flatten the dough really well and cut it into 12 equal-sized pieces with your dough scraper. If you want them all to be exactly the same size, weigh them out at about 55g (2oz) each.

Recipe continued overleaf

8. Fold and roll each piece of dough into a tight ball (see page 24), lining them up in order on the work surface.

9. At this point, I give the doughnuts a roll with a rolling pin to make them a puck shape so that they are easier to fry. Starting with the first one you shaped, roll each ball to flatten very slightly, then line them up on your oiled trays.

Resting: 1–1½ hours

10. Brush the tops of the doughnuts lightly with oil, cover loosely with cling film and rest for 1–1½ hours.

11. When the doughnuts are nearly ready, heat the oil for deep-frying in your deep-fat fryer or deep pan to 180°C (350°F).

12. Place the sugar for coating the doughnuts in a bowl.

Frying: 20–30 minutes

13. Set a wire rack over a tray.

14. Carefully lower 3 or 4 doughnuts at a time, one by one, into the hot oil and fry for 30 seconds on one side, then turn over and fry for 30 seconds on the other side. This initial frying seals the outside, making sure the raw top side doesn't BALLOON while the other side cooks. Flip again and cook for another 2 minutes, then turn a final time and cook for 2 minutes. Lift out with a spider or slotted spoon and drain on the rack. While still hot, toss each doughnut in turn in the sugar to coat and place back on the wire rack.

—— **TIP** ——

SIZE MATTERS

These doughnuts are on the slightly smaller side for a reason … they are fried SO BRIEFLY that it's important they are 'baked' to the middle in such a short time. As tempting as it is to make them MASSIVE – the bigger the better, right? – the chances are that they may not have a chance to bake through before the outside burns, and the last thing you want is to bite into your doughnut and find raw dough in the middle. So best to keep them this size and have 2.

LEMON & RASPBERRY CHEESECAKE DOUGHNUTS

MAKES 12 DOUGHNUTS

Lemon and raspberry were MADE for each other. Zesty, fragrant, sweet, sour, sharp, they deliver a flavour explosion, and here I've brought together a few different ways to use them to create a multi-dimensional doughnut. We have a creamy zesty filling, fresh raspberries in all their (slightly squished) glory, a raspberry and lemon icing for the top and, as a finishing touch, a sprinkling of gingernut crumb for a little heat and crunch.

1 batch of Doughnuts, fried and cooled (see page 219)

For the cheesecake filling
100ml (3½fl oz) whipping cream
50g (1¾oz) icing (confectioners') sugar
180g (6½oz) full-fat cream cheese
finely grated zest of 1 lemon

For the raspberry and lemon icing
20g (¾oz) raspberries
15g (1 tablespoon) lemon juice
160g (5½oz) icing (confectioners') sugar

For the white icing
60g (2oz) icing (confectioners') sugar
10g (2 teaspoons) water

To finish
240g (8½oz) raspberries, lightly crushed
60g (2oz) gingernut biscuits, about 6, chopped into a coarse crumb

Pictured on page 227

Making the cheesecake filling

1. In a large mixing bowl, whip the cream and icing sugar together with a balloon whisk or handheld electric mixer until thick and fluffy.
2. In a separate bowl, beat the cream cheese with the lemon zest with a spatula to soften it nicely.
3. Fold one-third of the whipped cream into the cream cheese with a metal spoon to loosen it, then fold in the remaining cream.
4. Fill a piping bag fitted with a medium star nozzle with your filling and pop it in the fridge for an hour or so to firm up.

Preparing the icings

5. For the raspberry and lemon icing, in a bowl, crush the raspberries with the back of a spoon, then add the lemon juice and icing sugar and mix until smooth and speckled with raspberry seeds.
6. For the white icing, in a separate bowl, mix the icing sugar and water together until smooth. Place in a piping bag fitted with a fine plain nozzle.

Putting it all together

7. Slice each doughnut in half horizontally.
8. Dip the tops of the lids into the raspberry and lemon icing and place on a wire rack. Drizzle over the white icing and top with a pinch of gingernut crumb.
9. Pipe your cream cheese decoratively round the edges of the bottom halves and then fill in the middle. Top with a tablespoonful of the crushed raspberries. Pop the lids on top. Finally, sprinkle a little of the gingernut crumb round the edges.

HAZELNUT PRALINE CREAM DOUGHNUTS

MAKES 12 DOUGHNUTS

Not overly sweet, this delicate, fluffy cream offers a MASSIVE toasted hazelnut hit. When I'm making caramel at home, there is no messing around, since after all it's hotter than the sun (probably) – no stirring, no tossing, no nonsense. For the praline here, we toast our nuts, make the caramel and then pour it over the top, minimizing the risk of burning fingers. Job done!

50g (1¾oz) blanched hazelnuts (filberts)
50g (1¾oz) golden caster (superfine) sugar
150ml (5fl oz) whipping cream
½ batch (150g/5½oz) of Crème Pâtissière, cooled (see page 224)
1 batch of Doughnuts, fried and cooled (see page 219)

Pictured on page 227

Making the hazelnut praline

1. Preheat your oven to 180°C fan/400°F/Gas Mark 6. Line a small baking tray with baking parchment.

2. Spread the hazelnuts in a single layer on your lined tray and toast for 12–15 minutes or until golden brown. Set the tray aside to cool.

3. Put the sugar into a small frying pan (skillet) and place over a medium heat. Keep your eyes peeled as the sugar slowly melts, gently swirling the pan to get rid of any lumps. Continue cooking the sugar until it turns a deep golden-brown colour, then pour it over the nuts. Let the praline and the empty pan cool.

4. Chop your praline into small pieces. Reserve half for later and blitz the other half to a fine powder in a mini food processor.

Making the hazelnut cream

5. In a large mixing bowl, whip your cream with a balloon whisk or handheld electric mixer until thick and fluffy.

6. In another bowl, beat your crème pâtissière with a spatula.

7. Fold one-third of the whipped cream into the crème pâtissière with a large metal spoon to loosen it. Then fold in the remaining cream and finally fold in the praline powder.

8. Now taste because your hazelnut cream is wicked delicious.

Putting it all together

9. Working with one at a time, make a hole in the side of a doughnut with the handle of a dessertspoon or a knife, all the way to the middle. Fill a piping bag fitted with a medium star nozzle with the cream, and with the doughnut on its side, insert the nozzle into the hole on the topmost side of your doughnut. Pipe in the cream, drawing out the bag as you go, then pipe a little extra on the top. Sprinkle a little of your reserved chopped praline on the top.

10. You'll have a good 30g (1oz) of cream for each doughnut, so you could pop each doughnut on your scales and set them to zero, then fill and return to the scales to get your quantity of cream inside and ensure you have enough for them all.

MAPLE & PECAN GLAZED RING DOUGHNUTS & HOLES

MAKES 10 RINGS AND 10 HOLES

One of the all-time greatest flavour combinations, here we have ring doughnuts encased in a light maple syrup glaze topped with crunchy, sweet and slightly salty pecans baked faff-free in the oven. As delicious as it is, I firmly believe that the glazed ring doughnut evolved as a principle of practicality. Think about it: it has a LOT of surface area, making it faster to dry out than a round doughnut, so sealing it with a glaze helps to lock in the moisture. And you get to enjoy the holes too!

1 batch of Doughnut
   Dough (see page 219
   and method here)
strong white bread flour,
   for dusting
sunflower oil, for oiling

For the pecans
40g (1½oz) icing
   (confectioners') sugar
10g (2 teaspoons) water
100g (3½oz) pecans
pinch of sea salt flakes

For the glaze
150g (5½oz) icing
   (confectioners') sugar
75g (2½oz) maple syrup
15g (1 tablespoon) water

Pictured on page 226–227

Toasting the pecans

1. Preheat your oven to 180°C fan/400°F/Gas Mark 6. Line a baking tray with baking parchment.
2. In a large mixing bowl, mix the icing sugar and water together. Add the pecans and toss to coat in a thin layer of icing. Space well apart on your lined tray and salt.
3. Bake for 12–15 minutes until golden, turning halfway. Turn the oven off, crack open the door and let them dry out for 15 minutes. Remove from the oven and cool. Chop half and keep the rest whole.

Making the ring doughnuts

4. Follow the method on page 219 to take your doughnut dough up to just before dividing. Once you have turned your dough out sticky side up, press flat with your fingertips and fold and roll it back into a ball (see page 24). Cover with an upturned bowl and rest on the work surface for 15 minutes. Oil a large baking tray lightly.
5. Dust the dough with flour and roll it out with a rolling pin to a circle about 25–30cm (10–12in) wide and about 1.5cm (½in) thick. Using an 8cm (3in) cutter, mark out 8 doughnuts from this first roll before cutting them all out and cut a hole in the middle of each with a 3cm (1in) cutter.
6. Place the doughnuts and holes on your oiled tray. Roll up the remaining dough and let it rest for 4–5 minutes. Roll it out into an oval shape the same thickness as before and cut out another 2 doughnuts and holes. Tray them up with the rest, brush the tops lightly with oil and cover loosely with cling film, then continue with the method (see page 220) to rest, deep-fry and drain the doughnuts, but fry the holes for only 2–3 minutes, turning them all the time.

Glazing and topping

7. Mix your glaze ingredients in a large mixing bowl. Dunk each doughnut and hole in the glaze to coat. Lift from the bowl and allow the excess glaze to drip before returning it to the rack. Top with pecans and pecan pieces, then let the glaze dry for 5–10 minutes.

APPLE, CUSTARD & CINNAMON FINGER DOUGHNUTS

MAKES 12 DOUGHNUTS

There was NO WAY I could write a book WITHOUT including an apple and custard doughnut recipe. And what a great way to introduce you to one of the MOST VERSATILE fillings/custards/creams ever – the EPIC crème pâtissière. Actually easy to make, so delicious and with so many uses, this isn't the only time you'll see it used in this doughnut section.

1 batch of Doughnut
   Dough (see page 219
   and method here)
strong white bread flour,
   for dusting

For the cinnamon sugar
75g (2½oz) golden caster
   (superfine) sugar
2g (1 teaspoon) ground
   cinnamon

For the crème pâtissière
3 medium egg yolks (60g/2oz)
50g (1¾oz) golden caster
   (superfine) sugar
25g (1oz) plain (all-purpose)
   flour
250ml (8½fl oz) full-fat milk
½ teaspoon vanilla
   bean paste

For the apple filling
6 eating apples, cored, peeled
   and chopped (420g/15oz
   prepared weight)
80g (2¾oz) golden caster
   (superfine) sugar
juice of 1½ lemons

Pictured overleaf

Finishing the doughnuts

1. Follow the method on page 219 to take your doughnut dough to the dividing and shaping stage where you shape it into 12 tight balls. Line them up on the work surface, dust lightly with flour and rest for 10 minutes to make the next part easier.

2. Dust the work surface lightly with flour. Working with one at a time, slide your dough scraper underneath a dough ball and flip it upside down onto the dusted surface. Press flat with your fingertips, then roll it up into a sausage. Line them up on the 2 oiled baking trays and continue with the method to rest and deep-fry the doughnuts. Mix the sugar and cinnamon together in a bowl, then toss the hot doughnuts in the cinnamon sugar before cooling.

Making the crème pâtissière

3. In a large mixing bowl, whisk the egg yolks and half the sugar together with a balloon whisk. Add the flour and whisk that in too. Set aside.

4. Place the milk, remaining sugar and vanilla in a heavy medium-sized saucepan over a medium heat and bring only just to the boil.

5. Pour half of the hot milk mixture into the egg yolk mixture, whisking to combine, then whisk in the rest.

6. Pour the mixture back into the pan and slowly bring to simmering point over the medium heat until thickened, stirring all the time. Keep the heat steady and stir for another 2 minutes to cook out the flour.

7. Pour into a bowl or container, cover with cling film touching the surface to avoid any skin forming and let it cool before refrigerating to firm up.

Making the apple filling

8. Put the chopped apple into a small saucepan with the sugar and lemon juice, cover with a lid and slowly bring to the boil. Cook, stirring occasionally, until the apple is soft and the liquid has reduced around the apple. Mix to break down the apples slightly, thickening up the purée while keeping it chunky. Set aside to cool.

Filling the doughnuts

9. Cut a slit down the middle of each sugared doughnut hot dog style. Your crème pâtissière will be firm from the fridge, so beat it in a bowl with a spatula before putting it into a piping bag fitted with a medium star nozzle.

10. Open up your doughnuts and pipe a generous line of crème pâtissière down the middle to one side, then spoon the apple down the other side. Repeat for all the doughnuts.

———————————— **TIP** ————————————

YOU DON'T HAVE TO WAIT . . .

If you are eating these straight away, they are UNBELIEVABLE eaten warm, so just let your crème pâtissière cool enough to be able to handle easily in a piping bag, fill up your doughnuts and eat them straight away.

DOUGHNUT OFFCUTS WITH S'MORES DIP

SERVES 2

When you've cut your 10 doughnuts and holes (see page 223), you'll have some dough left over ... DO NOT throw it away! These churros-inspired offcuts and dip are the perfect way to use them up and they take hardly any time at all.

leftover dough from making
    Maple & Pecan Glazed
    Ring Doughnuts & Holes
    (see page 223)
strong white bread flour,
    for dusting
sunflower oil, for deep-frying
    and oiling

For the s'mores dip
75g (2½oz) good-quality
    milk chocolate, chopped,
    or chocolate chips
75g (2½oz) good-quality
    dark chocolate, chopped,
    or chocolate chips
100g (3½oz) marshmallows
    (I used GIANT ones
    cut in half)
½ a batch of Cinnamon Sugar
    (see page 224)

1. Preheat your oven to 200°C fan/425°F/Gas Mark 7 and preheat the oil for deep-frying in a deep-fat fryer or deep pan to 180°C (350°F). Oil a baking tray lightly.

2. Mix the chocolates for the dip together and place in an enamel baking dish about 14 x 18cm (5½ x 7in). Top with the marshmallows and set aside.

3. Use your dough scraper to cut the leftover doughnut dough into small pieces. Dust the work surface lightly with flour and roll them with your palms on the work surface into long and thin skinny pencil shapes, then line them up on your oiled tray.

4. Bake your s'mores dip for 8–10 minutes.

5. Meanwhile, carefully deep-fry your doughnut pencils in manageable batches for 1½ minutes, turning all the time with a spider or slotted spoon. Drain on kitchen paper, toss in the cinnamon sugar and serve WARM with your s'mores dip straight from the oven.

WHITE CHOCOLATE ICE CREAM, DOUGHNUT CROUTONS & COMPOTE

SERVES 4

Croutons don't ALWAYS have to be savoury. These sweet and buttery, crunchy on the outside yet chewy on the inside doughnut nuggets just call out for cool ice cream and a sharp berry compote. Serve warm from the oven for a pretty impressive dessert, and save your leftover doughnuts from being binned! You can, of course, buy the ice cream, but this might just be the easiest no-churn, no-faff ice cream base ever.

For the ice cream
200ml (7fl oz) whipping cream
100ml (3½fl oz)
    condensed milk
75g (2½oz) white
    chocolate, chopped

For the compote
150g (5½oz) raspberries
150g (5½oz) blueberries
150g (5½oz) blackberries
juice of 1 orange (90ml/3fl oz)
35g (1¼oz) golden caster
    (superfine) sugar

For the doughnut croutons
2–3 stale plain Doughnuts
    (see page 219)
50g (1¾oz) unsalted
    or salted butter
4 tablespoons golden caster
    (superfine) sugar
pinch of ground cinnamon

Making the ice cream

1. In a large mixing bowl, whip the cream with a balloon whisk or handheld electric mixer until thick and fluffy, then whisk in the condensed milk really well. Fold in the chopped chocolate.
2. Pour the mixture into a small, lidded plastic container. Smooth the top, cover with the lid and freeze overnight.

Cooking the compote

3. Put all the compote ingredients into a large, heavy saucepan and mix together before slowly bringing everything to the boil. Stir once more, then simmer gently for 15–20 minutes to reduce.
4. Tip the compote out into a bowl or container to cool.
5. Have a taste of your compote and see how you feel about it. All berries at different times of the year will need more or less sugar, and I like mine to be quite sharp to contrast the sweet freshness of the ice cream and cut through the buttery croutons.

Making the croutons

6. Preheat your oven to 180°C fan/400°F/Gas Mark 6. Line a large baking tray with baking parchment.
7. Tear your doughnuts into large chunks and place them in a bowl. Melt the butter in a pan, pour half of it over the doughnut pieces and toss to coat them, then wipe them around the bowl to mop up the remaining butter like a sponge. Spread on your lined tray.
8. It's best at this point to bring your ice cream out of the freezer and let it soften at room temperature for 15 minutes or so.
9. Bake your croutons for 10–12 minutes until golden and crisp.
10. Meanwhile, mix the sugar and cinnamon in a small bowl.
11. Tip the croutons back into the buttery bowl, pour over the rest of the butter and toss. Add the cinnamon sugar and toss again to stick.

Putting it all together

12. Place your warm croutons on a plate with a couple of balls of the ice cream and a generous spoon of compote.

CHOCOLATE ORANGE KNOT BUNS

MAKES 12 KNOT BUNS

All recipes are refined with practise, and this one is a prime example, as it has featured heavily on the food festival circuit. Making a recipe work at a specific time of day for a demonstration in a tent outside whatever the weather is not the ideal scenario, but it's a great way to learn and improve on over time!

Delicious with a proper cup of tea, these buns are layered with a butter PACKED with orange zest and dark chocolate. A crunchy, nutty, salty, iced topping complements their soft sweetness, which is not only wicked tasty but also serves a purpose. Made out of the juice and pulp of the orange (double orange whammy!), the icing provides an additional orangey hit AND acts as a kind of 'airtight' seal to help the buns stay soft and moist inside.

If you can resist eating all of these on day one, they'll stay soft for a further day or two. Make a batch, eat them and share with friends and family when they are at their best.

EASY TO MAKE, FUN TO SHAPE, EASY TO BAKE / TOTAL TIME: 3¼–4½ HOURS

You'll need: a silicone spatula for creaming the frosting (or use a handheld electric mixer or stand mixer, but it's such a small amount)

100g (3½oz) warm milk, 25–30°C (77–86°F)
1 medium egg (50g/1½oz egg without the shell)
20g (¾oz) fresh yeast, crumbled, or 10g (½oz) fast-action dried yeast
250g (9oz) strong white bread flour, plus extra for dusting

35g (1¼oz) golden caster (superfine) sugar
4g (1 teaspoon) salt
35g (1¼oz) room-temperature unsalted butter, broken up into pieces

For the filling
50g (1¾oz) room-temperature unsalted butter
40g (1½oz) golden caster (superfine) sugar
finely grated zest of 2 oranges
50g (1¾oz) dark chocolate, chopped

For the icing
juice and pulp of 1 zested orange (used earlier) – scrape out the pulp from the squeezed-out halves
about 300g (10½oz) icing (confectioners') sugar (see method: step 18)

For the topping
50g (1¾oz) pumpkin seeds
pinch of salt
50g (1¾oz) cacao nibs
50g (1¾oz) pearl sugar nibs

Making the dough: 15–20 minutes

1. In a large mixing bowl, whisk together the milk, egg and yeast with a balloon whisk until the yeast has softened.

2. Add the flour, sugar and salt, then mix with a dough scraper until the mixture starts to come together into a rough dough. Add the butter and dimple it into the dough with your fingertips.

3. Turn your dough out onto a clean work surface and knead your dough without any additional flour for 10 minutes. It will get sticky, but be patient, using your scraper to tidy up every once in a while, and the dough will come together.

Resting and preparing the filling: 1½–2 hours

4. Shape the dough into a ball and place it back in the bowl. Sprinkle the top with a little flour, cover with an upturned bowl and rest at room temperature for 1½–2 hours.

5. Meanwhile, in a mixing bowl, beat together the butter, sugar and orange zest with the silicone spatula (or handheld or stand mixer) until aerated and super-soft so that it's easy to spread. Set aside.

Filling and shaping: 10–15 minutes

6. Line 2 large baking trays with baking parchment.

Recipe continued overleaf

7. Dust the work surface well with flour and use your dough scraper to turn the dough out upside down onto it, sticky side up.

8. Dust the top of the dough and press it flat with your fingertips, then roll it out with a rolling pin into a 35cm (14in) square.

9. Use your dough scraper to spread the filling evenly all over the dough, right to the edges. Sprinkle the chocolate all over the filling as evenly as you can, then press down with your palms to stick it to the filling. Fold the dough in half from the top edge and press gently with your palms just enough to flatten slightly, neaten it up and stick the halves together.

10. Use a knife or dough scraper to cut the dough vertically into 4 wide strips. Then cut each strip into 3 more strips, one per bun.

11. Working with one at a time, hold a strip of dough at each end and carefully stretch it lengthways and twist it. Wrap one end round the other in a circle twice, then pass the end of the strip underneath and finally wrap it once more over the top. Tuck the end underneath. It's not essential that you do your knots exactly like mine, so feel free to have a play, but you'll find that doing them the same as each other makes a big difference to the overall look of your rolls.

12. Place the buns on your lined trays with plenty of room inbetween them to expand.

Resting: 1–1½ hours
13. Cover your buns loosely with cling film dusted with flour and rest for 1–2 hours until risen and lighter, softer and much more delicate to the touch.

14. Towards the end of resting, preheat your oven to 180°C fan/400°F/Gas Mark 6 with 2 shelves in the middle and a deep roasting tray on the oven floor. Half fill a kettle.

Baking: 10–15 minutes
15. Boil the kettle.

16. Place your baking trays on the oven shelves and carefully pour the hot water into the tray below. Bake your knot buns for 10–15 minutes until golden. Slide a knife underneath and lift a bun, and if the underside is golden, then it's ready, but if it's still a little pale, return it to the oven for 2 minutes at a time until they are done.

17. Let the buns cool on a wire rack.

Preparing the icing and topping:
15–20 minutes
18. Weigh the orange juice and pulp, then multiply that number by 4 for your quantity of icing sugar. Mix together in a bowl until thoroughly combined.

19. Toast your pumpkin seeds in a small, dry frying pan (skillet) over a medium heat until they start popping. Keep toasting for 30 seconds or so and add the salt, then sprinkle with just enough water to sizzle and dissolve the salt so that it will stick to the seeds – too much water and your seeds will boil and become chewy. Cook away the water and dry out the seeds, then continue to toast until golden. Tip out onto a plate to cool.

20. Mix your toasted seeds with the cacao nibs and pearl sugar in a bowl.

21. Working with one at a time, first dunk a bun upside down into the icing, lift it out and allow any excess to drip back into the bowl before dipping it into your topping mixture. Place it upright back on the wire rack and rest until the icing dries and goes crunchy.

BLUEBERRY, ORANGE & HONEY PLAIT

MAKES 1 LARGE PLAIT

My kids LOVE fruit bread, so if there's any left for me, I'll enjoy it with a freshly brewed coffee. Alternatively, if you're a little bit fancy (like me!), you can turn it into warm French toast and top it with thick natural yoghurt, torn figs, a drizzle of honey and some crunchy toasted pecans. Now you're talkin'!

It's risky putting something so wet like blueberries into bread dough, and if this dough were to be baked in a loaf tin, the increased moisture from the berries as they cook would puff it up SO BIG that the loaf would crumble under its own weight when it cooled. So, this four-strand plait design not only looks stunning, but it serves a vital purpose.

Best on day one, still good on day two and day three and onwards it's time for toast.

=== PERHAPS A LITTLE STICKY TO MAKE, FUN TO SHAPE, ===
EASY TO BAKE / TOTAL TIME: 3¾–5 HOURS

115g (4oz) warm milk, 25–30°C (77–86°F)
1 medium egg (50g/1¾oz egg without the shell), plus 1 egg, beaten, for glazing
14g (½oz) fresh yeast, crumbled, or 7g (¼oz) fast-action dried yeast

250g (9oz) strong white bread flour, plus extra for dusting
4g (1 teaspoon) salt
35g (1¼oz) honey, plus extra for glazing
grated zest of 1 orange

35g (1¼oz) room-temperature unsalted butter, broken up into pieces
100g (3½oz) blueberries
pearl sugar nibs, for sprinkling

Making the dough: 20–25 minutes

1. In a large mixing bowl, whisk together the milk, egg and yeast with a balloon whisk until the yeast has softened.

2. Add the flour, salt, honey and orange zest, then mix with a dough scraper until the mixture starts to come together into a rough dough. Add the butter and dimple it into the dough with your fingertips.

3. Turn your dough out onto a clean work surface and knead without any additional flour for 10 minutes. It has the potential to be slippery and buttery here, but keep your scraper handy to tidy up every once in a while and the dough will come together nicely.

4. Cover the dough with a clean cloth and rest on the work surface for 5–10 minutes or so to make the next stage easier.

Adding the fruit: 2–5 minutes

5. Dust the work surface lightly with flour and roll the dough out with a rolling pin into a 15cm (6in) circle. Sprinkle 75g (2½oz) of the blueberries evenly all over the dough right to the edge, then press down with your palms to stick them to the dough.

6. Roll up your dough into a loose sausage. Then turn it 90 degrees, press it flat with your fingertips and roll up again into a short sausage.

Resting: 1½–2 hours

7. Shape the dough into a ball and place it back in the bowl. Sprinkle the top with a little flour, cover with an upturned bowl and rest at room temperature for 1½–2 hours.

Recipe continued overleaf

Dividing and pre-shaping: 5–10 minutes

8. Dust the work surface lightly with flour and use your dough scraper to turn the dough out upside down onto it, sticky side up.

9. Use your fingertips to flatten the dough gently into a circle. Cut it into 4 equal-sized wedges with your dough scraper. If you want them all to be exactly the same size, weigh them out at about 140g (5oz) each.

10. Starting at the pointy end, roll up each wedge of dough into a loose sausage.

Resting: 10 minutes

11. Cover with a clean cloth and rest for 10 minutes to relax the dough ready for the next stage.

Shaping: 5–10 minutes

12. Line a large baking tray with baking parchment.

13. Working with one at a time, flatten a dough sausage and roll it up into a sausage again, then roll it with your palms on the work surface until it is about 40–45cm (16–17¾in) long. At this point some blueberries might burst, but this is part of the game! Do your best to be delicate but firm enough to roll your sausages out nice and long, dusting any sticky patches as you go.

14. Line up the 4 strands vertically and pinch the tops together to join them. Working with the strands in 2 pairs and starting with the right pair, fold the right strand over the left. Repeat with the left pair, folding the right strand over the left. Next, take the 2 strands now in the middle and fold the left over the right. Repeat to the end: right over left, right over left, then left over right in the middle.

15. Press the ends together to stick and tuck them underneath the plait. Place the plait on your lined tray.

Resting: 1–1½ hours

16. Cover your plait loosely with cling film dusted with flour and rest for 1 hour.

17. Towards the end of resting, preheat your oven to 180°C fan/400°F/Gas Mark 6 with a shelf in the middle and a deep tray on the oven floor. Half fill a kettle.

Baking and glazing: 30–35 minutes

18. Boil the kettle.

19. Stud your puffy plait with the remaining blueberries.

20. Place your baking tray gently on the oven shelf and carefully pour the hot water into the tray below. Bake your plait for 30–35 minutes. Slide a knife underneath it and lift to have a peep at the underside. If it's golden, it's done, but if it's a little pale in the middle, bake for another 3–5 minutes at a time until it's ready.

Finishing: 5 minutes

21. As soon as it's cool enough to handle, transfer your plait carefully to a wire rack. Place the lining paper underneath to catch any honey drips. Drizzle the top of your plait generously with honey while still hot, then use a pastry brush to brush it all over to give it a lovely sheen and sprinkle over some pearl sugar nibs.

TIP

IT'S ALL ABOUT THE HONEY

There are tons of different honeys available, each with their own nuances of flavour and fragrance that shine through in this sweet dough. So, take a good look and have a play with what's available in your area to really make this loaf your own.

BLUEBERRY FRENCH TOAST WITH MACERATED FIGS & YOGHURT

SERVES 2

Figs are delicious when they are ripe. Round here it's a bit of a guessing game, a lottery, as to whether you'll get good ones or not, but there is an answer if they're not quite right and it's this: macerating.

It's basically a process of soaking, in citrus juice and a sugar of some description, to soften and sweeten. There's no need to heat anything up or cook anything, they just need a little time. The figs then become really juicy and retain their natural shape instead of becoming a 'sauce'. You can make them in advance if you like – the night before for example – and they will be perfect at breakfast time.

Here I've used the Blueberry, Orange and Honey Plait to make French toast or, as I know it, Eggy Bread. But hey, we're writing a book here, so let's go with French toast.

---

2 medium eggs
100ml (3½fl oz) milk
1 tablespoon golden caster (superfine) sugar
4 stale slices of Blueberry, Orange and Honey Plait (see page 237), around 2.5cm (1in) thick
20g (¾oz) butter

For the figs
150g (5½oz) fresh figs
50g (1¾oz) blueberries
zest and juice of ½ orange
2 tablespoons honey

To serve
200g (7oz) Greek yoghurt

Macerate your figs: Ahead of time

1. Trim the stalky tip from your figs and discard. Cut them into quarters and place them in a large mixing bowl. Cut your blueberries in half and add them to the bowl too, along with the orange zest and juice and honey. Gently mix everything around to coat and tip the mixture into a small container or re-usable food bag. Squeeze all the air from the bag and seal up, then leave in the fridge for 2 hours or overnight.

For the French toast

2. In a baking tray, beat your eggs and milk together with the sugar. Dip in both sides of your bread slices and leave them in there to soak.
3. Warm the butter in a large heavy frying pan (skillet) until foaming and place your soaked bread slices into the pan. Cook gently for around 2½–3 minutes on each side until golden.
4. Divide your toast between 2 plates, top with a generous amount of yoghurt and a few good spoonfuls of your figs and blueberries. Finish with a drizzle of the fig juice.

HOT CROSS BUNS

MAKES 12 HOT CROSS BUNS

Bakes don't get any more traditional here in England than a hot cross bun. Sweet, sticky and fruity with PLENTY of mixed spice, no wonder these are one of the nation's favourites.

I used to make hot cross buns a lot for my in-laws, and each time they would say they were nice BUT … MORE fruit! It's tricky, though, to get in as much fruit as we possibly can without it weighing too heavily on the bun and stalling the rise. Here, I've pre-soaked the fruit, which you don't HAVE to do, but it does make them really juicy. It can make them a little trickier to incorporate into the dough, so make sure you drain and dry them off really well. But don't be tempted to soak them in booze. The dough might puff the first time round, but more than likely the second rise won't happen as the yeast gets a little tipsy after that and doesn't work so well.

Always best on day one, halve and toast them thereafter.

=== EASY TO MAKE, EASY TO BAKE / TOTAL TIME: 4–5½ HOURS, ===
PLUS OVERNIGHT SOAKING OF THE DRIED FRUIT

You'll need: a piping bag fitted with a small plain nozzle or a disposable bag with the tip snipped off

265g (9¼oz) warm milk, 25–30°C (77–86°F)
1 medium egg (50g/1¾oz egg without the shell)
25g (1oz) fresh yeast, crumbled, or 14g (½oz) fast-action dried yeast
500g (1lb 2oz) strong white bread flour, plus extra for dusting

60g (2oz) golden caster (superfine) sugar
8g (¼oz) salt
10g (2 tablespoons) mixed spice
2g (1 teaspoon) ground cinnamon
50g (1¾oz) room-temperature unsalted butter, broken up into pieces

For the filling
75g (2½oz) raisins
75g (2½oz) sultanas (golden raisins)
75g (2½oz) mixed candied peel

For the crosses
50g (1¾oz) strong white bread flour
50g (1¾oz) water
pinch of sugar

3 tablespoons marmalade, for glazing

Pre-soaking the dried fruit: Overnight
1. Place your raisins and sultanas in a bowl and pour over just enough water to cover. Soak at room temperature overnight.
2. Drain the soaked fruit and pat dry really well with kitchen paper, then mix with the peel. Set aside.

Making the dough: 20–25 minutes
3. In a large mixing bowl, whisk together the milk, egg and yeast with a balloon whisk until the yeast has softened.
4. Add the flour, sugar, salt and spices, then mix with a dough scraper until the mixture

starts to come together into a rough dough. Add the butter and dimple it into the dough with your fingertips.
5. Turn the dough out onto a clean work surface and knead without any additional flour for 10 minutes. It has the potential to be slippery and buttery here, but keep your scraper handy to tidy up every once in a while and the dough will come together nicely.
6. Cover the dough with a clean cloth and rest on the work surface for 5 minutes or so to make the next stage easier.

Recipe continued overleaf

Adding the fruit: 2–5 minutes

7. Dust the work surface lightly with flour and roll out the dough with a rolling pin into a 25–30cm (10–12in) circle. Sprinkle over half your fruit mixture evenly and dimple it into the dough with your fingertips. Fold the bottom third of your dough circle up and the top third down over it. Then press the dough with your fingertips to spread it out into a rectangle.

8. Sprinkle your remaining fruit mixture evenly over the dough and again dimple it in with your fingertips. Roll up the dough from one short side into a short sausage.

Resting: 1½–2 hours

9. Shape the dough into a ball and place it back in the bowl. Sprinkle the top with a little flour, cover with an upturned bowl and rest at room temperature for 1½–2 hours.

Dividing and shaping: 5–10 minutes

10. Line a large baking tray with baking parchment.

11. Dust the work surface lightly with flour and use your dough scraper to turn the dough out upside down onto it, sticky side up.

12. Use your fingertips and knuckles to flatten the dough slightly and cut it into 12 equal-sized pieces with your dough scraper. If you want them all to be exactly the same size, weigh them out at about 100g (3½oz) each.

13. Fold and roll each piece of dough into a tight ball (see page 24). Place them on your lined tray a finger-width apart so that they will join up as they rise.

Resting and preparing the cross mixture: 1½–2 hours

14. Cover your buns loosely with cling film dusted with flour and rest for 1½–2 hours.

15. Meanwhile, mix the ingredients for the crosses together in a bowl until smooth, then fill your piping bag with the mixture.

16. Towards the end of resting, preheat your oven to 180°C fan/400°F/Gas Mark 6 with a shelf in the middle and a deep roasting tray on the oven floor. Half fill a kettle.

Piping: 10 minutes

17. Carefully pipe a cross on the top of each bun.

Baking: 20–25 minutes

18. Boil the kettle.

19. Place the baking tray on the oven shelf and carefully pour the hot water into the tray below. Bake your buns for 20–25 minutes.

Glazing: 5 minutes

20. As soon as they are cool enough to handle, transfer your buns to a wire rack. Place the lining paper underneath the rack to catch any marmalade drips.

21. Stir up your marmalade in a bowl, then use a pastry brush to brush it liberally over the tops of the buns while still warm to make them nice and sticky. Let them cool completely.

TIP

MAKE THEM YOUR OWN...

Don't feel you have to make these buns EXACTLY as I do, as they are completely customizable. If you're not a fan of candied peel, feel free to use the grated zest of an orange and a lemon instead. You can swap out the raisins and sultanas for other dried fruits that you like – chopped prunes, apricots, figs or a mixture will all work well as long as you stick to similar quantities. Or try chopped chocolate or choc chips, especially with orange zest. Instead of the orange marmalade, depending on your choice of fruit, opt for lemon or lime marmalade, maple syrup or honey. Or if you don't like them sticky, a simple egg wash painted over the top before you bake them will bring them a lovely golden sheen.

HOT CROSS BUN 'PANCAKE' STACK

SERVES 2

'My, oh my…' were my words when I made these for the first time.

Sweet leftover Easter hot cross buns turned pancakes, packed with fruit and spice, layered with the incredibly British buttery clotted cream, fresh tangerine and golden syrup. A good fit for a Good Friday dessert or an Easter Monday breakfast or, perhaps, even both.

If you can't get clotted cream, try ice cream or a thick double.

---

2 leftover Hot Cross Buns
(see page 243)
2 medium eggs
100ml (3½fl oz) milk
40g (1½oz) butter
2 tangerines or other seedless
orange-like fruit
100g (3½oz) clotted cream
golden syrup (light treacle),
for drizzling
icing (confectioners') sugar,
for dusting

1. Slice each hot cross bun horizontally into 3 pieces.
2. Beat together the eggs and milk and pour it into a tray big enough to fit all 6 hot cross bun slices in one layer.
3. Add the hot cross buns, flip them in the egg mixture to coat both sides and leave to soak up the mixture for a couple of minutes.
4. In a large non-stick frying pan (skillet), heat half the butter until foamy. Add 3 slices of hot cross bun and cook until golden, around 2–2½ minutes on each side. Transfer to a plate to keep warm, wipe out the pan with kitchen paper, add the remaining butter and cook the rest of the hot cross bun slices in the same way.
5. Peel your tangerines and slice horizontally into 5 or 6 slices.
6. Layer up your hot cross bun pancakes on 2 plates, alternating hot cross bun, tangerine slices and clotted cream. Repeat until you have nothing left.
7. Finally, drizzle with syrup and dust liberally with icing sugar.

MORNING BUNS

MAKES 12 BUNS

So how can we make an enriched dough bread EVEN MORE delicious? The answer is LAMINATION, where we layer up the dough with butter inbetween each layer, which is how you get those layers in puff pastry and croissants. We use the exact same principle here to create a light, buttery, sweet, crispy on the outside, soft in the middle, layered morning bun.

An overnight rest brings amazing flavour to our dough AS WELL AS making it firmer and easier to layer in the butter. After which I have simplified the laminating process by using a stack 'n' slice technique to get MAXIMUM layers for MINIMUM faff, resulting in a slightly less refined, slightly more rustic but still very delicious bun, tossed in sugar after baking doughnut style.

These are called morning buns because they are MEANT to be eaten as fresh as possible, and if we were to get one from a bakery that would mean first thing in the morning. The GREAT BENEFIT to making these at home ourselves is that we get to enjoy them at that exact magical moment, fresh from the oven, cooled for just 10 minutes or so. A moment unattainable by any other means!

So, eat these on the day, and if you have any left over, freeze them in a reusable freezer bag, then bring them back to peak freshness straight from the freezer in the oven at 180°C fan/400°F/ Gas Mark 6 for 8–12 minutes. These are delicious just as they are, but if you'd like to take them to the NEXT LEVEL, make a hole in the middle with the end of a spoon and pipe them full of Crème Pâtissière (see page 224) as I have here.

===== EASY TO MAKE, TRICKY TO SHAPE, EASY TO BAKE / =====
TOTAL TIME: DAY ONE 1¼ HOURS; DAY TWO 3–5 HOURS

You'll need: a 12-hole muffin tray

180g (6½oz) warm milk, 25–30°C (77–86°F)
1 medium egg (50g/1¾oz egg without the shell)
16g (½oz) fresh yeast, crumbled, or 8g (¼oz) fast-action dried yeast

375g (13oz) strong white bread flour, plus extra for dusting
45g (1½oz) golden caster (superfine) sugar
5g (1 teaspoon) salt
35g (1¼oz) room-temperature unsalted butter

For laminating
120g (4¼oz) room-temperature unsalted butter
75g (2½oz) golden caster (superfine) sugar, plus 100g (3½oz) for dusting

DAY ONE

Making the dough: 15–20 minutes
1. In a large mixing bowl, whisk together the milk, egg and yeast with a balloon whisk until the yeast has softened.
2. Add the flour, sugar and salt, then mix with a dough scraper until the mixture starts to come together into a rough dough. Add the butter and dimple it into the dough with your fingertips.
3. Turn your dough out onto a clean work surface and knead without any additional flour for 10 minutes. It has the potential to be slippery and buttery here, but keep your scraper handy to tidy up every once in a while and the dough will come together nicely.

Resting: 1 hour
4. Shape the dough into a ball and place it back in the bowl. Cover the bowl with cling film and rest at room temperature for 1 hour.

Recipe continued overleaf

Overnight

5. Place the bowl in the fridge to rest until the following day.

DAY TWO

Laminating: 10–15 minutes

6. Remove your dough from the fridge – it should look a little more puffed up than yesterday, be firm to the touch and should smell incredible.

7. Dust the work surface lightly with flour and use your dough scraper to turn the dough out upside down onto it, sticky side up.

8. Dust the top of the dough with flour and use your fingertips to flatten it into a circle, then roll it out with a rolling pin into a 30cm (12in) square.

9. Use your dough scraper to spread a third (40g/1½oz) of the butter over the top two-thirds of the dough square, then sprinkle one-third (25g/1oz) of the caster sugar over the buttered part. Fold the bottom third up and then the top third down over it. Turn the rectangle of dough 90 degrees portrait-wise and press with your fingertips to stick the layers together. Roll again with your rolling pin until it measures about 45cm x 15cm (17¾ x 6in).

10. Repeat the process with your rectangle of dough, adding another 40g (1½oz) of the butter and 25g (1oz) of the sugar and then folding in 3, ending up with a square of dough. Press again to seal and roll to level it off nice and tidy.

Resting: 15 minutes

11. Cover your dough with an upturned bowl and rest for 15 minutes to make the next stage easier.

Dividing and shaping: 5–10 minutes

12. Roll the dough out with your rolling pin to a landscape rectangle about 30 x 40cm (12 x 15¾in). Spread the remaining butter all over the top and sprinkle with the last of the sugar.

13. Cut the dough vertically into 4 quarters and place each piece on top of each other to form a brick of dough, then press firmly with your fingertips to stick the layers together.

14. Transfer your dough to a chopping board and use a sharp serrated knife to saw the dough into 12 strips.

15. Working with one at a time, hold a strip of dough at each end and stretch it lengthways to 20–25cm (8–10in) long. Twist it from the ends, curl it around itself and place it in the bottom of a hole of your muffin tin so that it fits nice and snug. We really want to see all those layers in the finished buns, so when you are twisting up the dough, try to make sure there is as much of the cut side showing as possible.

Resting: 2–4 hours

16. Cover your buns loosely with cling film and rest until puffed up over the rim of your muffin holes like a … muffin! This can take anything between 2 and 4 hours, depending on how warm your kitchen is, and how cold your fridge was.

17. Towards the end of resting, preheat your oven to 200°C fan/425°F/Gas Mark 7 with a shelf in the middle and a deep tray on the oven floor. Half fill a kettle.

Baking: 15–20 minutes

18. Boil the kettle.

19. Place your muffin tray gently on the oven shelf and carefully pour the hot water into the tray below. Bake your buns for 15–20 minutes until golden. To check they are done, slide a knife underneath one of them and have a peep. If the underside is evenly golden, they are good to go. They will probably still be soft and that's okay, as they will crisp up when they cool.

Finishing: 5 minutes

20. As soon as they are cool enough to handle, transfer the buns to a wire rack. Place your dusting sugar in a large bowl. While still hot, toss each bun in turn in the sugar to coat it and place it back on the rack to cool.

TROPICAL FRUIT MORNING BUN MILLEFEUILLE

SERVES 4

If by any chance you ever have morning buns left over, definitely give this a go. Crispy, toasted, buttery, slightly chewy in the middle morning buns, layered with smooth, silky orange crème pâtissière, fresh tropical fruit and mint. Turning a simple bun into a glorious dessert.

4 Morning Buns
  (see page 249)
50g (1¾oz) butter
½ batch (150g/5½oz) of Crème
  Pâtissière (see page 224)
zest of ½ orange
100g (3½oz) mango
100g (3½oz) pineapple
1 passion fruit
1 tablespoon chopped
  fresh mint leaves
1 tablespoon golden caster
  (superfine) sugar
icing sugar and fresh mint
  leaves, to garnish

1. Preheat your oven to 180°C fan/400°F/Gas Mark 6 and slice your buns horizontally into 3 rounds, arranging them on a parchment-lined baking tray.

2. Melt the butter and use a pastry brush to brush all the pieces liberally. Toast in the oven for 12–15 minutes until golden, then transfer to a cooling rack to cool completely. Don't worry if they are not crispy when they come out, they will crisp as they cool.

3. Make your crème pâtissière and stir in the orange zest before leaving it to cool.

4. Cut your mango and pineapple into 1cm (½in) cubes and place in a mixing bowl. Scoop out the flesh of your passion fruit and add it to the bowl along with the chopped mint leaves and sugar. Mix everything together.

5. When you are ready to serve, fill a piping bag with your crème pâtissière.

6. Pipe a little dot onto 4 plates and place the base pieces of the bun croutes on the dot to hold it in place. Pipe a little crème pâtissière on the top of each piece, followed by a spoonful of your fruit. Add the middle morning bun slice and repeat with crème pâtissière and fruit. Top with the final piece, the original top, and dust well with icing sugar. Pop a little pile of any leftover fruit to the side, and garnish with some of the teeniest mint leaves.

CHRISTMAS STOLLEN

MAKES 2 STOLLEN

Stollen IS Christmas. That sweet, fruity, spicy softness, the little treat circle of marzipan in every slice, the soft blanket of snow draped over the top – you can almost hear the sleigh bells jingling.

SO OFTEN in classes I hear people saying they don't like marzipan as the flavour is too strong, and some even opt for leaving it out of their stollen altogether – initially, at least. But when we make it together ourselves and try it, we realize that it's a completely different beast to that yellow, slightly weird-tasting block you buy in the shops. It's almondy but in a natural way rather than overpoweringly so, and those people opting out soon opt back in when they discover what the real thing tastes like.

If you are making these as gifts for Christmas, do your best to deliver them on the day you made them, when they're at their best.

━━━━━━━━━━ EASY TO MAKE, EASY TO BAKE / TOTAL TIME: 4–5¼ HOURS, ━━━━━━━━━━
PLUS OVERNIGHT SOAKING OF THE DRIED FRUIT

100g (3½oz) warm milk,
  25–30°C (77–86°F)
1 medium egg (50g/1¾oz
  egg without the shell)
1 egg yolk (20g/¾oz egg yolk),
  the white reserved for the
  marzipan (see below)
15g (½oz) fresh yeast,
  crumbled, or 7g (¼oz)
  fast-action dried yeast
250g (9oz) strong white bread
  flour, plus extra for dusting
4g (1 teaspoon) salt
40g (1½oz) golden caster
  (superfine) sugar

4g (2 teaspoons) mixed spice
50g (1¾oz) room-temperature
  unsalted butter, broken
  up into pieces, plus
  50g/1¾oz for brushing
  the baked stollen

For the filling
50g (1¾oz) sultanas
  (golden raisins)
50g (1¾oz) dried apricots
50g (1¾oz) dried cranberries
50g (1¾oz) candied orange peel,
  chopped

For the marzipan
100g (3½oz) ground almonds
  (almond meal)
50g (1¾oz) golden caster
  (superfine) sugar
50g (1¾oz) icing (confectioners')
  sugar, plus extra for dusting
pinch of salt
1 egg white reserved
  from making the dough
  (see left)

Pre-soaking the dried fruit: Overnight
1. Place all your dried fruit in a bowl and pour over just enough water to cover. Soak at room temperature overnight.
2. Drain the soaked fruit and pat dry really well with kitchen paper, then mix with the peel. Set aside.

Making the dough: 20–25 minutes
3. In a large mixing bowl, whisk together the milk, whole egg and egg yolk and yeast with a balloon whisk until the yeast has softened.
4. Add the flour, salt, sugar and spice, then mix with a dough scraper until the mixture

starts to come together into a rough dough. Add the butter and dimple it into the dough with your fingertips.
5. Turn your dough out onto a clean work surface and knead without any additional flour for 10 minutes. It has the potential to be slippery and buttery here, but keep your scraper handy to tidy up every once in a while and the dough will come together nicely.
6. Cover the dough with a clean cloth and rest on the work surface for 5 minutes or so to make the next stage easier.

Recipe continued overleaf

Adding the fruit: 5–10 minutes

7. Dust the work surface lightly with flour and roll out the dough with a rolling pin into a 30cm (12in) circle. Sprinkle over half your fruit mixture evenly and dimple it into the dough with your fingertips. Fold the bottom third of your dough circle up and the top third down over it. Then press the dough with your fingertips to spread it into a rectangle.

8. Sprinkle your remaining fruit evenly over the dough and again dimple it in with your fingertips. Roll up the dough from one short side into a short sausage.

Resting: 1½–2 hours

9. Shape the dough into a ball and place it back in the bowl. Sprinkle the top with a little flour, cover with an upturned bowl and rest at room temperature for 1½–2 hours.

Making the marzipan: 5–10 minutes

10. Meanwhile, mix together the dry ingredients for the marzipan in a bowl. Then add the egg white and keep mixing until a dough forms.

11. Work the marzipan with your hands on the work surface until it has all come together. Cut it in half and roll each piece into a sausage about 12–15cm (4½–6in) long, dusting with flour along the way. Set aside at room temperature.

Dividing and pre-shaping: 2 minutes

12. Divide the dough in half with your dough scraper, about 370g (13oz) each depending on how much moisture your fruit absorbed. If you want the pieces of dough to be exactly the same size, weigh the dough as a whole, divide the weight by 2 and then weigh out each piece accordingly.

13. Fold and roll each piece of dough into a tight ball (see page 24).

Resting: 15 minutes
14. Line up your dough balls on the work surface, cover with an upturned bowl and rest for 15 minutes to relax ready for the next stage.

Shaping: 5–10 minutes
15. Line a large baking tray with baking parchment.
16. Dust the work surface with flour. Working with one at a time, slide your dough scraper underneath a dough ball to release it and flip it sticky side up onto the dusted surface. Roll it out into a 15–20cm (6–8in) circle with a rolling pin, then push the rolling pin down horizontally across the middle. Roll up and down slightly to create a flattened area in the middle about 10cm (4in) wide, with a plump bit of dough at the top and bottom.
17. Lay your marzipan sausage in the flat area and fold the top part of the dough over it so that the 2 plump parts meet. Press your fingertips down between the rolled-up marzipan and 2 two pieces of dough to seal the gap, then place on your lined tray. If you want, you can pinch the dough to seal it around the ends of the marzipan, but I like to leave them open and that way you get a crunchy golden piece of marzipan on the end slices. Space the 2 stollen well apart on the tray to give them plenty of room to expand.

Resting: 1–1½ hours
18. Cover the stollen with a cloth and rest for 1–1½ hours. They may not puff up as much as you may be expecting, but that's because a large part of them are made of marzipan, which obviously doesn't puff up! Touch the plump part of dough, and if it feels soft and delicate, you are good to bake.

19. Towards the end of resting, preheat your oven to 180°C fan/400°F/Gas Mark 6 with a shelf in the middle and a deep roasting tray on the oven floor. Half fill a kettle.

Baking and finishing: 25–30 minutes
20. Boil the kettle.
21. Place the baking tray on the oven shelf and carefully pour the hot water into the tray below. Bake your stollen for 25–30 minutes.

Finishing: 5 minutes
22. As soon as they are cool enough to handle, transfer the stollen to a wire rack. Place the lining paper underneath the rack to catch any butter drips. Dip a pastry brush into the extra soft butter and brush it all over while the stollen are still hot, then dust liberally with a thick blanket of icing sugar. Let them cool completely before slicing.

--- **TIP** ---

GET AHEAD WITH YOUR FILLING

The marzipan takes no time at all to make, but if you wish you can make it in advance, roll it up into sausages ready to use and keep them in the fridge where they will firm up. Then take them out as you are making your dough and leave at room temperature so that they are not cold when you fill your stollen.

CHAPTER SIX
SOURDOUGHS

MAKING BREAD
WITHOUT YEAST ...

To make sourdough bread is to make bread without yeast, and so the big four: Flour, Water, Salt and Yeast, become three: Flour, Water and Salt.

So how does it PUFF UP?

The answer is Natural Fermentation in your 'sourdough starter'. A mixture of flour and water, given TIME, will ferment, i.e. make bubbles. And that's what puffs up your dough. I know, it's mad, isn't it? And that's exactly why the Sourdough is the most highly prized of breads.

Remember in the Bread Principles section I mentioned the importance of TIME? Well, sourdough is the extreme example. Because it is risen by the natural yeasts nurtured within our starter, it takes AGES to puff in comparison to baker's yeast, for that is why baker's yeast exists, so we can make bread quicker. If we follow the principles previously mentioned, then the fact that sourdough takes so long to make MUST MEAN it is the most flavoursome of breads, capable of reaching heights of flavour that yeasted bread can only dream of, and that's exactly right. Although, it DOESN'T mean that it has to be SOUR ...

If you are put off by the slightly strange-tasting sourness of a supermarket-bought sourdough loaf, rest assured that yours won't come out like that. Often that flavour is 'put in', so that you feel like you're eating real-deal sourdough when in fact you're not. When I make mine, it's never sour. There are ways and means of developing that twang if that's what you like, but for me, it's not what I like.

Sourdough is the definition of effort rewarded. It takes a long time from start to finish, although the reality is that the actual 'doing' time is very, very small. The time makes incredible flavour, allows the flour to FULLY absorb the moisture, makes the crumb so much more moist and, as an ADDED BONUS, results in a longer shelf life due to better moisture retention in the final bread.

In this section I have included three different sourdoughs, all made from the same simple starter, to show you just how versatile it can be. You won't need to babysit your starter, feed it daily or any of that nonsense. Just make your bread on the semi-regular and all will be fine. Like I said before, we don't want to, and shouldn't NEED to, rearrange our lives around our bread.

Here are my recipes for the all-important pedestal loaf (see page 264) that we all want to crack, some tasty rosemary rolls (see page 271) and, as a complete contrast, a 100 per cent rye loaf (see page 281). You'll notice that within these recipes I use Organic Flours. When doing our best to nurture live natural yeasts, I feel it makes sense to use the best, most natural ingredients.

When you put your heart and soul into any bread, especially sourdough, it becomes even more unfathomable that we would do anything but our best to use up every slice, every crust and every crumb. The dishes here are simple ones. Dishes to celebrate the bread you've worked so hard to create. Use leftovers for incredibly crispy breadcrumbs and croutons and crispbreads for dips (see page 273).

I've explained sourdough making as carefully as I can here because once you truly get it, when you UNDERSTAND the process, the seemingly overwhelming task at hand turns into actually quite a simple and straightforward task. So, read it through a couple of times before you start, let it marinate well in your brain for a while, perhaps watch some of my video tutorials, and welcome to the sourdough club. The home of the best loaf of bread you'll ever make.

RYE SOURDOUGH STARTER

ABOUT 200G (7OZ) STARTER

All sourdough starters have a history behind them – a romantic tale of travelling across the globe and changing hands from generation to generation in many cases. In others, the origins of a starter are unclear or are even hotly debated. Whatever the case, your starter is unique to you, so hey, start your own history!

When your starter is alive and breathing, write on it the date it was born. In years to come, your descendants may tell their own tales about that very moment.

To make a starter you need four things: flour (rye in this recipe), water, time and warmth. If one of these elements is missing, it won't work, but once you bring them together, making it is SO EASY. And once you have your starter alive and kicking, you need never repeat this process ever again, as long as you don't wash out your pot by accident!

TOTAL TIME: 4 DAYS

You'll need: a tall, ideally round, lidded container like a jar or a plastic pot (avoid preserving jars with rubber seals that are completely airtight, as pressure will build up inside at times and they may explode)

100g (3½oz) organic wholemeal rye flour

100g (3½oz) warm water, about 30°C (86°F)

DAY ONE

1. In your jar or pot, mix together 25g (1oz) each of flour and warm water. Smell this mixture now – it will have a grassy smell to it. Put the lid on and leave it on the kitchen side.

DAY TWO

2. Add another 25g (1oz) each of flour and warm water and mix together. Put the lid back on and leave it on the kitchen side until tomorrow.

DAY THREE

3. Repeat the process.

DAY FOUR

4. Repeat the process once more.

5. In the warm months, your starter will show signs of life on day four, sometimes even by day three! But if yours is slow to get going, make sure you are keeping it warm. It will smell acidic, sometimes really strong like nail polish, but never particularly unpleasant. When it's

bubbling and increasing in volume, you'll have about 200g (7oz) of happy and excited starter all ready to bake the double loaf recipe that follows. Your first batch will be a bit experimental, but go for it and get that one out of the way, and begin the journey to the best sourdough of your life!

6. Scoop out your sourdough starter and use it in the recipe, leaving just the scrapings clinging to the sides of the jar for next time, and put the jar in the fridge. Each time you make sourdough after that, you'll need to build up your scrapings by adding flour and water to your jar the day before you make your dough, then you'll be left with just the scrapings in your jar again ready to build up for your next loaf. If you bake once a week or even once every fortnight, your starter will be happy in its jar without any need for feeding at all. Just feed it when you need it. Every once in a while, transfer your scrapings into a clean jar.

SOURDOUGH LOAF

MAKES 2 LOAVES

This is THE ONE that everybody wants to make, and wants to make perfectly! That crispy crust, open texture inside, complex flavour and highly prized 'ear' where your loaf busts open on the top are completely possible to achieve at home with … wait for it … PRACTISE.

Making a sourdough loaf is a LONG-TERM journey. Every single loaf you make will teach you something new that your future self will benefit from. It's a lesson in care and attention and persistence. There are no two ways about it: great bread takes time and effort, but it is SO WORTH IT.

Sourdoughs are often wet and sloppy and difficult to manage because, after all, fermentation happens faster in a more liquid environment. But for beginners, it really doesn't help and it doesn't HAVE to work that way. This recipe has been specially devised by a home baker to be PRACTICAL for OTHER home bakers, with a manageable dough and a somewhat simplified process. It is still a long process, but the work involved is minimal. If your first loaves don't go exactly to plan, please promise me you'll bake at least three more. By then you'll definitely see an improvement. The recipe makes two loaves, which I ALWAYS recommend, as you're doubling up the result from the same long process AND getting double the shaping practise. But if you would like to make just one, simply halve all the ingredient quantities and skip the dividing stage.

EASY TO MAKE, TRICKY TO MASTER / TOTAL TIME: DAY ONE 5 MINUTES; DAY TWO 7 HOURS; DAY THREE 1¼–2 HOURS

You'll need: 2 oval banneton proving baskets about 30cm (12in) long and 16cm (6¼in) wide with or without liners (see method); baking or pizza stone; 2 narrow wooden peels or 1 large; grignette; spray bottle filled with water

For the starter
100g (3½oz) organic wholemeal rye flour
100g (3½oz) room-temperature water
Rye Sourdough Starter scrapings (see page 263)

For the dough
200g (7oz) excited Rye Sourdough Starter (take this from your jar and leave the scrapings in the fridge for next time)
620g (1lb 6oz) room-temperature water
900g (2lb) strong white bread flour, plus extra for dusting
16g (½oz) salt

DAY ONE

If you already have 200g (7oz) of excited starter from building your starter in the first place, skip straight to Day Two.

Feeding your starter: 5 minutes
1. The evening before you want to make the dough, add the flour and water to your jar of starter scrapings. Scrape down the sides to level off the mixture and mark on the side of the jar with a pen or elastic band where the mixture comes up to. If it has been a while since you baked (2 weeks or more), your starter might have become a little sleepy and require a couple of feeds to get it going, in which case feed half in the morning and half in the evening to help wake it up.

Resting: Overnight
2. Leave your starter at room temperature overnight, or 8–12 hours, until bubbling and at least doubled in volume.

Recipe continued overleaf

DAY TWO

Making the dough: 5–10 minutes
3. Take the 200g (7oz) of starter out of your jar and put it in a large mixing bowl. Add the water, flour and salt, then mix together for a minute or so until well combined into a dough.

Resting: 30 minutes
4. Spray the top of the dough with water, cover with a clean cloth and let it rest and soak for 30 minutes.

First fold: 5 minutes
5. Spray the work surface and the top of your dough with water. Turn the dough out upside down onto the wet surface. Grasp a bit of the dough edge, stretch it out and fold it over onto the dough. Repeat all the way round the dough, making about 10–12 folds, until you have a ball.

Resting: 2 hours
6. Turn the dough over, smooth side up, and place it back in the bowl. Spray the top with water, cover again and rest for 2 hours.

Second fold: 2 minutes
7. The dough should have puffed up slightly already.
8. Spray the work surface and the dough again with water. Turn the dough out as before and repeat the first fold process BUT this time make only 6 to 7 folds.

Resting: 2 hours
9. Turn the dough smooth side up and place it back in the bowl. Spray the top with water, then cover and rest as before.

Third fold: 2 minutes
10. You should now see clear signs of the dough rising.
11. Repeat the second fold process as before.

Resting: 1 hour
12. Turn the dough smooth side up and place it back in the bowl. Spray and cover as before BUT this time rest for 1 hour.

Dividing and pre-shaping: 5 minutes
13. Dust the work surface with flour. Turn your dough out upside down onto it and cut it in half with your dough scraper.
14. Fold each piece of dough into a loose ball (see page 24).

Resting: 1 hour
15. Line up your dough balls on the work surface, cover with the cloth and rest for 1 hour.

Final shaping: 5 minutes
16. The aim here is to create a tight structure without deflating the dough too much, so be delicate with the folds but still create tension.
17. Dust the work surface lightly with flour. Working with one at a time, slide your dough scraper underneath a dough ball to release it and flip it sticky side up onto the dusted surface. Let it relax into a circle. Grasp each side in turn, stretch it out very slightly and fold over the dough, one on top of the other. Starting from the top edge, roll up the dough towards you into a sausage and stick it onto the sticky patch of dough closest to you, pressing the seam to seal.
18. Dust each loaf well with flour, as well as your oval banneton baskets, and place one in each basket, seam side up. You can instead add liners and dust those well before adding your loaves, which will make turning them out easier, but you won't get those characteristic decorative lines on the loaves.

Resting: Overnight
19. Rest your loaves, uncovered, in the fridge to prove nice and slowly overnight.

DAY THREE

20. When you are ready to bake, remove your loaves from the fridge and let them rest on the kitchen side while the oven preheats. They should show clear signs of inflation, not hugely increased in volume but a distinct plumpness. If they appear not much different to when you put them in the fridge, leave them for an hour or so at room temperature for a puff booster.

21. Preheat your oven to 230°C fan/485°F/Gas Mark 9 with a baking or pizza stone on the middle shelf and a deep roasting tray on the oven floor. Half fill a kettle.

Slashing: 5 minutes

22. Boil the kettle.

23. Dust your 2 individual wooden peels or large peel with flour and turn the loaves out onto them/it. Hold a grignette at a shallow angle and make a LONG straight slash from end to end of each loaf.

Baking: 45 minutes

24. Slide your loaves onto the hot stone in the oven. Carefully pour the hot water into the tray below. Bake your loaves for 15 minutes, then turn the oven down to 200°C fan/425°F/ Gas Mark 7 and bake for a further 30 minutes.

25. Remove the loaves from the oven with your peel and let them cool completely on a wire rack before slicing.

TIP

EXTRA SHELF LIFE ... NATURALLY!

Sourdough is a long process from start to finish. This gives the dough loads of time for flavour and structure to develop, and for the flour to absorb all the moisture. The result is a bread that is more moist and capable of holding onto that moisture for longer, MEANING... the bread will stay fresh for longer too.

ROASTED RATATOUILLE & GOAT'S CHEESE BRUSCHETTA

SERVES 2

Courgettes? Okay. Aubergine? Okay. Peppers? Yeah, okay, there's nothing ground-breaking here, but sometimes these 'Med veg' get a bad rap and I think it's because they are not cooked well. When people describe their distaste, I hear the words 'watery' or 'spongy' and these all scream 'undercooked' to me. Cooked well, for a long time, they become intensely tasty, sweet even. Add a touch of garlic and dress with red wine vinegar and they are completely transformed.

A thick slice of stale Sourdough Loaf (see page 264) will make for the crunchiest bruschetta base here, whether it's toasted in a toaster or charred on a griddle pan.

100g (3½oz) ripe goat's cheese
1 aubergine (eggplant)
1 courgette (zucchini)
2 (bell) peppers, orange or red
200g (7oz) red and yellow cherry tomatoes on the vine
3 garlic cloves, plus 1 for the bruschetta
1 tablespoon chopped fresh rosemary leaves
3 tablespoons olive oil, plus extra for drizzling
2 tablespoons pine nuts
3 tablespoons chopped fresh flat-leaf (Italian) parsley leaves and stalks
2 tablespoons red wine vinegar
2 slices of stale Sourdough Loaf (see page 264)
sea salt and cracked black pepper

1. Preheat the oven to 180°C fan/400°F/Gas Mark 6 and remove your goat's cheese from the fridge to come up to room temperature.
2. Top and tail your aubergine and slice it lengthways down the middle into 2 halves. Turn each half cut side down and slice in half again. Chop into 3cm (1¼in) pieces and place into a large mixing bowl. Top and tail your courgette, slice in half lengthways down the middle, chop into 3cm (1¼in) chunks, add them to the bowl.
3. Slice the sides, top and bottom from the peppers. Discard the seeds and stalk. Cut the flesh into 3cm (1¼in) squares and add them to the bowl with the tomatoes, left whole but picked from their vine.
4. Grate in your garlic, add the chopped rosemary, a generous pinch of salt and the olive oil. Toss everything together to coat well in the oil and spread in one layer on a large parchment-lined roasting tray. Wipe out your bowl with kitchen paper and set aside for later.
5. Roast for 1 hour, checking every once in a while to make sure the edge pieces aren't burning while the middle ones remain uncooked. If they are, give them a little mix along the way.
6. At some point, on a small tray, toast your pine nuts as well in the oven for 8–12 minutes until golden.
7. Remove the veg from the oven and set aside. Chop your parsley and add it to the bowl from earlier, along with the red wine vinegar.
8. Add your vegetables to the bowl, toss together gently so as not to smash your vegetables up too much, taste, adjust the seasoning if you need to and set aside.
9. Toast your sourdough in a toaster, or grill or char in a griddle pan. Rub each piece with a cut garlic clove and drizzle with olive oil.
10. Place each slice on a plate and divide your vegetables between the 2 slices. Break up your goat's cheese over the top. Sprinkle with the toasted pine nuts and finish with a drizzle of olive oil and a pinch of black pepper.

SOURDOUGH ROSEMARY & POTATO ROLLS

MAKES 8 MINI BATARD-SHAPED ROLLS

Sourdough doesn't HAVE to be a big loaf. In fact, theoretically, ANY sort of bread can be sourdough.

Take these crusty fragrant rolls, for example, which are made moist and bouncy with the addition of mashed potato. They don't TASTE of potato but it certainly adds a little something. Once you have fed your starter on day one, on day two you'll be making the dough AND baking the rolls, since the slightly larger quantity of starter helps things happen a little faster here compared to the sourdough loaf.

These are of course best enjoyed on the day they are made, preferably warm with butter, but are also great for part-baking, freezing and bringing back to life in the oven at a later date (see my tip on page 48, baking initially for 10–12 minutes).

========== EASY TO MAKE, EASY TO BAKE / TOTAL TIME: DAY ONE 1–1¼ HOURS; ==========
DAY TWO 5¼–6 HOURS

You'll need: a baking or pizza stone (2 if you have them, to bake all 8 rolls at once); large wooden peel; grignette; spray bottle filled with water

For the starter
Rye Sourdough Starter scrapings (see page 263)
75g (2½oz) organic wholemeal rye flour

75g (2½oz) room-temperature water
1 large or 2 medium baking potatoes

For the dough
150g (5½oz) excited Rye Sourdough Starter (take this from your jar and leave the scrapings in the fridge for the next time)

225g (8oz) room-temperature water
425g (15oz) strong white bread flour, plus extra for dusting
8g (¼oz) salt
2 teaspoons chopped fresh rosemary leaves
100g (3½oz) baked and mashed potato (see left)

DAY ONE
Feeding your starter
1. If you already have 150g (5½oz) of excited starter from building your starter in the first place, skip straight to Day Two. If not, follow the instructions to feed your starter and rest overnight, or for 8–12 hours, on page 263.

Preparing the potato: 1–1½ hours
2. Preheat your oven to 180°C fan/400°F/Gas Mark 6. Score a cross in the top of your potato(es) and bake for 1–1½ hours until cooked through. Let them cool, then peel and mash or pass through a potato ricer. Weigh out 100g (3½oz) and set aside.

DAY TWO
Making the dough: 5–10 minutes
3. Take the 150g (5½oz) of starter out of your jar and put it into a large mixing bowl. Add the remaining dough ingredients, then mix together for a minute or so until well combined into a dough. It's quite a stiff dough, so you may find the easiest way to combine everything is to knead it on the work surface for 30 seconds or so, then return it to the bowl.

Resting: 30 minutes
4. Spray the top of the dough with water, cover with a clean cloth and let it rest and soak for 30 minutes.

Recipe continued overleaf

First fold: 5 minutes

5. Spray the work surface and the top of your dough with water. Turn the dough out upside down onto the wet surface. Grasp a bit of the dough edge, stretch it out and folding it over onto the dough. Repeat all the way round the dough, making about 10–12 folds, until you have a ball. Expect this dough to be quite tight.

Resting: 1½ hours

6. Turn the dough over, smooth side up, and place it back in the bowl. Spray the top with water, cover again and rest for 1½ hours.

Second fold: 2 minutes

7. Spray the work surface and the dough again with water. Turn the dough out as before and repeat the first fold process BUT this time make only 6 to 7 folds.

Resting: 1 hour

8. Turn the dough smooth side up and place the dough back in the bowl. Spray the top with water, then cover again and rest for 1 hour.

Dividing and pre-shaping: 5 minutes

9. Dust the work surface with flour. Turn the dough out upside down onto it and cut it into 8 equal-sized pieces with your dough scraper, about 110g (4oz) each if you're counting.
10. Fold and roll each piece into a ball (see page 24).

Resting: 15 minutes

11. Line up your dough balls on the work surface, cover with the cloth and rest for 15 minutes.

Final shaping: 5–10 minutes

12. Dust the work surface lightly with flour. Working with one at a time, turn a dough ball upside down and press it out into a circle with your fingertips. Now just like for a batard (see page 191), grasp each imaginary top corner, stretch them out and then fold them into the middle of the dough. Fold down the point at the top. Roll up the dough from the top to the bottom into a tight sausage, building tension as you go, then press the seam to stick it together. Roll the sausage a little with your palms on the work surface to even up and make the ends pointy like a lemon shape.
13. Cut 2 squares of baking parchment and place 4 rolls on each, seam side down.

Resting: 1½–2 hours

14. Dust your rolls with flour, cover with a cloth and rest for 1½–2 hours.
15. Towards the end of resting, preheat your oven to 230°C fan/485°F/Gas Mark 9 with a baking or pizza stone on the middle shelf (or 2 if you have them) and a deep roasting tray on the oven floor. Half fill a kettle.

Slashing: 5 minutes

16. Boil the kettle.
17. Use the grignette to slash the tops of your rolls swiftly and confidently at a shallow angle from one end to the other.

Baking: 15–20 minutes

18. Slide your peel underneath the paper and then slide the rolls AND the paper in one go onto the hot stone (or stones) in the oven. (If you only have one stone, don't worry as your rolls are fast to bake and the second batch will happily sit at room temperature while the first are baking.) Carefully pour the hot water into the tray below. Bake your rolls for 15–20 minutes until golden and crisp.
19. Let them cool completely on a wire rack.

SOURDOUGH CRISPBREADS & THE BEST DIPS IN THE WORLD

SERVES 3–4

You can make a crispbread out of pretty much anything. Here we are using our Sourdough Loaf (see page 264) or Rosemary & Potato Rolls (see page 271) to make the crispiest crispbreads on the planet, then serving the bread with two of my favourite dips. A creamy warm bean dip with black olive tapenade and a roasted pepper and hazelnut romesco. Serve as a starter, pre-dinner nibbles or pair with a salad or two.

FOR THE CRISPBREADS

leftover Sourdough Loaf (see page 264)
    or Sourdough Rosemary & Potato Rolls
    (see page 271)
olive oil
sea salt flakes

1. Slice your bread into 5mm (¼in) slices, enough to arrange over 2 large parchment-lined baking trays in a single layer. Drizzle with olive oil and season with sea salt flakes.
2. Bake in the oven at 180°C fan/400°F/ Gas Mark 6 for 12–15 minutes until golden. Turn off the oven, crack the door open and leave to cool in the residual heat until completely crisp.
3. These keep well in an airtight container or bag for a week or 2.

BUTTER BEAN DIP WITH BLACK OLIVE & MINT TAPENADE

4 tablespoons olive oil, plus extra to drizzle
2 garlic cloves, thinly sliced
400g (14oz) tinned butter (lima) beans
juice of ½ lemon
100g (3½oz) kalamata olives
25g (1oz) capers
½ garlic clove, finely grated
1 anchovy fillet, finely grated
1 tablespoon chopped fresh mint leaves
1 teaspoon red wine vinegar
sea salt and cracked black pepper

1. Put 3 tablespoons of the olive oil and the thinly sliced garlic into a medium-sized saucepan. Bring to a medium heat on the stove and gently sizzle for 2 minutes.
2. Drain your beans and add them to the pan along with enough water to cover the beans and lemon juice. Bring to a simmer. Cook for 15–20 minutes until the beans are soft.
3. While it is cooking, make the tapenade. In a mini food processor, roughly chop the olives and capers. Tip them into a mixing bowl. Add the garlic, anchovy, chopped mint, red wine vinegar and the remaining olive oil. Mix together.
4. Stir and mash the beans when they are ready. Add some water if needed to make it a loose and chunky dip. Season with salt to taste.
5. Serve your dip warm, topped with the tapenade. Drizzle with olive oil and season with cracked black pepper.

ROASTED RED PEPPER & HAZELNUT ROMESCO

4 plum-sized tomatoes
3 red (bell) peppers
4 garlic cloves, peeled
olive oil
35g (1¼oz) blanched, skin-off hazelnuts (filberts)
1 tablespoon red wine vinegar
1 tablespoon chopped fresh flat-leaf (Italian)
    parsley leaves and stalks
a few fresh flat-leaf (Italian) parsley leaves,
    to garnish
salt

1. Roughly chop the tomatoes and the flesh from your red peppers and place them in a large mixing bowl with the whole garlic cloves. Toss with enough olive oil to make them shine all over and season with salt. Make sure the garlic is tucked in underneath some of the tomatoes or peppers so that it roasts up nicely, becoming soft and sweet as opposed to dry and burnt.
2. Spread out on a parchment-lined roasting tray and roast in the oven at 180°C fan/400°F/Gas Mark 6 for 40 minutes until soft and sweet.
3. While your vegetables are roasting, you can roast your hazelnuts. Spread them out on a smaller tray and pop them in the oven too. They will take around 12–15 minutes to get nice and golden.

4. Tip your nuts into a food processor and process until they are roughly chopped, then remove some and set them aside to garnish. Add your roasted vegetables and garlic to the processor along with 2 tablespoons of olive oil and the red wine vinegar. Blend to a coarse consistency. Add your parsley and stir it through.
5. Taste the sauce and adjust the seasoning if you need to. Garnish with some parsley leaves, a sprinkling of the chopped hazelnuts that you kept to one side, and a drizzle of olive oil.

—————— **TIP** ——————

NOTES ON TEXTURE

I didn't peel the peppers or tomatoes in this recipe and that's a personal choice because I wanted a rustic, textured dip. If you prefer a more refined dip, you can remove the skins before blending or blend until smooth and pass through a sieve, pressing the purée with the back of a ladle.

PECORINO CHUNKS, SULTANAS, FENNEL SYRUP & TOASTED WALNUTS

SERVES 2

WAY back in the olden days after service in the restaurant I worked in, I would pass a Sardinian restaurant on the way home late at night. I pestered the chef to give me a job in her family-run restaurant SO MUCH that one day she finally did. When I got there, I learnt so much about pasta, risotto, fish and seafood but, as always, it was often the simplest of dishes that would intrigue me.

In the evening, the staff would often have a cold beer and a Sardinian snack: salamis, cheeses, something small, normally quite simple and always so tasty.

One time, the chef simply chunked up some Parmesan and drizzled it with bitter Sardinian honey and that was it. It blew my mind, and not only because up until then I'd only ever seen Parmesan grated or shaved but NEVER chunked, but because it was so tasty that years later the combination has stayed with me and evolved into this dish. I hope you like it.

This recipe makes way more sultanas than you need, but they will keep well in the fridge for a couple of weeks and are great to have around for cheeseboard emergencies.

150ml (5fl oz) water
150g (5½oz) golden caster (superfine) sugar
1 teaspoon fennel seeds
150g (5½oz) sultanas
50g (1¾oz) walnuts
180g (6½oz) pecorino cheese
Sourdough Rosemary & Potato Rolls (see page 271)

For the sultanas: Ahead of time
1. Put the water, sugar and fennel seeds in a medium-sized saucepan and bring to the boil.
2. Remove the syrup from the heat and tip in the sultanas. Give them a mix and leave them in the pan to cool. Transfer to a container and refrigerate to plump up overnight.
3. Toast the nuts
4. Spread the walnuts on a tray in a single layer and toast in the oven at 200°C fan/425°F/Gas Mark 7 for 8–10 minutes until golden. Set aside to cool and then chop roughly.

Bringing it all together
5. When you are ready to serve the cheese, use the tip of a knife to crack the pecorino into small chunks. Arrange over a plate or board and scatter with some sultanas. Drizzle a little extra fennel syrup over the top, making sure every chunk gets a bit, and sprinkle over some chopped walnuts. Serve with the rolls.

ROASTED CARROT & SHALLOT SOUP WITH TOASTED HAZELNUT & FETA

SERVES 4

OH LOOK … just like in our risotto, there is no vegetable dust here. Instead, we extract FLAVOUR from our ingredients in the best way possible because there is plenty in there, we just need to know HOW to make it SING.

The carrots and shallots are slow-roasted until soft, sweet and golden, then simmered in milk with herbs to INFUSE the flavours into them before whizzing them up at the end. The principle is a simple one and if carrots don't float your boat, you can do the same with sweet potatoes or butternut squash. Serve with rolls.

150g (5½oz) banana shallots
   (large shallots)
600g (1lb 5oz) carrots
3 tablespoons olive oil,
   plus extra for drizzling
4 garlic cloves, peeled
25g (1oz) softened butter
10g (½oz) fresh thyme sprigs
50g (1¾oz) hazelnuts (filberts)
900ml (30fl oz) whole milk
100g (3½oz) feta cheese
sea salt and cracked
   black pepper
Sourdough Rosemary
   & Potato Rolls
   (see page 271)

1. Preheat your oven to 175°C fan/400°F/Gas Mark 6.
2. Top, tail, peel and halve the shallots, then place them in a large bowl. Top, tail and chop your carrots into chunks and add them to the bowl too.
3. Add the olive oil, garlic cloves, softened butter, half the thyme and a pinch of salt and toss everything together really well. Spread it out on a large parchment-lined roasting tray and just before you bake, make sure the garlic is tucked in underneath instead of out in the open where it will burn.
4. Roast in the oven for 1 hour, tossing the veg every once in a while to make sure everything is evenly browned. At the same time, spread the hazelnuts on a tray and toast for 10–15 minutes until golden. Cool, chop roughly and set aside for later.
5. Take the carrots and shallots from the oven. Remove just enough to garnish your 4 bowls later on, then all the rest can go into a large saucepan. Cover with 600ml (20¼fl oz) of milk and slowly bring to the boil.
6. Toss in the rest of your thyme and simmer for 20–30 minutes.
7. Remove from the heat and leave to cool slightly before blending till smooth. Add some of the reserved milk at this point to adjust the consistency as you like it.
8. Pass the soup through a sieve to get rid of any woody bits of herb that haven't blended, leaving a deliciously silky soup in the bowl beneath. Taste and season with salt if you need to.
9. Serve in bowls, garnishing with the reserved vegetables, chopped hazelnut and crumbled feta. Drizzle with oil and sprinkle a pinch of cracked black pepper over each bowl.

RYE, CARAWAY & BLACK TREACLE SOURDOUGH

MAKES 1 MEDIUM LOAF

Rye flour makes HEAVY bread, but that's not a BAD thing! You see, although rye flour does contain gluten in some form, there is absolutely zero strength in a rye dough and therefore no structure to be built. No kneading, no folding, no shaping – you literally mix it up, pop it in its tin and wait for it to puff.

Because of this, a 100 per cent rye loaf can never get as light and fluffy as a bread made with strong white bread flour. However, every bread has its place and this one is no different. Its deliciousness lies in its wholesomeness, nuttiness and substantial richness enhanced by black treacle and fragrant caraway. It's not a combination that I've invented by any means – it's a classic because it works so well.

This loaf is so ridiculously easy to make that it brings us the freedom to give it a shot without much to lose. And it makes the most excellent crispbreads too (see page 273).

=== EASY TO MAKE, EASY TO BAKE / TOTAL TIME: DAY ONE 5 MINUTES; DAY TWO 4–5 HOURS ===

You'll need: a 450g (1lb) loaf tin – mine measures 13 x 7.5cm (5 x 3in) base, 16 x 10cm (6¼ x 4in) top, 7.5cm (3in) deep; spray bottle filled with water ready BEFORE you mix the dough, as rye flour sticks like glue

For the starter
Rye Sourdough Starter scrapings (see page 263)
50g (1¾oz) organic wholemeal rye flour
50g (1¾oz) room-temperature water

For the dough
vegetable oil or butter, for greasing
100g (3½oz) excited Rye Sourdough Starter (take this from your jar and leave the scrapings in the fridge for the next time)
150g (5½oz) room-temperature water
200g (7oz) organic wholemeal rye flour, plus extra for dusting
4g (1 teaspoon) salt
15g (½oz) black treacle
3g (½ tablespoon) caraway seeds

DAY ONE
Feeding your starter
1. If you already have 100g (3½oz) of excited starter from building your starter in the first place, skip straight to Day Two. If not, follow the instructions to feed your starter and rest overnight, or for 8–12 hours, on page 263.

DAY TWO
Preparing the tin: 2 minutes
2. Grease your loaf tin lightly with oil or butter.

Making the dough: 5 minutes
3. Take the 100g (3½oz) of starter out of your jar and put it into a large mixing bowl. Add the water and mix together. Add the remaining dough ingredients and mix into a thick paste.

Shaping: 5 minutes
4. Spray the dough and your hands thoroughly with water until everything is really slippery.

Recipe continued overleaf

Scoop the dough out of the bowl into your hands and pat into a smooth rectangular shape. Lower it into your greased tin and resist the urge to smooth down the top – if it's domed up, you're more likely to get those decorative cracks as it rises.

Resting: 3½–4 hours

5. Dust the top of the loaf really well with rye flour, cover with a clean cloth and rest for 3½–4 hours.

6. Towards the end of resting, preheat your oven to 200°C fan/425°F/Gas Mark 7 with a shelf in the middle and a deep roasting tray on the oven floor. Half fill a kettle.

Baking: 30–40 minutes

7. Boil the kettle.

8. Place the loaf tin on the oven shelf and carefully pour the hot water into the tray below. Bake your loaf for 30–40 minutes.

9. Pop the loaf out of the tin, and if the underside feels soft and cakey, return to the tin and bake for another 10 minutes or until crusty on the base.

10. Let the loaf cool completely on a wire rack.

TIP

REST IS FOR THE BEST

ALL baked breads are at their best after they've rested because resting gives all that moisture and steam inside a chance to settle and the crumb to turn from sticky and doughy to nicely moist. As this bread is made out of 100 per cent wholemeal flour, it really benefits from resting for AGES before you crack into it, so rest it overnight after you've baked it to enjoy the next day when it will have transformed from a difficult-to-cut, gummy texture to a sliceable and delicious loaf.

RYE BREAD OPEN SANDWICH WITH SMOKED SALMON & CRISPY CAPERS

SERVES 2

When I read a menu, the words 'open sandwich' always crack me up! Depending on how you look at it, it's either the bottom half of a sandwich or untoasted toast. However, wholesome rye bread like the one used here might be a bit much if it was two slices put together, so, hey, I guess the open sandwich has its place.

Here, I've topped the bread with a classic combo: smoked salmon and cream cheese with fresh cucumber ribbons, lemon juice and dill, loaded with crispy fried capers because, yes, that IS a thing and if you haven't tried them before, once you do, you'll realise …

---

4 tablespoons cream cheese
2 teaspoons chopped fresh
 dill, plus extra to garnish
2 tablespoons capers
olive oil
½ cucumber
1 teaspoon lemon juice
2 slices of Rye, Caraway &
 Black Treacle Sourdough,
 taken from the LONG edge
 (see page 281)
100g (3½oz) smoked salmon
2 lemon wedges, to garnish
sea salt and cracked
 black pepper

1. Mix together the cream cheese and dill and set aside.

2. Drain your capers really well on kitchen paper. Heat 3 tablespoons of olive oil in a small frying pan to a medium heat. Add the capers and fry for 2–2½ minutes, in which time they will open up and go crispy golden brown. Remove from the oil and drain the excess oil on kitchen paper.

3. Peel the cucumber into ribbons with a peeler and place them in a large mixing bowl. Dress with the lemon juice, 1 teaspoon of olive oil and a pinch of salt. Toss together well.

4. Spread the cream cheese onto your rye bread slices. Pile high with alternating layers of smoked salmon and cucumber ribbons. Sprinkle over your crispy capers and finish with a little extra chopped dill and cracked black pepper. Serve with a lemon wedge.

INDEX

ACKNOWLEDGEMENTS

Transforming random scribbled notes and sketches into this book you hold in your hands has been a MASSIVE task, the single BIGGEST achievement of BWJ to date and I could never have brought it to you all by myself …

I'd like to thank:

Andrew for the amazing photography and overall shoot day merriment, Anna for seeing the beauty in the simplest of things, Hattie for your incredible eye for the finest of details, Lucie and Laura for sharing my vision, wholeheartedly embracing my thoughts and bringing everything to life, Alex and Emma for your design finesse, Jo, Kay and Elise for making sure that what makes sense in my head, makes sense to everybody else! And to my wife Sara, Mum, Brother and family, thank you, for believing and supporting me in all that I do without question.

And finally, a HUGE THANKS to you, the reader, for you are quite simply the reason BWJ exists, and I am so proud to be a part of your bread-making journey. It is my hope that you find in bread what I have: a sense of calm in a busy world, a feeling of great achievement, satisfaction and that you continue to make it, eat it, share it, ENJOY it forever.

Jack :-)

Ebury Press, an imprint of Ebury Publishing, 20 Vauxhall Bridge Road, London SW1V 2SA

Ebury Press is part of the Penguin Random House group of companies whose addresses can be found at global.penguinrandomhouse.com

Penguin Random House UK

Copyright © Bake with Jack 2022
Photography © Andrew Hayes-Watkins 2022

Jack Sturgess has asserted his right to be identified as the author of this Work in accordance with the Copyright, Designs and Patents Act 1988

First published by Ebury Press in 2022

www.penguin.co.uk

A CIP catalogue record for this book is available from the British Library

ISBN 9781529109702

Design: Smith & Gilmour
Photography: Andrew Hayes-Watkins
Food Styling: Hattie Arnold
Prop Styling: Anna Wilkins

Colour origination by Altaimage Ltd, London
Printed and bound in China by C&C Offset Printing Co., Ltd

The authorised representative in the EEA is Penguin Random House Ireland, Morrison Chambers, 32 Nassau Street, Dublin D02 YH68

MIX
Paper | Supporting responsible forestry
FSC® C018179

Penguin Random House is committed to a sustainable future for our business, our readers and our planet. This book is made from Forest Stewardship Council® certified paper.

Recipes tested in a UK fan oven, please note that oven temperatures may vary.